BEACON ISLAMIC STUDIES SERIES

BEACON

ISLAMIC STUDIES SERIES

First published in the UK by Beacon Books and Media Ltd
Earl Business Centre, Dowry Street, Oldham, OL8 2PF, UK.

www.beaconbooks.net

ISBN: 978-1-912356-92-8 Paperback

Cataloging-in-Publication record for this book is available from the British Library.

Cover design by Raees Mahmood Khan

THE PRINCIPLES OF ISLAMIC JURISPRUDENCE

ACCORDING TO THE ḤANAFĪ SCHOOL

أصول الشاشي

ADAPTED FROM UṢŪL ASH-SHĀSHĪ BY NIZĀM AD-DĪN ASH-SHĀSHĪ

TRANSLATED BY TAHIR MAHMOOD KIANI | EDITED BY BILAL BROWN

BEACON BOOKS

BEACON ISLAMIC STUDIES SERIES

The *Beacon Islamic Studies Series* provides a structured framework for teaching Islamic studies, offering comprehensive coursebooks designed to engage students of all levels. From foundational principles to advanced topics, our series empowers institutions and teachers to deliver high-quality lessons that meet a consistent educational standard. This coursebook features:

- **Large Margins for Annotations**: Ample space for students to jot down their thoughts, questions, and insights right next to the text.
- **Points to Note Sections**: 'Points to Note' sections draw attention to complex ideas or crucial information, ensuring that important concepts are not overlooked.
- **End-of-Chapter Questions**: Questions at the end of each section test comprehension and provoke deeper exploration.
- **Lesson Break Icons**: Book icons in the margin suggest optimal points for the beginning and end of lessons.
- **Terminology Boxes**: Definitions of key terms and phrases.

BEACON

ISLAMIC STUDIES SERIES

CONTENTS

UNIT ONE

1.1: Types of Ḥukm (Ruling) 2

1.2: ʿAzīmah (Regular Act) and Rukhṣah (Dispensation) 3

UNIT TWO

2.1: Khāṣṣ (Specific) and ʿĀmm (General) 6

2.2: Muṭlaq (Unrestricted) and Muqayyad (Restricted) 12

2.3: Mushtarak (Homonymous), Mu'awwal (Construed), Mufassar (Elaborated) 15

2.4: Ḥaqīqah (Literal) and Majāz (Metaphorical) 18

2.5: Istiʿārah (Metaphor) 22

2.6: Ṣarīḥ (Explicit) and Kināyah (Implicit) 25

2.7: Mutaqābilāt (counterparts) 27

2.8: Their Antonyms 31

2.9: Diversion from the Original Meanings of the Words 34

2.10: Textual Implications (Mutaʿallaqāt an-Nuṣūṣ) 38

2.11: Amr (The Imperative) 44

2.12: The Ma'mūr Bihī (Enjoined) and Time-Constriction 49

2.13: Ma'mūr Bi-hī Being Ḥasan 55

2.14: Adā' (Due Performance) and Qaḍā' (Delayed Performance) 57

2.15: Division of Qaḍā' (Delayed Performance) 62

2.16: Nahy (The Proscription) 64

2.17: Deduction of Textual Inferences 68

2.18: Meaningful Particles 74

2.19: Bayān (Explanation) 100

UNIT THREE

3.1: Types of Report (Khabar) of the Messenger of Allah ﷺ 110

UNIT FOUR

4.1: Legal Status of Ijmāʿ 120

4.2: Ranks of Ijmāʿ 120

4.3: Kinds of Ijmāʿ 121

4.4: Ijmāʿ ʿAdam al-Qā'il bi'l-Faṣl and its Types 123

UNIT FIVE

5.1: Reports from the Prophet ﷺ on the Legal Status of Qiyās 130

5.2: Conditions for the Validity of Qiyās 131

5.3: Legal Qiyās (Qiyās Sharʿī) 138

5.4: Objections Against Qiyās 144

UNIT SIX

6.1: Inference (Istidlāl) Without an 'Illah (Effective Cause) 152

6.2: Istiṣḥāb (Presumption of Continuity) 153

6.3: Lack of Evidence is Proof for repelling (Dafʿ) 153

UNIT SEVEN

7.1: The Reality of the Sabab (Reason) 156

7.2: Asbāb (Reasons) for Legal Commands 159

UNIT EIGHT

8.1: The Types of Impediments 164

Glossary 167

UNIT **ONE**

THE PRINCIPLES OF ISLAMIC JURISPRUDENCE

(Uṣūl al-Fiqh)

The word *uṣūl* is the plural of the word *asl* (meaning 'principle' or 'foundation').

The *uṣūl* is a framework wherein discussions take place around principles through which we derive rulings pertaining to the Sharīʿah for our everyday lives. It comprises of the following benefits:

i. It is an act of worship itself.

ii. Instills confidence in students of knowledge and those who specialise in Islamic law.

iii. Helps to minimise contradiction between evidences through application of rules of interpretation.

iv. Provides a methodological framework.

The agreed upon principles of Islamic jurisprudence are four:

i. The Book of Allah ﷻ,

ii. The Sunnah of the Messenger of Allah ﷺ,

iii. *Ijmāʿ* (scholarly consensus), and

iv. *Qiyās* (analogical extrapolation).

Therefore, there must be discussion of each one of these categories in order that the method of deriving legal rulings is known.

1.1: TYPES OF ḤUKM (RULING)

Farḍ (Obligatory)

Farḍ (فَرْضٌ) literally means 'to decree'. The ordained actions of the sacred law are its decrees, inasmuch that they do not entertain any increase or decrease. In the Sharīʿah, [*farḍ*] is that which is established by definitive evidence (*dalīl qaṭʿī*) wherein lies no doubt. Its ruling (*ḥukm*) is to bind [oneself] to act upon it and have firm belief in it.

Wājib (Incumbent)

Wujūb (وُجُوبٌ) is 'to fall', i.e. that which falls upon the person without him having any choice. It is [also] said that it [= the word *wujūb*] is from [the word] *wajabah* (وَجَبَةٌ) which means 'indecision', by which [the word] *wājib* is named, and that is because it occurs [in an undecided state] between the *farḍ* and the *nafl* (supererogatory). Hence, it becomes *farḍ* to act upon it, such that it is not permissible to omit it, and [it is] *nafl* to have belief in it, such that it is not binding upon us to have convincing belief in it. In the Sharīʿah, it is that which is established by proof that has an uncertainty in it, such as an elaborated verse [of the Qur'an], or a sound solitary report.

Its ruling (*ḥukm*) is what we have mentioned afore.

Sunnah (Recommended/Encouraged)

Sunnah is an expression for the preferred well-trodden path in the affairs of *dīn*, irrespective of whether it is from the Messenger of

Allah ﷺ or from his [Noble] Companions (Allah be pleased with them). The Prophet ﷺ said:

عَلَيْكُمْ بِسُنَّتِي وَسُنَّةِ الْخُلَفَاءِ مِن بَعْدِيْ، عَضُّوْا عَلَيْهَا بِالنَّوَاجِذِ

'Adhere to my way and the way of the Caliphs after me; cling to it aggressively [literally: with your molar teeth].'[1]

Its ruling (*ḥukm*) is that the person is demanded to revive it [= the Sunnah] and he is blameworthy for omitting it, except when he omits it due to an excuse.

Nafl (Supererogatory)

Nafl is an expression for excess. Spoils [of war] are called *nafl* because they are in excess of the objective of the military campaign. In the Sharī'ah, it is an expression for whatever is in excess of the *farḍ* and the *wājib*. Its ruling (*ḥukm*) is that the person is rewarded for doing it but he is not culpable for omitting it. *Nafl* and *taṭawwu'* are synonyms [in the legal sense].

TERMINOLOGY

Dalīl qaṭ'ī: Definitive evidence
Farḍ: Obligatory
Wājib: Incumbent
Sunnah: Recommended/ Encouraged
Nafl/Taṭawwu': Supererogatory
'Azīmah: Regular act

QUESTIONS

1. What is the literal meaning of *farḍ*?
2. *Nafl* is an expression for excess. True or false?
3. How is *sunnah* defined?
4. *Wājib* is derived from definitive evidence. True or false?

❖

1.2: 'AZĪMAH (REGULAR ACT) AND RUKHṢAH (DISPENSATION)

'Azīmah (Regular Act)

'Azīmah is intention when it is done with utmost conviction, and hence, we [= the Ḥanafī jurists (Allah have mercy on them)] said: Indeed, the intention (*'azm*) to have sexual intercourse is a revocation in the category of *ẓihār* (injurious comparison), because it is like it [= the intended act] [already] exists, and so it is permitted to regard it as [already] existing when the indications [also] suggest. Hence, if someone said: 'أَعْزِمُ (*a'zimu* - I have a firm resolve),' he becomes one who has taken an oath.

In the Sharī'ah, it is an expression for whatever commands we bind ourselves to, initially. They are called *'azīmah* because they are done with utmost conviction due to the conviction of their *sabab*, which [in itself] is that the One giving the command is the One to

1 At-Tirmidhī, *al-Jāmi' al-Kabīr*, Kitāb al-'Ilm, Ch. Mā Jā fi'l-Akhdh bi's-Sunnah wa Ijtināb al-Bid'ah, Ḥadīth 2676, p.1921; Abū Dāwūd, *as-Sunan*, Kitāb as-Sunan, Ch. Fī Luzūm as-Sunnah, Ḥadīth 4607, p.1561; Ibn Mājah, *as-Sunan*, Kitāb as-Sunnah, Ch. Ittibā' Sunnat al-Khulafā ar-Rāshidīn al-Mahdiyyīn, Ḥadīth 42, p.2479; al-Ḥanbalī, *Jāmi' al-'Ulūm wa'l-Ḥikam*, etc.

whom [our] obedience is obligatory, with the ruling that He is our God, and we are His slaves.

The types of *ʿazīmah* are those that we [have already] mentioned among the *farḍ* and the *wājib*.

Rukhṣah (Dispensation)

As for *rukhṣah* (dispensation), it is an expression for ease and simplicity. In the Sharīʿah, it is to convert an affair from difficulty to ease by virtue of a [valid legal] excuse in the [legally] responsible person.

Its types vary according to the difference in their *sababs* and they are the [legal] excuses of people. The upshot is: in punishments, they are interpreted of two types:

i. One of the two is the *rukhṣah* (dispensation) of the act with the unlawfulness maintained, in the status of the waiver [of punishment] in the area of crime. This is similar to pronouncing words of disbelief with the tongue while the heart remains in contentment of faith when under duress, and [like] insulting the Holy Prophet ﷺ, destroying the property of a Muslim, and killing a person wrongfully.

   Its ruling is that if he remains patient [and refrains from committing the wrong] to the extent that he is killed, he shall be rewarded for his abstaining from the unlawful act out of reverence for the proscription from the Lawgiver ﷻ.

ii. The second type is the transformation of the nature of the act so that it becomes permissible in one's favour. Allah ﷻ said:

فَمَنِ ٱضْطُرَّ فِى مَخْمَصَةٍ غَيْرَ مُتَجَانِفٍ لِّإِثْمٍ ۙ فَإِنَّ ٱللَّهَ غَفُورٌ رَّحِيمٌ

'And whoever is compelled by severe hunger, not wilfully inclining to sin, then certainly Allah is Most-Forgiving, Ever-Merciful.' Qur'an, 5:3

   This is like the coercion to eat carrion and drink wine. Its ruling is that if one abstains from consuming it until he is killed, he shall be sinful for resisting something permitted, and he becomes like someone who commits suicide.

QUESTIONS

1. The *farḍ* and the *wājib* are among the *ʿazīmah*. True or false?
2. Linguistically, *ʿazīmah* is intention when it is done with utmost conviction. True or false?
3. What does *rukhṣah* (dispensation) mean linguistically?
4. Give an example of a *rukhṣah* (dispensation).

THE BOOK OF **ALLAH** ﷻ

2.1: KHĀṢṢ (SPECIFIC) AND ʿĀMM (GENERAL)

Khāṣṣ (Specific)

Khāṣṣ (specific) is a word devised for a known meaning or for a known article, individually. Such as our saying:

i. 'Zayd' to specify an individual,[2]

ii. 'Man' to specify a type [of group from humans],[3] or

iii. 'Human' to specify a genus [of creatures].[4]

ʿĀmm (General)

ʿĀmm (general) is every word that comprises[5] a group of individual entities:

i. either literally, as we say, 'مُسْلِمُوْنَ - Muslims', and 'مُشْرِكُوْنَ - Polytheists', or

ii. figuratively, as we say, 'مَنْ - Whoever', and 'مَا - Whatever'.

The Ruling of the *Khāṣṣ* from the Book of Allah ﷻ

The ruling of the *khāṣṣ* when from the Book of Allah ﷻ is an obligation to act upon it unreservedly.

If a solitary report (*khabar al-āḥād*)[6] or *qiyās* (analogical extrapolation) conflicts with it, both of them are acted upon[7] provided they can be combined without any alteration to the ruling of the *khāṣṣ*, otherwise the Book is acted upon and that which is against it is discarded.

EXAMPLE

Its example is in the saying of Allah ﷻ:

وَٱلْمُطَلَّقَٰتُ يَتَرَبَّصْنَ بِأَنفُسِهِنَّ ثَلَٰثَةَ قُرُوٓءٍ

'Divorced women must wait with themselves for three menstrual periods.'
Qur'an, 2:228

Indeed, the word 'ثَلَاثَة - three' is *khāṣṣ* in determining a known number, and so it is incumbent to act by it.

If the word 'قُرْء - *qur'*' was taken to mean 'طُهْر - *ṭuhr*',[8] as Imam ash-Shāfiʿī (Allah have mercy on him) has suggested, on account of

2 This is *khāṣṣ al-fard*, also known as *khāṣṣ al-ʿayn*.

3 This is *khāṣṣ an-nawʿ*.

4 This is known as *khāṣṣ al-jins*.

5 According to this definition, the comprisal of devised words is of two types: i. literal – the *ʿāmm* comprises its individuals in word and form, like the words cars and houses, etc., ii. figurative – the *ʿāmm* comprises its individuals in the figurative sense without any recourse to its word or form, like the words the car and the company, etc.

6 *Khabar al-āḥād* (solitary report): a category of narrations that do not reach the level of *mutawātir* (continuously mass-transmitted).

7 The *khāṣṣ* and the solitary report or *qiyās*.

8 طُهْر (*ṭuhr*) is the state of purity between two periods of menstrual bleeding.

the word 'طُهْر - ṭuhr' being masculine whereas the word 'حَيْض - ḥayḍ (menstruation)' is not, the Book of Allah ﷻ has mentioned a plural with the word in its feminine form.[9] This proves that it is the plural of a masculine word, which is 'طُهْر - ṭuhr'.

This obliges the omission of acting upon the *khāṣṣ* because whoever takes it to mean 'طُهْر - ṭuhr' cannot obligate three periods of purity, but rather only two periods of purity and a portion of the third (which is that wherein the divorce took place). Thus, what derives from this is:

i. the ruling of retracting the divorce in the third menstrual period or its elapsing,
ii. the validity or invalidity of marrying someone else,
iii. the ruling of withholding or freeing [the divorcée],
iv. [the ruling of providing] lodging and maintenance,
v. [the ruling of] divorce at the instance of the wife (*al-khulʿ*),
vi. the issuance of [another] divorce,
vii. the husband marrying her sister,
viii. [marriage to] four women other than her, and
ix. the many rulings of inheritance.

EXAMPLE

Likewise, is the saying of Allah ﷻ:

قَدْ عَلِمْنَا مَا فَرَضْنَا عَلَيْهِمْ فِيٓ أَزْوَٰجِهِمْ

'We know what We enjoined upon them concerning their wives.'
Qur'an, 33:50

It is *khāṣṣ* in a legal determination. Acting upon it shall not be omitted because it is reckoned to be a financial agreement, and so it shall be reckoned with financial agreements; thus, the determination of the *mahr* shall be delegated to the opinion of the couple, as suggested by Imam ash-Shāfiʿī (Allah have mercy on him).

Imam ash-Shāfiʿī (Allah have mercy on him) has deduced the following based on this:

i. Devotion to optional worship is better than being occupied with marriage.
ii. He permitted ending the marriage with divorce howsoever the husband sees fit, collectively or separately.
iii. He permitted the issuance of three in one go.
iv. He rendered the marriage agreement rescindable by way of *khulʿ* (divorce at the instance of the wife in exchange for wealth).[10]

9 In Arabic grammar of numerals, if the object that is counted is between 3 to 10, the word used for the number will be opposite to the gender of the counted object, i.e. if the noun for the counted object is masculine, the number appears in the feminine and vice versa.

10 This is known to be the Ḥanbalī stance, not the Shāfiʿī stance.

TERMINOLOGY

Khāṣṣ: Specific
ʿĀmm: General
Ijmāʿ: Scholarly consensus
Qiyās: Analogical extrapolation
Khabar al-āḥād: Solitary report

Likewise, the saying of Allah ﷻ:

فَلَا تَحِلُّ لَهُۥ مِنۢ بَعْدُ حَتَّىٰ تَنكِحَ زَوْجًا غَيْرَهُۥ ۗ

'She shall no longer remain lawful for him unless she marries a partner other than him.' Qur'an, 2:230

is *khāṣṣ* in the validity of marriage coming from the woman. Thus, acting upon it is not abandoned because of that which has been reported from the Prophet ﷺ:

أَيُّمَا اِمْرَأَةٍ نَكَحَتْ نَفْسَهَا بِغَيْرِ إِذْنِ وَلِيِّهَا فَنِكَاحُهَا بَاطِلٌ، بَاطِلٌ، بَاطِلٌ.

'Any woman who marries herself without the consent of her guardian, her marriage is void, void, void!'

The Disagreements Arising from This Issue

From this, arises the disagreement in:

i. the lawfulness of sexual intercourse,

ii. the obligation of the *mahr* and maintenance and providing lodging,

iii. the effectiveness of divorce, and

iv. marriage after the issuance of three divorces in accordance with what his early disciples have suggested, as opposed to what the later scholars have adopted.

QUESTIONS

1. There are five principles of Islamic jurisprudence that are agreed upon. True or false?
2. Discuss the main differences between the *khāṣṣ* (specific) and the *ʿāmm* (general).
3. What happens when a solitary report (*khabar al-āḥād*) or analogical extrapolation (*qiyās*) conflict with the *khāṣṣ* of the Qur'an?
4. Is it incumbent to act upon the *khāṣṣ?*
5. Discuss two disagreements that arise from the way that Imam ash-Shāfiʿī (Allah have mercy on him) and Imam Abū Ḥanīfah (Allah have mercy on him) use the *khāṣṣ* (specific) in verse 2:230.

❖

ʿĀmm and Its Types

As for the ʿ*āmm*, it has two types:

i. ʿ*Āmm* from which a portion has been specified, and

ii. ʿ*Āmm* from which nothing has been specified.

The Ruling of the Second Type

As for the ʿ*āmm* from which nothing has been specified, it is unquestionably of the status of *khāṣṣ* in terms of the obligation to act upon it.

EXAMPLE

Based on this, we say: When the hand of the thief is amputated after the stolen item perishes whilst in his possession, there is no compensation due from him because the amputation is the punishment for everything the thief had committed.

Indeed, the word 'مَا - *mā*' is ʿ*āmm*. It incorporates everything that emanated from the thief; if compensation was obliged then that punishment [i.e. compensation] would be all-inclusive. Thus, acting upon it is not to be abandoned by analogy with expropriation (*ghaṣb*).

Evidence of مَا being ʿĀmm

The evidence that the word 'مَا - (*mā*)' is ʿ*āmm* is that which Muhammad[11] mentioned: When a master says to his slave-woman, 'إِنْ كَانَ مَا فِيْ بَطْنِكِ غُلَامًا فَأَنْتِ حُرَّةٌ (If whatever is in your womb is a boy then you are free),' and then she gives birth to a boy and a girl, she is not freed.

Similarly, we say in the words of Allah ﷻ:

فَٱقْرَءُوا۟ مَا تَيَسَّرَ مِنَ ٱلْقُرْءَانِ ۚ

'So, recite whatever of the Qur'an is easy.' Qur'an, 73:20

So it is ʿ*āmm* for 'whatever is easy from the Qur'an', and it is necessary not to restrict the permission to reciting only Sūrat al-Fātiḥah.

It came in a report that he [= the Prophet Muhammad ﷺ] said:

لَا صَلَاةَ إِلَّا بِفَاتِحَةِ الْكِتَابِ.

'There is no prayer without the Fātiḥah.'

However, we act upon both of these in such a manner that the ruling of the Book does not change; that we take the report to mean 'incompleteness', so that general recitation becomes an obligation (*farḍ*) by the ruling of the Book and reciting al-Fātiḥah becomes incumbent (*wājib*) by the ruling of the report.

Likewise, we say in the words of Allah ﷻ:

---

11 Imam Muhammad (Allah have mercy on him).

وَلَا تَأْكُلُوا مِمَّا لَمْ يُذْكَرِ ٱسْمُ ٱللَّهِ عَلَيْهِ

'Do not eat [the meat] over whatever the name of Allah has not been pronounced.' Qur'an, 6:121

This gives cause to the unlawfulness of deliberately omitting pronouncement of the name of Allah ﷻ.

It came in a report that the Prophet ﷺ was asked regarding the deliberate omission of pronouncing the name of Allah ﷻ, and so he replied:

كُلُوْهُ فَإِنَّ تَسْمِيَةَ اللّٰهِ تَعَالَى فِيْ قَلْبِ كُلِّ امْرِئٍ مُسْلِمٍ.

'Eat it, for the pronouncement of the name of Allah ﷻ is present in the heart of every Muslim.'[12]

It is not possible to bring about an amalgamation between the two because if lawfulness [of the slaughtered animal] was established by deliberately omitting it [= the pronouncement of the name of Allah ﷻ] then that would establish lawfulness by unintentionally omitting it, ﷻ and this way the ruling of the Book would be erased. Thus, the report is omitted.

Likewise, is the saying of Allah ﷻ:

وَأُمَّهَٰتُكُمُ ٱلَّٰتِيٓ أَرْضَعْنَكُمْ

'And your mothers who breastfed you.' Qur'an, 4:23

This verse necessitates, by its generality, the unlawfulness of marrying the woman who breastfed him.

It appeared in a report:

لَا تُحَرِّمُ الْمَصَّةُ وَلَا الْمَصَّتَانِ وَلَا الْإِمْلَاجَةُ وَلَا الْإِمْلَاجَتَانِ.

'Breastfeeding once or twice does not render [marriage] unlawful, and nor does feeding once or twice.'

Amalgamation is not possible between the two, so the report is abandoned.

The Ruling of the First Type

As for the *ʿāmm* from which a portion has been specified, its ruling is that it is incumbent to act upon the remainder with the possibility of further specification.

When evidence stands to specify the remainder, then it is possible to specify it with a solitary report (*khabar al-āḥād*) or via *qiyās* (analogical extrapolation) until there remain only three, after which specifying it is not allowed, and so it is incumbent to act upon it.[13]

That is permitted because if the specifier – that which excludes a portion from the whole – excludes some unknown portion, the possibility is established for each specified individual because:

---

12 *Musannaf Abd ar-Razzaq*, bab at-tasmiyah ind adh-dhabh.

13 This is because if less than three people practise it, it shall not remain *ʿāmm* (general). The minimum amount required for plural in Arabic is three.

i. it is permitted for it to remain under the ruling of *ʿāmm*, and

ii. it is permitted for it to enter the evidence of being specific.

Both sides are equal in relation to the specified individual. Thus, if legal evidence is established that it is a part of the whole that is included in the evidence of being specific then the probability of it being specific is weightier. However, if the specifier excludes a known portion from the whole, it is permitted for it to be explained by an *ʿillah* (effective cause) that exists in this specified individual. Therefore, when legal evidence stands to prove the existence of that *ʿillah* in anything other than that specified individual, then the probability of it being specific shall be given preference and it shall be acted upon with the possibility of specification of the remainder.

QUESTIONS

1. There are four types of *ʿāmm* (general). True or false?
2. How do we treat the *ʿāmm* that has not been specified?
3. If a thief has their hand amputated after the stolen item perishes, why is no compensation due from the thief?
4. How do we treat the *ʿāmm* from which a portion has been specified?
5. Can the *ʿāmm* that has been specified be further specified?

❖

The difference between the two is in their expression i.e. whether that word considers or entertains the possibility of a group(s) or not in its meaning:

- If it does not: specific (such as male or human).
- If it does: general (such as Muslims and disbelievers).

The general can be divided into two types:

i. Nothing is specified from it.

ii. Part of it is specified (*takhṣīs*).

POINTS TO NOTE

- Legal reasoning in Islamic law requires being able to differentiate between the general (*ʿāmm*) and the specific (*khāṣṣ*).
- The need to identify linguistic patterns.
- While the general (*ʿāmm*) and the specific (*khāṣṣ*) are distinguishable conceptually, they do not always appear in the grammatical forms of words.
- Scholars have developed methods to distinguish between the general (*ʿāmm*) and the specific (*khāṣṣ*).

2.2: MUṬLAQ (UNRESTRICTED) AND MUQAYYAD (RESTRICTED)

Muṭlaq (Unrestricted)

Our scholars went with the view that when the unrestrictedness of the *muṭlaq* statement from the Book of Allah ﷻ is possible to act on, then adding to it, by way of solitary reports or analogical reasoning, is impermissible.

EXAMPLE

Its example is in the saying of Allah ﷻ:

فَٱغْسِلُوا۟ وُجُوهَكُمْ

'Then wash your faces.' Qur'an, 5:6

The command given is unrestricted washing. Thus, the conditions of intention, sequence, continuity, and pronouncing the basmalah, cannot be added to with reports. However, the report is applied in a manner that the ruling of the Book does not change by it. Thus, it may be said that unrestricted washing is an obligation by the ruling of the Book, and the intention is a *sunnah* by the ruling of the report.

Likewise, we say regarding the words of Allah ﷻ:

ٱلزَّانِيَةُ وَٱلزَّانِى فَٱجْلِدُوا۟ كُلَّ وَٰحِدٍ مِّنْهُمَا مِا۟ئَةَ جَلْدَةٍ

'The fornicatress and the fornicator, flog each one of them [with] a hundred stripes.' Qur'an, 24:2

The Book ﷻ has rendered the hundred lashes a *ḥadd* (divine statutory)[14] punishment for fornication. Thus, banishment cannot be added as a *ḥadd* punishment to it due to the saying of the Prophet ﷺ:

اَلْبِكْرُ بِالْبِكْرِ جَلْدُ مِائَةٍ وَّتَغْرِيْبُ عَامٍ.

'The [fornication of a] virgin with a virgin [warrants] one hundred lashes and banishment for one year.'

Therefore, the report will be acted upon in a manner that the ruling of the Book does not change by it, that is, lashing will be the legal *ḥadd* punishment based on the ruling of the Book, and banishment will be politically legislated[15] based on the ruling of the report.

Likewise, in the saying of Allah ﷻ:

وَلْيَطَّوَّفُوا۟ بِٱلْبَيْتِ ٱلْعَتِيقِ

'And they must circle the Ancient House.' Qur'an, 22:29

---

14 *Ḥadd* offences (pl. *ḥudūd*), i.e. punishments for contraventions of the limits, are the rights of Allah ﷻ alone and no one is permitted to vest these rights.

15 Politically legislated refers to the opinion of the ruler or any other political supreme body or individual of the state. Banishment shall apply according to the opinion of such ruler or governing body. (Al-Qudūrī, *Mukhtaṣar*, p.542).

This is *muṭlaq* in mentioning the circumambulation of the House, which is why the condition of wudu is not added to it by way of the report.

However, it is acted upon in a manner that the ruling of the Book does not change by it; that is, unrestricted circumambulation is *farḍ* based on the ruling of the Book and wudu is *wājib* based on the ruling of the report. Hence, repairing the binding deficiency due to omission of the *wājib* wudu is done with a slaughter.

Likewise, is the saying of Allah ﷻ:

وَٱرْكَعُوا۟ مَعَ ٱلرَّٰكِعِينَ

'And bow with those who bow.' Qur'an, 2:43

This is *muṭlaq* in mentioning the bowing posture (*rukūʿ*), so the condition of *ta'dil*[16] is not added to it because of the report.[17]

However, the report is acted upon in a manner that the ruling of the Book does not change by it; that is unrestricted bowing is *farḍ* based on the ruling of the Book and the *ta'dil* is *wājib* based on the ruling of the report.

It is on this basis we said that it is permitted to perform wudu with saffron water and with all water in which something pure became mixed with then one of its properties changed[18] because the condition of resorting to *tayammum* is due to the absence of unrestricted water and this is still unrestricted water. Indeed, the restriction of the genitive construction did not remove the name 'water' from it; rather, it confirmed it, hence it enters under the ruling of unrestricted water and the condition of it remaining on the description of 'Water sent down from the sky' is a restriction of this *muṭlaq*.

From this is derived the ruling for:

i. saffron water,

ii. soap water, and

iii. saltwort[19] water, etc.

Impure water is excluded from this issue based upon the saying of Allah ﷻ:

وَلَٰكِن يُرِيدُ لِيُطَهِّرَكُمْ

'But He wants to purify you.' Qur'an, 5:6

whereas impurity does not give the benefit of purification.

With this indication, it is known that ritual impurity (*ḥadath*) is a condition for wudu to be incumbent, for surely it is impossible to achieve purity without there being ritual impurity.

Imam Abū Ḥanīfah (Allah have mercy on him) said:

16 *Ta'dil* is to complete each pillar of the prayer for a satisfactory amount of time.

17 Al-Bukhārī, *al-Jāmiʿ aṣ-Ṣaḥīḥ*, Kitāb aṣ-Ṣalāh.

18 The properties of water are three: colour, flavour and odour.

19 A plant that the Arabs would burn/dry, grind and then use as a cleaning agent.

“

TERMINOLOGY

ʿIllah: Effective cause

Ghaṣb: Expropriation

Muṭlaq: Unrestricted

Muqayyad: Unrestricted

Ẓihār: A pre-Islamic method of divorce by resembling one's wife or a part of her to an unmarriageable female relative

Ḥadd: Divine statutory punishment

Aṣb: Expropriation

”

'When a man who commits *ẓihār* (injurious comparison)[20] has sexual intercourse with his wife during [the expiation of] feeding, he does not restart the feeding afresh, because the Book is *muṭlaq* with regards to the feeding, and so the condition of not having sexual contact[21] cannot be added to it, using analogy with fasting,[22] but the *muṭlaq* continues upon its unrestrictedness and the *muqayyad* upon its restrictedness.'

Likewise, we say that the slave for the expiation of *ẓihār* and expiation of an oath is *muṭlaq*; the condition of faith is not added to it using analogy with the expiation for homicide.[23]

Contention 1

If it was said: Indeed, the Book obliges wiping an unrestricted portion when wiping the head, and you have restricted it to the extent of the forelock by basing it on a report.

Contention 2

The Book is *muṭlaq* in the ending of the major prohibition by marriage, but you have restricted it to sex after the second marriage using the *ḥadīth* of Rifāʿah's wife.

Response to Contention 1

We say: The Book is not *muṭlaq* with regards to wiping, because surely the ruling of the *muṭlaq* is that when the one practising it does so in any of its entities, he is deemed to have duly fulfilled the command, but the one practising any portion of it here is in essence not complying with what has been commanded because if he wipes over a half or two-thirds then the whole of it will not be obligatory.[24] With this, the *muṭlaq* (unrestricted) differed from the *mujmal* (ambiguous).

Response to Contention 2

As for the restriction of consummation of marriage, some have said: The word 'نِكَاحْ - *nikāḥ*' in the scripture means sexual intercourse, because the contract is deduced from the word 'زَوْجْ - *zawj* (partner).' With this the question no longer remains.

Also, some said: The restriction of consummation of marriage is proven by the report, and they deemed to be one of the *mash'hūr* (well-known reports),[25] thus restricting the Book with solitary reports is not binding upon them.

---

20 *Ẓihār*: The husband's unlawful comparison of his wife, equating her with the back of his own mother and thereby prohibiting intercourse with her.

21 This includes kissing, touching, fondling and sexual intercourse.

22 The one who makes the injurious comparison and is fasting for two consecutive months for expiation shall begin fasting the two months anew if he has sexual contact with his wife during that period.

23 The expiation in quasi-intentional (*shibh al-'amd*) and unintentional (*al-khaṭa'*) homicide is to free one Muslim slave.

24 This proves that the Qur'anic verse is not unrestricted. Moreover, the ḥadīth reported by al-Mughīrah ibn Shu'bah (Allah be pleased with him), that the Prophet ﷺ arrived at the camp of a tribe and urinated. He then performed wudu and wiped over his forelock and his leather socks.

25 *Mash'hūr* report: It is a ḥadīth that is reported by a large number of narrators

QUESTIONS

1. When can the *muṭlaq* be restricted?
2. How do Ḥanafīs respond to the contention that ending of major prohibition and separation has been restricted by a ḥadīth?
3. Why is wudu not a condition for the validity of *tawāf* in the Ḥanafī school?
4. Banishment of the fornicator is established by the *muṭlaq* of the Qur'an. True or false?

❖

2.3: MUSHTARAK (HOMONYMOUS), MU'AWWAL (CONSTRUED), AND MUFASSAR (ELABORATED)

Mushtarak (Homonymous)

Mushtarak is that which is devised for two different meanings, or for several meanings of differing nature.

EXAMPLE

Its example is our saying: 'جَارِيَةٌ - *jāriyah*'; it incorporates 'a slave-girl' as well as 'a boat', and: 'المُشْتَرِي - *al-mushtarī*'; it incorporates 'someone who accepts a sales transaction' as well as 'a planet in the sky (i.e. Jupiter)'.

And our saying: 'بَائِنٌ - *bā'in*'; it implies 'البَيْن - *al-bayn* (separation)' as well as 'البَيَان - *al-bayān* (explanation)'.

The Ruling of the Mushtarak

The ruling of the *mushtarak* is that when one meaning becomes distinguished as the intended meaning, consideration of the intention of any other meaning is omitted.

For this reason, the scholars (Allah have mercy on them) have unanimously agreed that the meaning of the word 'قُرُوْءٌ - *qurū*" that is mentioned in the Book of Allah ﷻ, is taken to mean 'حَيْضٌ - *ḥayḍ* (menses)' – as is our orientation, or to mean 'طُهْرٌ - *ṭuhr* (purity)' – as is the orientation of Imam ash-Shāfi'ī (Allah have mercy on him).

Abū Ḥanīfah and Imam Muhammad (Allah have mercy on them) said: When someone bequeaths to the 'مَوَالِي – *mawālī* (masters or freedmen)'[26] of such-and-such a tribe, and that tribe has *mawalī* in the upper degree [i.e. masters] as well as *mawālī* in the lower degree [i.e. freedmen], then he dies, the bequest is void in relation

---

but not reaching the quantum for it to become *mutawātir* (continuously mass-transmitted).

26 موالي (*mawālī*) is the plural for مولى (*mawlā*), and, being a homonym, it carries the meaning of 'master' in the upper degree, as well as 'freedman' in the lower degree.

> **TERMINOLOGY**
>
> *Mushtarak*: Homonymous
> *Mu'awwal*: Construed
> *Mufassar*: Elaborated
> *Mawālī*: Freed slave; slavemaster

to both degrees based on the impossibility of their amalgamation, and the absence of preponderance.

Abū Ḥanīfah (Allah have mercy on him) said: When someone says to his wife, 'أَنْتِ عَلَيَّ مِثْلُ أُمِّي (You are like my mother to me),' he does not commit injurious comparison (*ẓihār*), because the utterance is *mushtarak* between 'reverence' and 'prohibition'. Hence, the perspective of 'prohibition' shall not be preponderant except with an intention.

Due to this we said: It is not incumbent to repay with like-for-like in recompense for hunting game, basing it on the saying of Allah ﷻ:

فَجَزَآءٌ مِّثْلُ مَا قَتَلَ مِنَ ٱلنَّعَمِ يَحْكُمُ بِهِۦ

'... then compensation is from domestic flocks similar to what one has killed.' Qur'an, 5:95

That is because 'مِثْل - *mithl* (like/similar to)' is *mushtarak* (homonymous) between the practical similarity and the theoretical similarity (which is the price). In this scripture theoretical similarity is intended by 'مِثْل - *mithl* (like/similar to)' for the killing of a pigeon or a sparrow, etc. by agreement, and thus practical similarity is not added, because there is no generality in the *mushtarak* whatsoever, so consideration of the practical similarity is omitted due to the impossibility of amalgamation.

Mu'awwal (Construed)

Thereafter, when one aspect of the *mushtarak* is preponderant with overwhelming inclination of the mind, it becomes *mu'awwal* (construed).

The Ruling of the Mu'awwal

The ruling of the *mu'awwal* is obligation to act upon it albeit with the possibility of error.

EXAMPLE

Its example in legal rulings is what we said: When one does not specify the payment in the sale, it is according to the predominant currency of the land.[27] This is by the method of construing the meaning (*ta'wīl*). If there are different currencies, the sale is invalid, due to what we mentioned.[28]

Some Inferences

Taking 'الأقراءُ - *al-aqrā"* to mean 'حَيْضٌ - *ḥayḍ* (menstruation)', taking 'نِكَاحٌ - *nikāḥ*' in the verse[29] to mean 'وَطْءٌ - *waṭy* (sexual intercourse)' and taking allegorical statements during a discussion of divorce to mean 'طَلَاقٌ - *ṭalāq* (divorce)' are of this type.[30]

27 See al-Qudūrī, *Mukhtaṣar*, p.157.

28 Ibid.

29 Qur'an: فَلَا تَحِلُّ لَهُۥ مِنۢ بَعْدُ حَتَّىٰ تَنكِحَ زَوْجًا غَيْرَهُۥ

'She shall no longer remain lawful for him unless she marries a man other than him.' (Qur'an, 2:230).

30 See al-Qudūrī, *Mukhtaṣar*, p.412.

Due to this, we said: The debt that inhibits one from paying *zakāh* resorts to the easier of the two types of wealth in order to clear the debt.

Imam Muhammad (Allah have mercy on him) inferred from this hence he said: When one marries a woman for the *niṣāb*[31] when he owns the *niṣāb* of sheep and the *niṣāb* of dirhams, the debt is resorted to the dirhams, such that when one year passes on them both *zakāh* is obliged on him from the *niṣāb* of the sheep but not of the dirhams.

Mufassar (Elaborated)

If one of the meanings of the *mushtarak* is preponderant by an explanation from the part of the speaker, it becomes *mufassar*.

The Ruling of Mufassar

Its ruling is that it is incumbent to act upon it with certainty.

EXAMPLE

Its example occurs when one says: 'I owe so-and-so ten dirhams of Bukhara currency,' then his words 'of Bukhara currency,' are an elaboration for him.[32]

Had it not been so, it would resort to the predominant currency of the land by the method of *ta'wīl*.[33] Thus, *mufassar* is preferred, and therefore, the predominant currency of the land is not due.

POINTS TO NOTE

- *'Āmm* is expressed once and includes a group of individuals based on a single meaning assigned to it by the Arabs.
- *Mushtarak* was assigned by the Arabs multiple times for different meanings at different periods, so it carries only one of those meanings at different periods at any one time.

QUESTIONS

1. What is the ruling of the *mu'awwal*?
2. Give an example of the *mufassar*.
3. How does something become *mufassar*?
4. The word *jāriyah*, meaning 'slave-girl', also means 'boat'. True or false?
5. If someone says to their wife, 'You are like my mother to me', what is the outcome?

31 The minimum amount of property obliging payment of *zakāh*.

32 These words make it *mufassar*.

33 By *ta'wīl*, it becomes *mu'awwal*.

2.4: ḤAQĪQAH (LITERAL) AND MAJĀZ (METAPHORICAL)

Ḥaqīqah (Literal)

Every word that the semanticist composed corresponding to a thing is *ḥaqīqah* for that thing.

Majāz (Metaphorical)

If it is used otherwise, then it is *majāz* not *ḥaqīqah*.

The Ruling of Ḥaqīqah and Majāz

Thereafter, *ḥaqīqah* and *majāz* do not come together as an intention from one word in one state.

EXAMPLE

Due to this, we said: When what is intended is that which is placed in a 'صَاعٌ - *ṣā*ʿ',[34] by his statement ﷺ:

لَا تَبِيْعُوا الدِّرْهَمَ بِالدِّرْهَمَيْنِ وَلَا الصَّاعَ بِالصَّاعَيْنِ

'Do not sell one dirham for two dirhams, nor one ṣāʿ [of measured product] for two ṣāʿs.'[35]

then consideration of the *ṣā*ʿ in and of itself is omitted, inasmuch as that the sale of one (*ṣā*ʿ) for two is permitted.[36]

And when 'وِقَاعٌ - *wiqā*ʿ (sexual intercourse)' is intended by the verse of 'مُلَامَسَةٌ - *mulāmasah* (making sexual contact),'[37] then consideration of intending 'touching with the hand' is omitted.

Imam Muhammad (Allah have mercy on him) said: When one bequeaths to his freedmen[38] – when he has freedmen whom he has manumitted and his freedmen also have freedmen[39] whom they have manumitted – the bequest is for his freedmen [i.e. the primary freedmen], and not for the freedmen of his freedmen [i.e. the secondary freedmen].

In *as-Siyar al-Kabīr*:[40] If the combatants in a war seek protection for their fathers, grandfathers are not included in that protection, if they seek protection for their mothers, protection is not established for grandmothers.

---

34 *Ṣā'* is a dry volumetric measure equal to 3.362 litres (Ḥanafī) and it is used in *ḥaqīqah* as a standard for a specific measuring tool, but as *majāz* it refers to whatever is measured in it.

35 Similar wording of the ḥadīth has been narrated in the *Musnad* of Imam Ahmad (109/2), in al-Bukhari (2178), Muslim (1585) and Ibn Majah (2256).

36 When the thing measured in it is of a different category.

37 Qur'an: أَوْ لَٰمَسْتُمُ ٱلنِّسَآءَ

'... or you have made sexual contact with [your] women ....' Qur'an, 4:43; 5:6.

38 In this case, they shall be the primary freedmen.

39 In this case, they shall be the secondary freedmen.

40 *As-Siyar al-Kabīr*: This is Imam Muḥammad ash-Shaybānī's (131 AH/749 CE – 189 AH/805 CE) magnum opus, in his *ẓāhir ar-riwāyah*, discussing and highlighting the rules and laws of military conduct.

Upon this, we said: If one bequeaths for the female virgins of such-and-such a tribe, the woman who lost her virginity in a sinful manner does not enter the ruling of the bequest.

If one bequeaths for the children of so-and-so – when that person has children and grandchildren – the bequest is for his children and not his grandchildren.

Our companions (Allah have mercy on them) have said: If one swears an oath that he will not engage in 'نِكَاحٌ - *nikāḥ*' with such-and-such a woman who is a female non-relative then it means the marriage contract inasmuch as that if he commits unlawful sexual intercourse (*zinā*) with her, he does not violate his oath.

Contention 1

If one says: When someone swears an oath that he will not set foot inside the house of so-and-so, he violates his oath if he enters it barefoot, wearing shoes, or mounted.

Contention 2

Likewise, if he swears an oath that he will not live in the house of so-and-so, he violates it if the house is the property of that person, or if it was on rent or on loan. This is an amalgamation of *ḥaqīqah* and *majāz*.

Contention 3

Likewise, if he says that this slave shall be a freeman the day so-and-so arrives, and then that person arrives by night or by day, he violates his oath.[41]

Response to Contention 1

We said: 'To set foot in' has become *majāz* for entry, based upon the ruling of custom (*ʿurf*), and entry does not vary in either state.[42]

Response to Contention 2

'The house of so-and-so' has become *majāz* for the house that is a dwelling for him, and therefore, it does not differ whether he owns the property or he rents it.

Response to Contention 3

And 'day' in the issue of arrival denotes unrestricted time, because when the word 'day' is ascribed to an action that is not continuous, it denotes absoluteness of the time, as is well known.[43]

Hence, the violation of the oath occurs in this manner and not by an amalgamation of *haqīqah* and *majāz*.

TERMINOLOGY

Ḥaqīqah: Literal

Majāz: Metaphorical

Ḥaqīqah Mustaʿmalah: Employed Literal Meaning

Mutaʿadhdhirah: Unfeasible

ʿUrf: Customary practice

Wiqāʿ: Sexual intercourse

---

41 The advent of that specific person manumits the slave of the oath-taker.

42 The *ḥaqīqah* or *majāz* – whether one enters barefoot, wearing shoes, or mounted.

43 As opposed to him ascribing it to an action that is continuous like 'wearing' or 'riding', for e.g. one would say 'I wore the garment for a day' or 'I drove the car for two days.' Hence, in this scenario it means a 24-hour period.

Types of Ḥaqīqah

Thereafter, *ḥaqīqah* is of three types:

i. *muta'adhdhirah* – متعذّرة (unfeasible),[44]

ii. *mahjūrah* – مهجورة (abandoned),[45] and

iii. *musta'malah* – مستَعمَلة (employed).[46]

The Ruling of Ḥaqīqah Muta'adhdhirah (Unfeasible Literal Meaning) and Ḥaqīqah Mahjūrah (Abandoned Literal Meaning)

In the first two types, by agreement, the *majāz* is applied.

Example of Ḥaqīqah Muta'adhdhirah

An example of *muta'adhdhirah* occurs when one swears an oath that he will not eat from this particular tree or from this particular pot – for it is certainly unfeasible to eat the tree or the pot – then it applies to the fruit of the tree or to whatever is in the pot, such that if he eats the tree *per se* or the pot *per se* by taking the trouble, he does not violate his oath.

Based on this we said: When one swears an oath that he will not drink from 'this well', it applies to 'scooping', such that if we hypothesised that he sipped directly from it by taking the trouble, he does not violate his oath by an agreement.

Example of Ḥaqīqah Mahjūrah

An illustration of *mahjūrah* is if one swears an oath that he will not set foot inside the house of so-and-so, then the intention of literally 'setting foot' is abandoned according to custom.

It is on this principle that we said: Appointing an advocate for a lawsuit in and of itself applies to the unrestricted response to the litigant, such that it allows the agent to answer with 'yes' just as it allows for him to answer with 'no' because appointing an advocate for a lawsuit in and of itself is abandoned by the Sharī'ah[47] and customarily.

The Ruling of Ḥaqīqah Musta'malah (Employed Literal Meaning)

If the *ḥaqīqah* is *musta'malah* and does not have a conventional *majāz*, then the *ḥaqīqah* is inarguably the most appropriate.

If, however, it does have a conventional *majāz*, then the *ḥaqīqah* is the most appropriate – according to Abū Ḥanīfah (Allah have mercy on him), but according to Abū Yūsuf and Muhammad (Allah have mercy on them), acting upon the generality of the *majāz* is the most appropriate.

---

44 *Muta'adhdhirah*: that *ḥaqīqah* which cannot be achieved normally.

45 *Mahjūrah*: that *ḥaqīqah* which is not used by people even though it may be easily achievable.

46 *Musta'malah*: that *ḥaqīqah* which is used by people and is easily achievable.

47 This is because the Sharī'ah has prohibited dispute.

Example of Ḥaqīqah Mustaʻmalah

Its example is if one swears an oath that he will not eat from this ear of wheat, it applies to the actual wheat itself – according to Abū Ḥanīfah (Allah have mercy on him), such that if he eats bread produced from it, he does not violate his oath – according to him (Allah have mercy on him), but according to Abū Yūsuf and Muhammad (Allah have mercy on them), it applies to what the ear of wheat implies according to the generality of the *majāz*. Thus, he violates his oath by eating it, as well as by eating the bread produced from it.

Likewise, if he swears an oath that he will not drink from the Euphrates, it applies to sipping from it directly – according to Abū Ḥanīfah (Allah have mercy on him), but according to Abū Yūsuf and Muhammad (Allah have mercy on them), it applies to the conventional *majāz*, which is drinking its water in any manner.

Majāz is Substitute to Ḥaqīqah

Thereafter, according to Abū Ḥanīfah (Allah have mercy on him) the *majāz* is a substitute to the *ḥaqīqah* in terms of the wording, whereas, according to Abū Yūsuf and Muhammad (Allah have mercy on them), it is a substitute to the *ḥaqīqah* in terms of the ruling, such that if the *ḥaqīqah* is possible *per se*, but acting upon it is impeded due to an impediment, it will end up as the *majāz*, otherwise the statement becomes null. According to Abū Ḥanīfah (Allah have mercy on him) it will end up as the *majāz* even if the *ḥaqīqah* is not possible *per se*.

EXAMPLE

Its example occurs when one says about his slave who is older than him in age: 'This is my son,' it is not applied to the *majāz* – according to Abū Yūsuf and Muhammad (Allah have mercy on them) – due to the impossibility of the *ḥaqīqah*. According to Abū Ḥanīfah (Allah have mercy on him)], it is applied to the *majāz* – such that the slave is freed.[48]

Moreover, on this principle the ruling is derived about one's statement: 'I owe him a thousand,' or 'This wall owes a thousand,' or his saying, 'My slave is free,' or 'My donkey is free.'

Response to a Contention

It is not incumbent based on this if one says about his wife, 'This is my daughter,' when she has a well-known parentage from someone else, such that she does not become unlawful to him. Furthermore, it is not rendered *majāz* for divorce, irrespective of whether the woman is younger than him in age or older because this wording (if its meaning was valid) would have been inconsistent with marriage, so it would be inconsistent with its ruling – which is divorce; and there is no *istiʻārah* (metaphor) with a presence of inconsistency.

48 The *majāz* is a substitute to the *ḥaqīqah* in wording and therefore the latter may take the meaning of the former, in which case the slave shall be set free.

As opposed to one's saying, 'This is my son,' because filiation does not negate the establishment of ownership for the father, but rather, ownership is established for him [the father] and then he [the son] is set free from him [the son].

POINTS TO NOTE

- Literal: A word that corresponds to what it is expressed for. "Lion" corresponds to an animal that is a predator. "Salāh" corresponds to a specific form of worship.
- Metaphorical: A word used for a meaning other than what it was coined for because there is some relationship, such as "lion" to describe a strong or brave person. Ruling: Its meaning is affirmed for what it is expressed whether specific or general.

QUESTIONS

1. What happens if a person swears an oath that he will not drink from the Euphrates? Discuss both views.
2. Give an example of the *ḥaqīqah mahjūrah*.
3. How do Ḥanafīs respond to the contention that when someone swears an oath that he will not set foot inside the house of so-and-so, he violates his oath if he enters it barefoot, wearing shoes, or mounted?
4. The *ḥaqīqah* and *majāz* do not come together as an intention from one word in one state. True or false?

❖

2.5: ISTIʿĀRAH (METAPHOR)

Types of Istiʿārah

Know that *istiʿārah* (metaphor) in the rulings of the Sharīʿah is consistent in two ways:

i. one of the two is due to the existence of a connection between the *ʿillah* (cause) and the *ḥukm* (ruling), and
ii. the second is due to the existence of a connection between the pure *sabab* (reason) and the *ḥukm*.

The Ruling of the First Type

The first of the two necessitates the soundness of the *istiʿārah* from both ends.[49]

49 Both ends refer to the *ʿillah* (effective cause) and the *ḥukm* (ruling).

The Ruling of the Second Type

The second necessitates the soundness of it from one of the two ends, and that is the *istiʿārah* of the *aṣl* (principal case) for the *farʿ* (novel case).

Example of when there is a connection between the ʿillah and the ḥukm

The example of the first type occurs when one says: 'إِنْ مَلَكْتُ عَبْدًا فَهُوَ حُرٌّ (If I take ownership of a slave, he is free),' and then he becomes the owner of half a slave – whom he sells – and then he becomes the owner of the other half, he will not be set free, and that is because the whole of the slave did not come together into his ownership.

But if one says: 'إِنْ اِشْتَرَيْتُ عَبْدًا فَهُوَ حُرٌّ (If I buy a slave, he is free),' and then he buys a half a slave – whom he sells – and then he buys the other half, the second half is set free.

If, by 'ownership' he meant 'purchasing', or by 'purchasing' he meant 'ownership', his intention is valid by way of *majāz*, and that is because purchasing is the *ʿillah* (cause) of the ownership whereas ownership is its *ḥukm*,[50] and so the *istiʿārah* is common between the *ʿillah* and the effect (*maʿlūl*) from both ends. However, if there is anything that causes a reduction in his right, it will not be attested to in a court ruling specifically due to notion of accusation – not because the *istiʿārah* is invalid.[51]

Example of when there is a connection between the sabab and the ḥukm

The example of the second type occurs when one says to his wife: 'حَرَّرْتُكِ (I have freed you),' and by that he means divorce. It is valid, because 'freeing' in reality obliges the abandonment of the ownership of sexual pleasure by way of the abandonment of the ownership of personage. Thus, it is the pure *sabab* (reason) for the removal of sexual enjoyment, and so it is permitted to be used metaphorically for divorce, which is a remover of the ownership of sexual enjoyment.

Response to the Contention

And it cannot be said that: If it was rendered *majāz* for divorce then the divorce that occurs by it must be revocable (*ṭalāq rajʿī*) like explicit divorce, because we say that we do not render it *majāz* for divorce, but rather for removal of the ownership of sexual enjoyment, and this is [only the case] for irrevocable divorce (*ṭalāq bā'in*), since the revocable divorce does not remove ownership of sexual enjoyment – according to us.

TERMINOLOGY

Istiʿārah: Metaphor
Aṣl: Principal case
Farʿ: Novel case
Hibah: Gift
Dār al-ḥarb: Countries under the authority of the disbelievers
Ṭalāq rajʿī: Revocable divorce
Ṭalāq bā'in: Irrevocable divorce
ʿIllah: Cause
Maʿlūl: Effect

50 Purchasing causes ownership and ownership is the effect brought about by purchasing.

51 For example, one says, 'I said "I have purchased," by which I meant "I have become the owner of."' In a court of law, he will not be attested to because this contains an element of accusation that he wants to retain a half of his slave.

The Aṣl (Principal Case) is Not Established by the Farʿ (Novel Case)

If one says to his slave-woman: 'طَلَّقْتُكِ (I have divorced you),' and by that he intends emancipation, it is not valid; because the *aṣl* (principal case) may be established by the *farʿ* (novel case), but as for the *farʿ* (novel case) it cannot be established by the *aṣl* (principal case).

Based on this we say: Marriage is established by the wording of 'هِبَة - *hibah* (gifting)', 'تَمْلِيك - *tamlīk* (transferral of ownership)' and 'بَيع - *bay*ʿ (sale)', because gifting, in reality, necessitates the ownership of personage, and the ownership of personage in slave-women necessitates ownership of sexual enjoyment. Therefore, gifting is the pure *sabab* (reason) for the establishment of ownership of sexual enjoyment, and so it may be used as metaphor for 'نِكَاح - *nikāḥ* (marriage)'. Likewise, are the wording of 'تَمْلِيك - *tamlīk* (transferral of ownership)' and 'بَيع - *bay*ʿ (sale)'.

However, this cannot be done in reverse, such that a sale or a gift cannot be concluded with the words 'نِكَاح - *nikāḥ* (marriage)'.

When Intention is Not Necessary

Thereafter, in every scenario where the repository is fixed for a kind of *majāz*, intention is not needed in it.

Contention

It cannot be said: When the possibility of *ḥaqīqah* is a stipulation for the validity of the *majāz* – with Imam Abū Yūsuf and Imam Muhammad (Allah have mercy on them) – how can the *majāz* be applied in the case of 'نِكَاح - *nikāḥ* (marriage)' being concluded with the word 'هِبَة - *hibah* (gift)', being that transferring the ownership of a freewoman through sale or gift is impossible?

Response to the Contention

We say: It is possible in general like when the freewoman apostatises and takes herself to enemy territory (*dār al-ḥarb*) and then is captured.[52]

This is the equivalent of the example of 'touching the sky' and similar to it.[53]

QUESTIONS

1. In what two ways is *istiʿārah* (metaphor) in the rulings of the Sharīʿah consistent and applicable?
2. Give an example of when there is a connection between the *ʿillah* and the *ḥukm*.
3. If a man says to his wife, 'I have freed you', what is the outcome?

52 She is now treated as a slave-woman who may be bought and sold.

53 This occurs when a person swears an oath that they will 'touch the sky' or 'change this stone into gold'; they need to make expiation of the oath immediately due to it being normally impossible. Due to it being conceivable by way of a miracle, the person must make expiation for not fulfilling the oath.

2.6: ṢARĪḤ (EXPLICIT) AND KINĀYAH (IMPLICIT)

Ṣarīḥ (Explicit)

Ṣarīḥ is a word in which intent is obvious, such as one's saying: 'بِعْتُ (I sold),' and 'اِشْتَرَيْتُ (I bought),' and other examples of it.

The Ruling of Ṣarīḥ

Its ruling is that it obliges the establishment of its meaning in any manner whatsoever,[54] be that by informing, by an attribute, or by a vocative. Part of its ruling is that it is independent of intention.

EXAMPLE

Based on this we said: When one says to his wife; i. 'أَنْتِ طَالِقٌ (You are divorced),'[55] ii. 'طَلَّقْتُكِ (I have divorced you),'[56] or iii. 'يَا طَالِقُ (O you who is divorced),'[57] the divorce occurs whether he intended divorce by it or not. Likewise, if one says to his slave: i. 'أَنْتَ حُرٌّ (You are free),' ii. 'حَرَّرْتُكَ (I have freed you),' or, iii. 'يَا حُرُّ (O you who is free).'

Based on this we said that *tayammum*[58] causes purification, because the saying of Allah ﷻ:

وَلَٰكِن يُرِيدُ لِيُطَهِّرَكُمْ

'*... but He [Allah] intends to purify you.*' Qur'an 5:6

is *ṣarīḥ* in acquiring purification by it.

Imam ash-Shāfiʿī (Allah have mercy on him)

Imam ash-Shāfiʿī (Allah have mercy on him) has two sayings in this regard:

i. one of the two is that it is purification that is acquired out of *ḍarūrah* (compulsive necessity), and

ii. the other is that it is not purification, rather it is a cover for impurity.

The Inference of the Rulings

Based upon this the following issues have been deduced in accordance with the two schools:

i. The permissibility of *tayammum* before the prayer time,

ii. The performance of two obligatory prayers with a single *tayammum*,

TERMINOLOGY

Ṣarīḥ: Explicit
Kināyah: Allusive/Implicit
Baynūnah: Separation by irrevocable divorce
Dalālat al-ḥāl: Contextual indication

NOTES

54 It is due to the clear meaning the word represents that it rules out any room for intention.

55 This is an example of description.

56 This is an example of report.

57 This is example of calling.

58 A type of purification usually performed with dry soil or sand when water is not available for use.

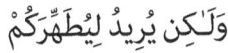

iii. Someone who performed *tayammum* leading those in prayer who have performed *wuḍū'*,

iv. The permissibility of *tayammum* even if one is not apprehensive about losing his life or a limb if he performed *wuḍū'*,

v. The permissibility of *tayammum* for the Eid and funeral prayers,

vi. The permissibility of *tayammum* with the intention of purification.

Kināyah (Implicit)

Kināyah is that in which meaning is concealed. *Majāz*, before becoming conventional, is in the rank of *kināyah*.

The Ruling of Kināyah

The ruling of the *kināyah* is the establishment of the ruling with it when the intention exists or by contextual indication (*dalālat al-ḥāl*). It is then imperative for there to be evidence (*dalīl*) whereby ambivalence is removed and by it one of the possible aspects becomes dominant.

It is due to this meaning that the words 'بَيْنُوْنَةٌ - *baynūnah* (separation)' and 'تَحْرِيْمٌ - *taḥrīm* (prohibition)' are termed *kināyah* in the category of divorce because of the denotation of ambivalence, and the concealment of what is intended,[59] not because it actually performs the act of divorce.

The ruling of implicit words branches out from this in relation to not having the jurisdiction of revoking the divorce.

The Ruling of Kināyah in Ḥadd[60] Cases

It is due to the existence of the denotation of ambivalence in the *kināyah* that punishments are not applied by them, such that if anyone confesses against himself in the category of *zinā* (unlawful sexual intercourse) and theft, the *ḥadd* is not applied to him unless he mentions a *ṣarīḥ* word.

Due to this idea, the *ḥadd* is not applied to the mute [who confesses] by gesture.

If one makes an accusation of *zinā* against a man, and the other replies, 'You have spoken the truth,' the *ḥadd* is not due on him because of the possibility of his affirmation to him for something else.

QUESTIONS

1. What is the ruling of the *ṣarīḥ*?
2. Does the *ṣarīḥ* need intention?

NOTES

59 This is because it is imperative for the intention or contextual indication to be present.

60 A stipulated form of corporal or capital punishment.

3. Why are *ḥadd* punishments not applied when the *kināyah* is used?
4. Name two issues that have been deduced based on the *ṣarīḥ*.

❖

2.7: MUTAQĀBILĀT (COUNTERPARTS)

By them we refer to: the *ẓāhir* (apparent), the *naṣṣ* (perspicuous), the *mufassar* (elaborated) and the *muḥkam* (unequivocal), with whatever is opposed to them of the *khafī* (obscure), the *mushkil* (complex), the *mujmal* (ambiguous), and the *mutashābih* (equivocal).

Ẓāhir (Apparent)

The *ẓāhir* is a word for every statement by which the intent is apparent to the listener by merely hearing it without contemplation.[61]

Naṣṣ (Perspicuous)

The *naṣṣ* is that for which the statement was contextualised.

EXAMPLE

Its example is in the saying of Allah ﷻ:

وَأَحَلَّ ٱللَّهُ ٱلْبَيْعَ وَحَرَّمَ ٱلرِّبَوٰا۟

'And Allah permitted trade and prohibited interest.' Qur'an 2:275

The verse was contextualised for clarification of the difference between trade and interest (*ribā*) as a refutation against what the non-Muslims claimed – in there to be parity between them both – such that they said:

إِنَّمَا ٱلْبَيْعُ مِثْلُ ٱلرِّبَوٰا۟

'Surely, trade is like interest.' Qur'an 2:275

The lawfulness of trade and unlawfulness of interest is recognised by merely listening. Therefore, this is *naṣṣ* in differentiating, *ẓāhir* in permissibility of trade and the prohibition of interest.[62]

Likewise, is the saying of Allah ﷻ:

61 The difference between the *ẓāhir* (apparent) and the *ṣarīḥ* (explicit) is that the former is a mere expression of what is intended without any internal or external influence whereas the *ṣarīḥ* (explicit) is contextual. For example, the word طلاق (*ṭalāq*) means 'to let go, release.' This is *ẓāhir* (apparent) but in the context of cessation of marriage, it means 'divorce'. This is *ṣarīḥ* (explicit), because the context of its expression is evident.

62 This verse of the Qur'an is a *naṣṣ* in differentiating between trade and interest, and it is *ẓāhir* in discriminating between the lawfulness of trade and the unlawfulness of interest.

“

TERMINOLOGY

Ẓāhir: Apparent
Naṣṣ: Perspicuous
Mufassar: Elaborated
Muḥkam: Unequivocal
'Ushr: A tenth of crops and fruits given as zakah
Walā': Attribution of the freed slave to the tribe of the slavemaster who freed them

”

فَٱنكِحُوا۟ مَا طَابَ لَكُم مِّنَ ٱلنِّسَآءِ مَثْنَىٰ وَثُلَٰثَ وَرُبَٰعَ

'Then marry those women who seem good to you; two, three, or four.' Qur'an 4:3

The statement was contextualised for clarification of the number, whereas unrestrictedness and permission [in marriage] is known by merely listening. Thus, it is *ẓāhir* in relation to the unrestrictedness, and *naṣṣ* in clarification of the number.

Likewise, the saying of Allah ﷻ:

لَّا جُنَاحَ عَلَيْكُمْ إِن طَلَّقْتُمُ ٱلنِّسَآءَ مَا لَمْ تَمَسُّوهُنَّ أَوْ تَفْرِضُوا۟ لَهُنَّ فَرِيضَةً

'There is no blame on you if you divorce women provided you have not touched them or appointed for them a portion.' Qur'an 2:236

is *naṣṣ* in the ruling of the one who has not designated a marriage payment for her, *ẓāhir* in the autonomy of the husband in divorce,[63] and an indication that marriage without the mention of the marriage payment is valid.

Likewise, his statement ﷺ:

مَنْ مَلَكَ ذَا رَحِمٍ مَحْرَمٍ مِنْهُ، عَتَقَ عَلَيْهِ

'Whoever becomes the owner of an unmarriageable relative, they are freed from them.'[64]

is *naṣṣ* in the right of the manumission for the close relative[65] and *ẓāhir* in establishing ownership for him.[66,67]

The Ruling of the Ẓāhir and the Naṣṣ

The ruling of the *ẓāhir* and the *naṣṣ* is an obligation to act on both of them, whether they are both *'āmm* or *khāṣṣ*, with the possibility of having the intention of something else; this is in the rank of the *majāz* with the *ḥaqīqah*.[68]

Based on this we said: If one purchases his close relative, inasmuch that he is freed from him, he stands to be the manumitter and the clientage (*walā'*)[69] belongs to him.[70]

---

63 The *ẓāhir* of this verse of the Qur'an explains to us the independence of the husband in issuing divorce to his wife.

64 The wording of the ḥadīth is slightly different; see Abu Dawud (3440) and al-Tirmidhi (1285).

65 The *naṣṣ* of this ḥadīth of the Messenger of Allah ﷺ states the right of the closely-related slave to the master to be manumitted.

66 The manumitter.

67 The *ẓāhir* (apparent) of this ḥadīth explains to us that someone acquires ownership who purchases a slave closely related to him.

68 The *ḥaqīqah* carries the possibility of a meaning in the *majāz*. Likewise, the *ẓāhir* (apparent) and the *naṣṣ* carry the possibility of the meaning of *takhṣīṣ* of the *'āmm*.

69 *Walā'* involves the master becoming one of the heirs of the slave and standing responsibility for any compensatory payments he might become due for causing damage, injury or even homicide. (al-Qudūrī, *Mukhtaṣar*, p.495). It also gives the manumitter the right to inherit from the one manumitted when the latter has no heir.

70 The manumitter.

NOTES

Appearance of the Disparity

The disparity between the two only appears when there is a contradiction. Due to this if he says to her: 'طَلِّقِي نَفْسَكِ (Divorce yourself),' and she replies, 'أَبَنْتُ نَفْسِي (I have rendered myself irrevocably divorced),' a revocable divorce occurs, because this is *naṣṣ* for divorce and *ẓāhir* for irrevocable divorce, so the preferred implementation is of the *naṣṣ*.[71]

Likewise, his statement ﷺ to the people of ʿUraynah:

اِشْرَبُوْا مِنْ أَبْوَالِهَا وَ أَلْبَانِهَا

'Drink of their [i.e. camel's] urine and their milk.'

is *naṣṣ* in explaining the reason for the cure, whereas it is *ẓāhir* in permitting the drinking of urine.

However, his statement ﷺ:

اِسْتَنْزِهُوْا مِنَ الْبَوْلِ، فَإِنَّ عَامَّةَ عَذَابِ الْقَبْرِ مِنْهُ

'Be careful regarding urine, for the most common punishment in the grave will be because of it.'

is *naṣṣ* in the obligation of avoiding urine, and so the *naṣṣ* takes precedence over the *ẓāhir*, and therefore it is not lawful to drink urine whatsoever.

His statement ﷺ:

مَا سَقَتْهُ السَّمَاءُ فَفِيْهِ الْعُشْرُ

'That which the sky irrigates, there is a tenth (ʿushr) in it.'

is *naṣṣ* in explaining the *ʿushr*.

However, his statement ﷺ:

لَيسَ فِي الْخَضْرَوَاتِ صَدَقَةٌ

'There is no ṣadaqah (zakāh) in vegetables.'

is construed (*mu'awwal*) to negate the *ʿushr* because *ṣadaqah* (charity) carries multiple meanings,[72] and so the first ḥadīth takes precedence over the second.

Mufassar (Elaborated)

The *mufassar* is that in which the intent of its wording becomes clear via an explanation from the speaker, such that likelihood of construed specification does not remain with it.[73]

---

71 In this illustration, the *naṣṣ* expresses explicit divorce, the choice of which she has been delegated, whereas her pronunciation of irrevocable divorce is merely the *ẓāhir* (apparent). The context of what she mentioned was made in the simple divorce that she was delegated and so we resort to the *naṣṣ* and not the *ẓāhir* (apparent).

72 The word *ṣadaqah* (charity) includes *zakāh*, *ʿushr*, *khums*, as well as supererogatory charity.

73 A similar discussion on the *mufassar* is made in reference to the *mushtarak* (homonymous) in 2.3., though that particular discussion is restricted to *mufassar* being in explanation to *mushtarak*, whereas here it is in its general form.

EXAMPLE

Its example is in the saying of Allah ﷻ:

فَسَجَدَ ٱلْمَلَٰٓئِكَةُ كُلُّهُمْ أَجْمَعُونَ

'And the angels prostrated, all of them, altogether.' Qur'an, 15:30

The word 'مَلَآئِكَةٌ (angels)' is *ẓāhir* in general, but the possibility of specification (*takhṣīṣ*) also remains. However, the door of specification is closed with the saying of Allah : 'كُلُّهُمْ - (all of them)'.

Thereafter remains the possibility of asynchrony in prostration, and so the door of *ta'wīl* is closed by the saying of Allah: 'أَجْمَعُوْنَ (altogether)'.[74]

[Its example] in legal aspects, occurs when one says: 'تَزَوَّجْتُ فُلَانَةً شَهْرًا بِكَذَا (I married so-and-so a woman for a month with such-and-such),' his saying, 'تَزَوَّجْتُ (I married)' is *ẓāhir* for 'نِكَاحٌ - *nikāḥ* (marriage)', but the possibility of 'مُتْعَةٌ - *mut'ah* (temporary marriage)'[75] remains, so he interpreted what was meant with his statement 'شَهْرًا (a month).'[76] Therefore, we say this is *mut'ah*, not *nikāḥ*.

If someone said: 'لِفُلَانٍ عَلَيَّ أَلْفٌ مِنْ ثَمَنِ هٰذَا الْعَبْدِ (I owe so-and-so a thousand [dirhams] from the payment of this slave),' or, '... أَوْ مِنْ ثَمَنِ هٰذَا الْمَتَاعِ... from the payment of this product),' his saying, 'عَلَيَّ أَلْفٌ (I owe a thousand),' is *naṣṣ* for the obligation of the thousand, except that the likelihood of *tafsīr* (elaboration) still remains; he explains what was meant with his statement, '... مِنْ ثَمَنِ هٰذَا الْعَبْدِ (... from the payment of this slave),' or '... مِنْ ثَمَنِ هٰذَا الْمَتَاعِ (... from the payment of this product),' so the *mufassar* takes precedence over the *naṣṣ*, inasmuch that he doesn't need to pay the money except when taking hold of the slave or the product.

Moreover, his saying, 'لِفُلَانٍ عَلَيَّ أَلْفٌ (I owe so-and-so a thousand),' is *ẓāhir* for confession and *naṣṣ* for the currency of the land. However, if he said, '... مِنْ نَقْدِ بَلَدِ كَذَا (... in the currency of such-and-such a land),' the *mufassar* takes precedence over the *naṣṣ*, and thus, the currency of the land is not binding upon him but rather the currency of such-and-such a land. Other illustrations are based on this.

Muḥkam (Unequivocal)

The *muḥkam* is that which exceeds[77] the *mufassar* inasmuch that opposition to it is not permitted whatsoever. Its example in the Book is:

إِنَّ ٱللَّهَ بِكُلِّ شَيْءٍ عَلِيمٌ

'Indeed, Allah knows all things.' Qur'an, 8:75

74 This verse of the Qur'an is *ẓāhir* (apparent) in the prostration of the angels, and it is *naṣṣ* in terms of their reverence of Prophet Ādam.

75 *Mut'ah:* This occurs when a man marries a woman saying to her that he has married her for, say, ten days, and he uses the word *mut'ah* or any of its variants. (al-Qudūrī, *Mukhtaṣar*, p.390.)

76 Lawful marriage (*nikāḥ*) is for life and not of a temporary nature. Hence, temporal specification of marriage (*mut'ah*) is prohibited.

77 In clarity.

إِنَّ ٱللَّهَ لَا يَظْلِمُ ٱلنَّاسَ شَيْـًٔا

'Indeed, Allah does not do any wrong to people.' Qur'an, 10:44

[Its example] in legal rulings is what we said regarding confession, that: 'لِفُلَانٍ عَلَيَّ أَلْفٌ مِنْ ثَمَنِ هٰذَا الْعَبْدِ (I owe so-and-so a thousand from the payment of this slave).' This wording is *muḥkam* in relation to it being binding as an exchange for the slave.

Other illustrations are based on this.

The Ruling of Mufassar and Muḥkam

The ruling of the *mufassar* and the *muḥkam* is the unequivocal obligation to act upon them both.

POINTS TO NOTE

- *Ẓāhir* is when the intent is 'apparent' to the listener without any need for reflection, whether it is general or specific. Even then, there is a possibility of the meaning being diverted, specified, or abrogated.
- *Naṣṣ* is discussion or speech which has been articulated for a specific purpose (as opposed to *ẓāhir*) and clarifies the *ẓāhir*. It exceeds the *ẓāhir* in clarity and preference is given to it if there is a clash.
- Something may be vague but then it is made clear. This is elaborated (*mufassar*). For example: 'Strike the adulteress and the adulterer *one hundred times...*' (24:2)

QUESTIONS

1. What is the ruling of the *mufassar* and the *muḥkam*?
2. How does the *mufassar* come about?
3. Define the meaning of *ẓāhir* (apparent).
4. The *ẓāhir* is at a stronger level than the *muḥkam*. True or false?
5. *Naṣṣ* takes precedence over the *ẓāhir*. True or false?

2.8: THEIR ANTONYMS

Thereafter, there are four other types contrary to these four: contrary to the *ẓāhir* is the *khafī*, contrary to the *naṣṣ* is the *mushkil*, contrary to the *mufassar* is the *mujmal*, and contrary to the *muḥkam* is the *mutashābih*.

Khafī (Obscure)

The *khafī* is that in which the intent is obscure due to an obstruction, not the form.

EXAMPLE

Its example is in the saying of Allah ﷻ:

وَٱلسَّارِقُ وَٱلسَّارِقَةُ فَٱقْطَعُوٓا۟ أَيْدِيَهُمَا جَزَآءً

'As for the thief, both male and female, cut off their hands.' Qur'an, 5:38

It is *ẓāhir* to mean 'thief (*sāriq*)', but it is *khafī* to mean 'pickpocket (*ṭarrār*)' and 'graverobber (*nabbāsh*)'.

Likewise, the saying of Allah ﷻ:

ٱلزَّانِيَةُ وَٱلزَّانِى فَٱجْلِدُوا۟ كُلَّ وَٰحِدٍ مِّنْهُمَا مِا۟ئَةَ جَلْدَةٍ

'The woman and the man guilty of illegal sexual intercourse, flog each of them a hundred stripes.' Qur'an, 24:2

is *ẓāhir* in the case of the fornicator (*zānī*), but *khafī* to mean 'sodomite'.

If someone takes an oath that he will not eat fruit, it is *ẓāhir* regarding that with which enjoyment is acquired,[78] but *khafī* in relation to grapes and pomegranates.[79]

The Ruling of Khafī (Obscure)

The ruling of the *khafī* is an obligation to investigate until the obscurity disappears.

Mushkil (Complex)

As for the *mushkil*, it is that which exceeds the *khafī* in obscurity, as though after the reality of something was obscure to the listener, it enters its semblances and similarities, inasmuch that its intent is not acquired except with investigation and then with contemplation until it can be distinguished from its similarities.

EXAMPLE

Its example in legal commands is: If someone takes an oath that he will not consume bread with a condiment, it is *ẓāhir* for vinegar and date syrup, but it is *mushkil* for meat, egg, and cheese, such that the meaning of 'إِيْتِدَامٌ - *ītidām* (to consume bread with a condiment)' is investigated then that meaning is contemplated to see whether or not it exists in meat, egg, and cheese or not.

---

78 'تَفَكَّهَ بِهِ : He enjoyed it: and [particularly] he enjoyed the eating of it.' (Lane, Edward William, *Arabic-English Lexicon*. London: Williams and Norgate, 1863. p. 2432)

79 General fruit is consumed for enjoyment, but certain fruits are not eaten on a general basis and especially not merely for the purpose of enjoyment, but rather for medicinal purposes or as delicacies. In this regard, they are not considered fruits as fruits are in the general sense, and therefore they do not fall into the category of fruits on a *ẓāhir* (manifest) basis but on a *khafī* (obscure) basis. Such differences between what constitutes fruit in the *ẓāhir* (manifest) and the *khafī* (obscure) sense varies from region to region, time to time, and season to season.

NOTES

Mujmal (Ambiguous)

Thereafter, beyond the *mushkil* is the *mujmal*. It is that which bears many aspects, so it is in a state wherein what was meant is not known without clarification from the speaker.

EXAMPLE

Its example in the legal rulings is the saying of Allah ﷻ:

وَحَرَّمَ ٱلرِّبَوٰاْۚ

'... and He prohibited interest.' Qur'an, 2:275

because the understood meaning of *ribā* (interest) is unrestricted excess, but it is not what is meant; rather, what is meant is 'excess that is free from an exchanged item in the sale of measured items of the same category,' and the wording has no indication of it, so what was meant is not attained by contemplation.

Mutashābih (Equivocal)

Thereafter, beyond the *mujmal* in obscurity is the *mutashābih*.

EXAMPLE

An example of the *mutashābih* are the abbreviated letters (*ḥurūf muqaṭṭaʿāt*) at the beginning of chapters.

The Ruling of Mujmal and Mutashābih

The legal ruling of the *mujmal* and the *mutashābih* is to have firm belief in the truthfulness of what is meant until clarification comes.

POINTS TO NOTE

- Obscurity due to an incidental reason: Obscure (خفي)
- Obscurity due to an expression: Complex (مشكل), Ambiguous (مجمل), Equivocal (متشابه)
- The *mushkil* is more ambiguous than the *khafī* because obscurity lies in the provision rather than external matter.
- The *mujmal* is more ambiguous than the *mushkil* and requires explanation from the lawgiver.
- Only Allah knows the meaning of the equivocal.

QUESTIONS

1. What is the ruling of the *mujmal* and the *mutashābih*?
2. If someone takes an oath that he will not eat fruit, how is it understood?

TERMINOLOGY

Khafī: Obscure
Mushkil: Complex
Mujmal: Ambiguous
Mutashābih: Equivocal
Sāriq: Thief
Ṭarrār: Pickpocket
Nabbāsh: Graverobber

3. Give an example of the *mutashābih*.
4. The *mushkil* exceeds the *khafī* in obscurity. True or false?
5. The meaning of the *khafī* can be understood. True or false?

❖

2.9: DIVERSION FROM THE ORIGINAL MEANINGS OF THE WORDS

Types

That which the original meaning of the word is diverted is of five types:

i. customary implication,
ii. implication in the statement *per se*,
iii. contextual implication,
iv. speaker's implication, and
v. abstract implication

Customary Implication (Dalālah al-'Urf)

The first type is customary implication. That is because establishment of legal rulings by words is only via the implication of the words according to the meaning intended by the speaker. Thus, if the meaning is conventional among the people, that conventional meaning is proof that outwardly it was what was intended by it, and therefore the ruling results from it.

EXAMPLE

Its example is if someone takes an oath that he will not purchase a head, it is according to what people are acquainted with, and so he does not violate the oath by purchasing the head of a sparrow or a pigeon.

Likewise, if someone takes an oath that he will not eat an egg, it is according to convention, so he does not violate the oath by consuming the egg of a sparrow or a pigeon.

With this, it becomes clear that diversion from the original meaning does not necessitate resorting to the *majāz*. In fact, it is permitted for the imperfect original meaning (*al-ḥaqīqah al-qāṣirah*)[80] to be established by it; an example of this is the restriction of the *'āmm* with *al-ba'ḍ* (a portion).

Likewise, if someone makes a vow (*nadhr*) to perform *Ḥajj*, or walk to the House of Allah ﷻ (i.e. the Ka'bah), or that he will strike the Ḥaṭīm of the Ka'bah with his garment, the *ḥajj* is binding upon him with known actions due to the presence of *'urf*.

---

80 *Ḥaqīqah qāṣirah* is the primary meaning of a word when its inclusive contents are restricted, such as when someone mentions the word 'car'. In general, it includes the cars of a train, balloon or airship, an elevator car or a chariot, etc. but according to customary use, it only denotes an automobile.

Implication in the Statement Per Se

The second type may occur when the original meaning is diverted by an implication in the statement *per se*.

EXAMPLE

Its example is when someone says, 'كُلُّ مَمْلُوكٍ لِي فَهُوَ حُرٌّ (Every slave of mine is free)', his *mukātab*[81] are not manumitted nor the one that part of him was manumitted, unless he includes them in his intention, because the word 'مَمْلُوكٌ - *mamlūk* (an owned slave)' is *muṭlaq;* it takes up the meaning of 'the *mamlūk* in every aspect', whereas the *mukātab* is not owned in every aspect therefore the master's; i. free disposal of him is not allowed, ii. it is not permitted for him to have sexual intercourse with the female *mukātab*, and iii. if the *mukātab* marries the daughter of his master and then the master dies, and the daughter inherits him, the marriage is not vitiated. Thus, when he is not owned in every aspect, he does not come under the unrestricted word *mamlūk*.

This is contrary to the *mudabbar*[82] and the *umm al-walad*[83] because ownership of them is perfect, due to this sexual intercourse with the female *mudabbar* and the *umm al-walad* is lawful, and the deficiency is in bondage only, such that it unequivocally ceases with death.

Upon this we said: If he manumits the *mukātab* as an expiation for his oath (*yamīn*) or his injurious comparison (*ẓihār*), it is permitted, but the manumission of a *mudabbar* or an *umm al-walad* is not permitted in these two scenarios because the obligation is 'emancipation' which is establishment of freedom by removal of bondage. Thus, if the bondage of the *mukātab* is perfect then his manumission is a manumission in all aspects, but because the bondage of the *mudabbar* and the *umm al-walad* is imperfect; the manumission is not a manumission in all aspects.

Contextual Implication

The third type may occur when the original meaning is diverted by an implication in the context of the statement.

EXAMPLE

He[84] said in *as-Siyar al-Kabīr*: When a Muslim says to a *ḥarbī*,[85] 'إِنْزِلْ (Dismount!),' and he dismounts, he is legally protected but if he says, 'إِنْزِلْ إِنْ كُنْتَ رَجُلًا (Dismount, if you are a man!),' and he dismounts, he is not legally protected. However, if the *ḥarbī* says, 'اَلْأَمَانَ ، اَلْأَمَانَ (Grant me legal protection!),' and the Muslim replies, 'اَلْأَمَانَ ، اَلْأَمَانَ (I granted you legal protection!),' he is legally protected. If the Muslim replies, 'اَلْأَمَانَ. سَتَعْلَمُ مَا تَلْقَى غَدًا (Legal protection?! You shall come to know what

TERMINOLOGY

Dalālah al-'Urf: Customary implication

Majāz: Metaphorical meaning

Hibah: Gift

Tamlīk: Transferral of ownership

81 Contracted slaves working towards emancipation.

82 A slave emancipated upon the death of his/her master.

83 A slave-woman bearing her master's child, who is also emancipated upon the death of her master.

84 Imam Muhammad, *al-Siyar al-Kabīr* 2/47.

85 A non-Muslim living in non-Muslim lands.

you shall encounter tomorrow),' or, 'لَا تَعْجَلْ حَتَّى تَرَى (Do not rush until you see [what you encounter]),' and he dismounts, he is not legally protected.

If someone says, 'اِشْتَرِ لِي جَارِيَةً لِتَخْدِمَنِيْ (Purchase a slave-woman for me so she can serve me),' and he purchases a blind or disabled woman, it is not permitted.

If he says, 'اِشْتَرِ لِيْ جَارِيَةً حَتَّى أَطَأَهَا (Purchase a slave-woman for me so I can have sexual intercourse with her),' and he purchases his sister via breastfeeding (*ukht min ar-raḍāʿ*), it is not on behalf of the principal (*muwakkil*).

Upon this we said, regarding the saying of the Prophet ﷺ:

إِذَا وَقَعَ الذُّبَابُ فِيْ طَعَامِ أَحَدِكُمْ فَامْقُلُوْهُ ثُمَّ انْقُلُوْهُ، فَإِنَّ فِيْ أَحَدِ جَنَاحَيْهِ دَاءٌ وَفِي الْأُخْرَى دَوَاءٌ، وَإِنَّهُ لَيُقَدِّمُ الدَّاءَ عَلَى الدَّوَاءِ

'When a fly falls into the food of any of you, you should immerse it in and then remove it because one of its two wings has a disease while the other has a cure, and it puts forward the disease before the cure.'

The context of the statement implies that the immersion is to remove the harm from us and not as a religious command; that is a right of the Sharīʿah, therefore it is not to establish an obligation.

And the saying of Allah ﷻ:

إِنَّمَا ٱلصَّدَقَٰتُ لِلْفُقَرَآءِ وَٱلْمَسَٰكِينِ

'Indeed, alms are only for the poor and the destitute... .' Qur'an, 9:60

immediately after His saying:

وَمِنْهُم مَّن يَلْمِزُكَ فِى ٱلصَّدَقَٰتِ

'And of them are those who blame you regarding the alms.' Qur'an, 9:58

implies that the mentioning of the categories is in order to remove their greed for alms by clarifying the recipients of them, therefore, removal from responsibility does not depend on payment to all of them.

Speaker's Implication

The fourth type may occur when the original meaning is diverted by an implication from the speaker.

EXAMPLE

Its example is the saying of Allah ﷻ:

فَمَن شَآءَ فَلْيُؤْمِن وَمَن شَآءَ فَلْيَكْفُرْ

'And whoever wills let him believe, and whoever wills let him disbelieve.'
Qur'an, 18:29

That is because Allah ﷻ is the All-Wise and disbelief is abhorrent, and the one who is wise does not command the abhorrent. Thus, the implication of the words is diverted away from the command due to the wisdom of the one who issues the command.

Based on this we said: When someone appoints an agent to purchase meat, if he is a traveller who dismounted along the way, it is in the meaning of cooked or roasted meat; but if he is a resident, it is in the meaning of raw meat.

Momentary Oath (Yamīn al-Fawr)

Of this type is the momentary oath (*yamīn al-fawr*).

EXAMPLE

Its example occurs when someone says, 'تَعَالَ ، تَغَدَّ مَعِي (Come, have breakfast with me),' and he replies, 'وَاللهِ ، لَا أَتَغَدَّى (By Allah! I will not have breakfast),' it resorts to the breakfast which he is invited to, inasmuch as if he has breakfast after that in his house, with him or with someone else on that particular day, he does not violate his oath.

Likewise, when a woman stands, intending to leave, and the husband says to her, 'إِنْ خَرَجْتِ ، فَأَنْتِ كَذَا (If you leave, then you are such-and-such),' the ruling is restricted to the present, inasmuch as if she leaves after that, he does not violate the oath.

Abstract Implication

The fifth type may occur when the original meaning is diverted by an implication in the repository of the statement, such that the repository does not accept the original meaning of the word.

EXAMPLE

Its example is: The enactment of the marriage of a freewoman with the words; 'بَيْعٌ - *bay*ʿ (sale)', 'هِبَةٌ - *hibah* (gift)', 'تَمْلِيكٌ - *tamlīk* (transferring ownership)', and 'صَدَقَةٌ - *ṣadaqah* (charity)', and someone saying about his slave, whose lineage is known to be from someone else, 'هٰذَا اِبْنِي (This is my son).'

Likewise, when someone says to his slave and he is older than the master, 'هٰذَا اِبْنِي (This is my son),' it is manumission in the sense of the *majāz* – according to Abū Ḥanīfah (Allah have mercy on him), contrary to the two,[86] on the basis of what we discussed – that the *majāz* is a substitute to the *ḥaqīqah* in terms of the word according to him,[87] but in terms of the ruling according to the two.

86 Imam Abū Yūsuf and Imam Muhammad (Allah have mercy on them).

87 Imam Abū Ḥanīfah (Allah have mercy on him).

POINTS TO NOTE

- *Umm al-walad:* A slave-woman bearing her master's child, who is also emancipated upon the death of her master.
- *Mudabbar*: A slave emancipated upon the death of his/her master.

QUESTIONS

1. Give an example of abstract implication.
2. Give an example of speaker's implication.
3. Give an example of the momentary oath.
4. Give an example of contextual implication.
5. Give an example of customary implication.

❖

2.10: TEXTUAL IMPLICATIONS (MUTAʿALLAQĀT AN-NUṢŪṢ)

By them, we mean:

i. the explicit meaning of the text (*ʿibārat an-naṣṣ*),
ii. its indicative meaning (*ishārat an-naṣṣ*),
iii. its inferred meaning (*dalālat an-naṣṣ*), and
iv. its exigent meaning (*iqtiḍā' an-naṣṣ*).

ʿIbārat an-Naṣṣ (Explicit Meaning)

As for *ʿibārat an-naṣṣ*, it is that for which the statement was contextualised and intentionally meant by it.

Ishārat an-Naṣṣ (Indicative Meaning)

As for *ishārat an-naṣṣ*, it is that which is established by the composition of the text without any excess, provided it is not evident in all aspects and the statement was not contextualised for it.

EXAMPLE

Its example is in the saying of Allah ﷻ:

لِلْفُقَرَآءِ ٱلْمُهَـٰجِرِينَ ٱلَّذِينَ أُخْرِجُوا۟ مِن دِيَـٰرِهِمْ وَأَمْوَٰلِهِمْ يَبْتَغُونَ فَضْلًا مِّنَ ٱللَّهِ وَرِضْوَٰنًا
وَيَنصُرُونَ ٱللَّهَ وَرَسُولَهُۥٓ ۚ أُو۟لَـٰٓئِكَ هُمُ ٱلصَّـٰدِقُونَ

'[It is] for the emigrating poor who were forced out of their homes, and [deprived of] their properties, seeking grace from Allah and His pleasure, assisting Allah and His Messenger. It is they who are the truthful.'
Qur'an, 59:8

Hence, indeed it was contextualised in explaining the rightful ownership of the booty, so it is *naṣṣ* in that regard, and their poverty is established by the composition of the text, so it is an indication that a non-Muslim's appropriation of a Muslim's property is a cause for the establishment of ownership for a non-Muslim, since if the properties remained in their ownership, then their poverty would not be established.

Inferences

Extracted from it is:

i. the ruling regarding the issue of appropriation,

ii. the ruling regarding the establishment of ownership for the trader by purchasing from them,

iii. his free management in selling, gifting and manumitting,

iv. the ruling establishing the spoils of war,

v. establishing the ownership of the Muslim soldier,

vi. the incapacity of the owner from expropriating it from his possession,

and other inferences from this.

Likewise, is the saying of Allah ﷻ:

أُحِلَّ لَكُمْ لَيْلَةَ ٱلصِّيَامِ ٱلرَّفَثُ إِلَىٰ نِسَآئِكُمْ ۚ هُنَّ لِبَاسٌ لَّكُمْ وَأَنتُمْ لِبَاسٌ لَّهُنَّ ۗ عَلِمَ ٱللَّهُ أَنَّكُمْ كُنتُمْ تَخْتَانُونَ أَنفُسَكُمْ فَتَابَ عَلَيْكُمْ وَعَفَا عَنكُمْ ۖ فَٱلْـَٔـٰنَ بَـٰشِرُوهُنَّ وَٱبْتَغُوا۟ مَا كَتَبَ ٱللَّهُ لَكُمْ ۚ وَكُلُوا۟ وَٱشْرَبُوا۟ حَتَّىٰ يَتَبَيَّنَ لَكُمُ ٱلْخَيْطُ ٱلْأَبْيَضُ مِنَ ٱلْخَيْطِ ٱلْأَسْوَدِ مِنَ ٱلْفَجْرِ ۖ ثُمَّ أَتِمُّوا۟ ٱلصِّيَامَ إِلَى ٱلَّيْلِ ۚ

'It is permitted for you, in the night of fasting, to go to your women. They are clothing for you and you are clothing for them. Allah knows that you have been deceiving yourselves, so He accepted your repentance and pardoned you. So now, have relations with them and seek what Allah has ordained for you, and eat and drink until the white thread becomes distinct from the black thread of dawn; then complete the fasting up to the night.' Qur'an, 2:187

Abstinence during the first portion of the morning is ascertained in the state of major ritual impurity (*janābah*), because from the necessity of lawfulness of sexual intimacy until the morning is that the first portion of the day is with the presence of major ritual impurity, and abstinence during that portion is fasting, the completion of which the person has been enjoined. Thus, this is an indication that major ritual impurity does not nullify the fast.

In addition, it is binding from this that rinsing the mouth and rinsing the nostrils does not negate continuance of the fast.

TERMINOLOGY

ʿIbārat an-naṣṣ: Explicit meaning

Ishārat an-naṣṣ: Allusive meaning

Dalālat an-naṣṣ: Inferred meaning

Iqtiḍā' an-naṣṣ: Exigent meaning

Ḍarūrah: Compulsive necessity

Inferences

Deduced from it are:

i. that whoever tastes something with his mouth, his fast is not vitiated – because if water is salty and one finds its taste when rinsing the mouth, the fast is not vitiated by it, and

ii. known from this is the ruling of a wet-dream, cupping and applying oil, because when the Book termed abstinence – proven by virtue of refraining from the three mentioned things[88] from the first portion of the morning – fasting, it is known that the integral of fasting is completed by refraining from the three things.

Based on this, the ruling of the issue of making intention at night is derived[89] because the intention of performing what is enjoined is only binding at the time of undertaking the command. The command is only undertaken after the first portion due to the saying of Allah ﷻ:

ثُمَّ أَتِمُّوا۟ ٱلصِّيَامَ إِلَى ٱلَّيْلِ ۚ

'Then complete the fasting up to the night.' Qur'an, 2:187

Dalālat an-Naṣṣ (Inferred Meaning)

As for *dalālat an-naṣṣ*, it is that which is known as an *ʿillah* (effective cause) – for the ruling determined by the text (*manṣūṣ ʿalayh*) – linguistically not via *ijtihād* nor juridical inference.

EXAMPLE

Its example is in the saying of Allah ﷻ:

فَلَا تَقُل لَّهُمَآ أُفٍّ وَلَا تَنْهَرْهُمَا

'So do not say to them, 'uff!' and do not repel them.' Qur'an, 17:23

Thus, someone who knows the modes of language, understands with the initial hearing that the prohibition of saying *'uff'* is to prevent harm from them.[90]

The ruling of this type is generality of the ruling determined by the text because of the generality of its *ʿillah*.

Because of this meaning, we professed the prohibition of hitting, vilifying, seeking service from the father based on hire, detainment for the reason of debt, and killing in retaliation.

---

88 The three things that one abstains from during fasting is; i. eating, ii. drinking, and iii. sexual intercourse.

89 The Shāfiʿī scholars (Allah have mercy on them) are of the view that the intention for fasting the following day must be made the night before, i.e. prior to dawn, whereas the Ḥanafī scholars (Allah have mercy on them) oppose this opinion and thereby allow the extension of making the intention up until midday of that particular day.

90 The parents.

Dalālat an-Naṣṣ is Akin to Scripture

Thereafter, *dalālat an-naṣṣ* is in the status of scripture, inasmuch that it is valid to establish punishment by *dalālat an-naṣṣ*.

EXAMPLE

Our companions said:[91] Expiation for having sexual intercourse is obligatory by scripture,[92] and for eating and drinking by *dalālat an-naṣṣ*.

On account of this meaning, it is said: The ruling revolves around that *ʿillah*.

Al-Imam al-Qāḍī Abū Zayd (Allah have mercy on him)[93] said: 'لَوْ أَنَّ قَوْمًا يَعُدَّوْنَ التَّأْفِيْفَ كَرَامةً ، لَا يَحْرُمُ عَلَيْهِمْ تَأْفِيْفُ الأَبَوَيْنِ (If a people consider saying *'uff'* a way of reverence, then it is not forbidden for them to say *'uff'* to parents).'

Likewise, we said regarding the saying of Allah ﷻ:

يَٰٓأَيُّهَا ٱلَّذِينَ ءَامَنُوٓاْ إِذَا نُودِىَ لِلصَّلَوٰةِ مِن يَوْمِ ٱلْجُمُعَةِ فَٱسْعَوْاْ إِلَىٰ ذِكْرِ ٱللَّهِ وَذَرُواْ
ٱلْبَيْعَ ۚ ذَٰلِكُمْ خَيْرٌ لَّكُمْ إِن كُنتُمْ تَعْلَمُونَ

'O you who believe, when the prayer is called to on Friday, hasten to the remembrance of Allah, and leave off trading. That is better for you, if you only knew.' Qur'an, 62:9

If we hypothesise a sale that does not prevent two contracting parties from hastening to the Friday prayer such that they are in a boat that is proceeding towards the mosque, the sale is not disapproved.

Based on this we said: When someone takes an oath that he will not hit his wife, and then he pulls her hair, bites her, or strangles her, he violates his oath if it is a manner of causing pain. However, if the scenario of hitting or hair pulling is found during mutual playing without causing pain, he does not violate his oath.

If someone takes an oath that he will not beat so-and-so, and then he beats him after his death, he does not violate his oath due to the absence of the objective of beating, which is to cause pain.

Likewise, if someone takes an oath that he will not speak to so-and-so, and then he speaks to him after his death, he does not violate his oath due to the absence of making someone understand.

With account of this meaning, it is said: When one takes an oath that he will not eat any meat, and then he eats the meat of fish or locust, he does not violate his oath, but if he eats the meat of swine or human, he violates his oath because someone who knows will

91 The Ḥanafī jurists.

92 Based on the ḥadīth of the companion who violated his fast in Ramadan by having sexual intercourse with his wife whilst fasting.

93 Al-Imam al-Qāḍī Abū Zayd: He is Abū Zayd, ʿAbdullāh ibn ʿUmar ibn ʿIsā, ad-Dabbūsī (367 AH/977 CE - d.430 AH/1039 CE). He was a Transoxianan Ḥanafī jurist who wrote *Ta'sīs an-Naẓar* (the first book on the difference in *fiqh* and its principles between imams Abū Ḥanīfah, Abū Yūsuf, Muḥammad, and others (Allah have mercy on them), and in which he included eighty-six legal maxims), and *Taqwīm al-Adillah fī Uṣūl al-Fiqh*.

know with the initial hearing that the bearing of this oath is just to avoid that which originates from blood, and therefore, it is to avoid consuming haematics.[94] Therefore, the ruling revolves around that.

Iqtiḍā' an-Naṣṣ (Exigent Meaning)

As for the *muqtaḍā* (the exigent), it is an augmentation to the scripture; the meaning of the scripture can only be ascertained with it, as though the scripture demanded it in order that its meaning is sound intrinsically.

EXAMPLE

Its example in legal rulings is someone saying: 'أَنْتِ طَالِقٌ (You are divorced).' This is a description of the woman, but the description demands the infinitive noun, and so it is as though the infinitive noun is present by way of *iqtiḍā'* (exigency).

Also, when someone says: 'أَعْتِقْ عَبْدَكَ عَنِّيْ بِأَلْفِ دِرْهَمٍ (Manumit your slave on my behalf for a thousand dirhams),' and he replies, 'أَعْتَقْتُ (I have manumitted [him]),' the manumission takes effect on behalf of the one giving the command and the thousand [dirhams] are due on him, but if the one giving the command intended expiation by it, then whatever he intends takes effect, and that is because his saying, 'أَعْتِقْهُ عَنِّيْ بِأَلْفِ دِرْهَمٍ (Manumit him on my behalf for a thousand dirhams),' entails the meaning of his saying [to be], 'بِعْهُ عَنِّيْ بِأَلْفٍ ، ثُمَّ كُنْ وَكِيْلِيْ بِالْإِعْتَاقِ فَأَعْتِقْهُ عَنِّيْ (Sell him to me for a thousand [dirhams], then become my agent in manumitting him and manumit him on my behalf).' Therefore, the sale is established by way of *iqtiḍā'* (exigency), and the acceptance is [also] established in that manner because it is an integral in the category of sale.

Because of this, Imam Abū Yūsuf (Allah have mercy on him) said: When someone says [to another], 'أَعْتِقْ عَبْدَكَ عَنِّيْ بِغَيْرِ شَيْءٍ Manumit your slave on my behalf for nothing [as consideration]),' and he replies, 'أَعْتَقْتُ (I have manumitted [him]),' the manumission takes effect on behalf of the one giving the command, and it results in it requiring the giving of a gift and forming agency, but taking possession is not needed because it[95] is in the status of acceptance in the category of sale, but we[96] say that acceptance is an integral in the category of sale; so when we establish the sale by way of *iqtiḍā'* (exigency), we establish acceptance by way of *ḍarūrah* (compulsive necessity), as opposed to possession in the category of gifting, for it[97] is not an integral in gifting in order so that the ruling for the gift by way of *iqtiḍā'* (exigency) would become a ruling for possession.

The ruling of the *muqtaḍā* (exigent) is that it is established by way of *ḍarūrah* (compulsive necessity), and so it is meted out to the extent of the *ḍarūrah* (compulsive necessity).

Thus we said: When one [i.e. husband to his wife] says, 'أَنْتِ طَالِقٌ (You are divorced),' and by it he intends three [divorcements], it is

94 What is meant here is animals that are warm-blooded.

95 Taking possession.

96 The Ḥanafī jurists opposing Imam Abū Yūsuf (Allah have mercy on them).

97 Possession.

not valid, because the divorce is implied as being mentioned by way of *iqtiḍā'* (exigency), and so it is meted out to the extent of the *ḍarūrah* (compulsive necessity), and the *ḍarūrah* (compulsive necessity) is fulfilled by one [divorce], and hence, it is implied as being mentioned in the meaning of one [divorce].

Extracted from this [principle] is the ruling in one's saying: 'إِنْ أَكَلْتُ (If I eat),'[98] and intended by it some food exclusive of other food, it is not valid, because eating requires food; this is established by way of *iqtiḍā'* (exigency). Thus, it is meted out to the extent of the *ḍarūrah* (compulsive necessity), and the *ḍarūrah* (compulsive necessity) is fulfilled by an unrestricted singular entity (*fard muṭlaq*), and the unrestricted singular entity is not specified because specification relies on generality [i.e. being *ʿāmm*].[99]

If one [husband] said [to his wife] after consummation of the marriage: 'إِعْتَدِّى (Enter the waiting period),' and by that he intends divorce, the divorce takes effect by way of *iqtiḍā'* (exigency), because to spend the waiting period (*ʿiddah*) requires the existence of divorce, and so the divorce is implied to exist out of *ḍarūrah* (compulsive necessity), and thus the occurrence [as divorce] is revocable (*rajʿī*) [divorce] because the description of irrevocable (*baynūnah*) [divorce] is beyond the extent of *ḍarūrah* (compulsive necessity) so it is not established by way of *iqtiḍā'* (exigency), and nothing takes effect but one [divorce], as we have mentioned [earlier].

POINTS TO NOTE

- *ʿIbārat an-naṣṣ* (explicit meaning) is what is normally understood as the context of that text even without thinking.

QUESTIONS

1. What is the difference between *ishārat an-naṣṣ* and *ʿibārat an-naṣṣ*?
2. If someone takes an oath that he will not speak to so-and-so, and then he speaks to him after his death, does he violate his oath? If not, why not? If so, why?
3. Give an example of *dalālat an-naṣṣ*.
4. If a man says to his wife 'You are divorced', can he intend three divorces?

❖

98 'Then my slave is free.'

99 Therefore, it is impossible for him to specify it with his intention.

	Sub-type	Types
Specific	خاص	وضع Coinage
General	عام	
Homonym	مشترك	
Construed	المؤوّل	
Literal	حقيقة	استعمال Use
Metaphorical	مجاز	
Explicit	صريح	
Metonymic	كناية	
Apparent	ظاهر	ظهور Clarity
Explicit	نص	
Explained	مفسر	
Firm	محكم	
Hidden	خفي	خفا Ambiguity
Problematic	مشكل	
Concise	مجمل	
Intricate	متشابه	
Explicit Meaning	عبارة النص	دلالة Indication
Alluded Meaning	إشارة النص	
Inferred Meaning	دلالة النص	
Required Meaning	اقتضاء النص	

Important note: The four types are mutually exclusive, but their subtypes are not, for example, a verse of the Qur'an could be specific, literal, and apparent and have an alluded meaning all at same time!

2.11: AMR (THE IMPERATIVE)

Linguistically, *amr* (imperative) is the saying of the speaker to another, 'إِفْعَلْ (Do it).'

In the Sharīʿah, it is 'the free disposal to make the action binding on someone'.

Some imams have mentioned that the intended [meaning] of *amr* is specific to this form [of wording] (*ṣīghah*).

But it is absurd for it to mean that 'the realistic [meaning] of the *amr* is specific to this form [of wording],' because Allah ﷻ is speaking in eternity – according to us – and His Speech is *amr* (imperative), *nahy* (proscription), *ikhbār* (information), and *istikhbār* (inquiry), and so it is impossible for this form [of wording] [= 'إِفْعَلْ (Do it)'] to exist in eternity.

It is also absurd for its meaning to mean the intended [meaning] of 'the *amr* of the one giving the command' is specific to this [particular] form [of wording], because the intended [meaning] of the *amr* by the Lawgiver is 'the obligation of the action on the person,' (which – according to us – is the meaning of being tested) and obligation has been established without this form [of wording]. Is it not that belief (*īmān*) is obligatory on one whom the invitation to faith has not reached without the advent of hearing?

Imam Abū Ḥanīfah (Allah have mercy on him) said: 'Had Allah ﷻ not sent a messenger, it would have been obligatory upon the sane to recognise Him with their intellects.'

Thus, this is taken as the intended [meaning] for *amr* is that it is specified with this [particular] form [of wording] [i.e. 'إِفْعَلْ (Do it)'] for the person in terms of the legal rulings, such that the action of the Messenger ﷺ is not in the status of his ﷺ saying, 'إِفْعَلُوْا (All of you do it),' and it is not binding to believe it to be obligatory.[100]

As for following him in his actions ﷺ, it is only obliged when there is persistence and absence of any evidence of specification [to him ﷺ alone].[101]

Amr Muṭlaq (Unrestricted Imperative)

Difference Between the Effects of Amr Muṭlaq (Unrestricted Imperative)

The scholars have differed regarding the *amr muṭlaq* (unrestricted imperative), i.e. [the *amr*] that is free from any contextual indicator that indicates to it being binding or non-binding.

Example of the Amr (Imperative) that is Attached with a Contextual Indicator

For example, the saying of Allah ﷻ:

وَإِذَا قُرِئَ ٱلْقُرْءَانُ فَٱسْتَمِعُوا۟ لَهُۥ وَأَنصِتُوا۟ لَعَلَّكُمْ تُرْحَمُونَ

'And when the Qur'an is recited, then listen carefully to it and be attentive, so that you may be shown mercy.' Qur'an, 7:204

And the saying of Allah ﷻ:

وَلَا تَقْرَبَا هَـٰذِهِ ٱلشَّجَرَةَ فَتَكُونَا مِنَ ٱلظَّـٰلِمِينَ

'And do not [you two] approach this tree, otherwise [the two of] you will be of the wrongdoers.' Qur'an 2:35

---

100 Some acts or omissions of the Messenger of Allah ﷺ are connected to his personal life that Muslims are not obliged to follow.

101 Adherence to the acts or omissions of the Messenger of Allah ﷺ is not an obligation as a fundamental requisite merely because he ﷺ practised or refrained from such an act. However, the act or omission is rendered an obligation if the Messenger of Allah ﷺ performed it on a regular basis without ever leaving it. Moreover, for such an act or omission to stand as an obligation on the Muslims in general, it must also be free of being specific to the Messenger of Allah ﷺ, such as his ﷺ marriage to more than four women in one time, the specific obligation on him ﷺ of *tahajjud* prayer, etc.

TERMINOLOGY

Amr: The imperative
Nahy: The proscriptive
Ism al-jins: Generic noun
Iṭlāq: Unrestrictedness
Taṣarruf: Free disposal/control

The Correct Opinion

The correct opinion of the school is that its effect is obligation (*wujūb*) unless there is evidence established against it, because the omission of [performing] the *amr* is disobedience,[102] just as adherence to it is obedience.[103]

Al-Ḥumāsī[104] said:

أَطَعْتِ لِآمِرِيْكِ بِصَرْمِ حَبْلِيْ

مُرِيْهِمْ فِيْ أَحَبَّتِهِمْ بِذَاكِ

فَهُمْ إِنْ طَاوَعُوْكِ فَطَاوِعِيْهِمْ

وَإِنْ عَاصَوْكِ فَاعْصِيْ مَنْ عَصَاكِ

Your commanders, to sever off the cords of tie with me, you obey,
The same command must you give them regarding their friends too,
For if then they obey you, so obey them you may,
But if they disobey, then disobey whoever disobeys you.

Disobedience to that which resorts to a right of the Shariʿah [i.e. a legal right,] is the reason for punishment. The verification of this is that the obligation of adherence to the *amr* is according to the jurisdiction of the one giving the command over the one who is addressed.

For this reason, if you directed the [expressive] form of the command to someone whose obedience to you is not binding upon him at all, then that does not oblige adherence, but if you directed it to a slave whose obedience to you was binding upon him, adherence is undeniably binding upon him, such that if he was to wilfully disregard it he would be liable to punishment in accordance with the common practice (*ʿurf*) and the Sharīʿah (i.e. the law).

On this [principle] that we know that the obligation of adherence is according to the jurisdiction of the one giving the command [over the one who is addressed].

Once this has been established, we say: Indeed, for Allah ﷻ is absolute ownership of every particle of the particles of the universe, and He ﷻ has disposal (*taṣarruf*) of it as He ﷻ wills and intends.

When it is established that whoever has imperfect ownership of a slave whose omission of [performing] the command becomes a reason for [him] being liable to punishment, then what is your opinion regarding the omission of [the performance of] a command of [the One] Who brought you into existence out of nothingness and showered upon you an abundance of bounties?

---

102 And disobedience is a sin.

103 And obedience is a virtue.

104 He is Khalid, one of the poets whose works have been included in the *Diwān al-Ḥumāsah*.

The Exigent of the Amr

The Imperative Does Not Necessitate Repetition

The imperative to perform an act does not necessitate [its] repetition.

EXAMPLE

It is due to this [principle] that we said: When one says [to his agent]: 'طَلِّقْ إِمْرَأَتِي (Divorce my wife),' and the agent divorces her, and thereafter the principal [= the divorcing husband] marries her [again], the agent may not divorce her a second time with the first command. If one said: 'زَوِّجْنِي إِمْرَأَةً (Marry me to a woman),' this does not incorporate marrying time after time. If one said to his slave: 'تَزَوَّجْ (Get married),' it only incorporates once because the command to perform an act is a demand to fulfil the act by way of brevity. [For example,] one's saying: 'اِضْرِبْ (Strike!),' is a summarised [way] of him saying, 'اِفْعَلْ فِعْلَ الضَّرْبِ (Do an act of striking!),' and brevity and elongation in speech are the same in ruling.

The Meaning of Genus (Jins) in the Amr

Also, the command to strike is a command from the genus (*jins*) of a known disposal (*taṣarruf*) [of capacity].

The Ruling of Ism al-Jins (Generic Noun)

The ruling of the *ism al-jins* (generic noun) is that it incorporates the minimum when applied in an unrestricted manner (*iṭlāq*),[105] and it [also] bears the possibility of the entire genus.[106]

EXAMPLE

Due to this, [principle] we said: When one swears an oath that he will not drink water, he violates [his oath] by drinking even a tiny drop of it, but if he intended by it all the waters of the world, then his intention is valid.[107]

It is due to this [principle] that we said: When someone says to her [= his wife], 'طَلِّقِي نَفْسَكِ (Divorce yourself),' and she replies, 'طَلَّقْتُ (I have divorced [myself]),' only one [divorce][108] takes effect, but if he intended three [divorcements], then his intention is valid.[109]

Likewise, if he says to another [i.e. his agent], 'طَلِّقْهَا (Divorce her),' it incorporates one [divorcement] when unrestricted, but if

---

105 An example of this would be someone divorcing his wife using words of divorce that are interpreted without qualification.

106 An example of this would be someone divorcing his wife using words of divorce that are interpreted generically. The difference between this and the previous example is that the words are interpreted according to the intention of the divorcing husband.

107 As in the previous two footnotes, the intention shall be taken into account.

108 This shall amount to one revocable divorce (*ṭalāq rajʿī*) (al-Qudūrī, *Mukhtaṣar*, p.422).

109 In this case, all three pronouncements of divorce shall take effect on her (al-Qudūrī, *Mukhtaṣar*, p.422).

he intended three [divorcements], his intention is valid. However, if he intends two [divorcements], it is not valid unless the wife is a slave-woman – because the intention of two [divorces] for her is the intention of the entire genus.[110]

If one says to his slave: 'تَزَوَّجْ (Get married),' it takes effect to marry one woman, but if he intends two then his intention is valid, because that is the entire genus in the case of a slave.[111]

The Issue of the Repetition of Worships

The act of repetition in acts of worship does not result from this,[112] for it is not established with the [solitary] *amr*, but rather by the repetition of its causes with which the obligation is established. The *amr* is the demand to fulfil whatever has been obligated as a duty due to a previous *sabab* (cause) and not due to the establishment of the origin of the obligation *per se*.

This is in the status of a man saying: 'أَدِّ ثَمَنَ الْمَبِيعِ (Pay the price of the goods),' or 'أَدِّ نَفَقَةَ الزَّوْجَةِ (Pay the maintenance of the wife).'

Thus, when an act of worship is obligated due to its cause then the *amr* is orientated] towards the fulfilment of that which is obligatory from it [= worship] upon the person.[113]

Thereafter, it is because the *amr* incorporates the genus that it incorporates the genus of whatever is obligatory upon him.

EXAMPLE

Its example is as is said: Indeed, the incumbent act during the time of *ẓuhr* is the *ẓuhr* [prayer] itself, and so the *amr* orientates to the fulfilment of that incumbent act. Then, when the time reoccurs, the incumbent [act] repeats.[114] Therefore, the *amr* incorporates that other incumbent act out of the *ḍarūrah* (compulsive necessity) of incorporating it as the entire genus that is incumbent on him, irrespective of whether it is fasting (*ṣawm*) or prayer (*ṣalāh*).

Thus, the repetition of the recurrent worship is in this manner and not in the manner that the *amr* necessitates repetition.

QUESTIONS

1. What is the meaning of genus in the *amr*?
2. What does the *amr* mean linguistically?

---

110 The maximum number of divorcements that can be issued to a slave-woman by the same husband are two that result in an irrevocable divorce (*ṭalāq bā'in*), unlike three for a freewoman.

111 The maximum number of women a slave can be married to at the same time are two, unlike four for the freeman.

112 Such as the repetition of the command for worship such as prayer and *zakāh*, etc.

113 An example of this is the prayer (*ṣalāh*); its incumbency repeats itself due to the repetition of its *sababs* (reasons or effective conditions), which are its times. The original incumbency of prayer is established by the *amr* (command), and the incumbency of its performance is repeated with the repetition of time.

114 This means that the incumbency becomes due whenever the time for the fulfilment of the incumbent act begins.

3. Repetition of the action is derived from the *amr*. True or false?
4. What is the necessary outcome of the *amr*?

❖

2.12: THE MA'MŪR BIHĪ (ENJOINED) AND TIME-CONSTRICTION

Ma'mūr bihī (the act that is enjoined) is of two types:

i. *Muṭlaq* ([time-]independent), and
ii. *Muqayyad* (constricted) by it [= time].

The Ruling of Muṭlaq (Time-Independent)

The ruling of *muṭlaq* ([time-]independent) is that the performance [of it] is incumbent on a deferred basis, provided one does not miss it during [his or her] lifetime.

Example of Muṭlaq (Time-Independent)

It is on this [principle] that Imam Muhammad (Allah have mercy on him) has said in *al-Jāmiʿ [al-Kabīr]:*[115] If one makes a vow (*nadhr*) that he will assume a month's duration of [religious] seclusion (*iʿtikāf*), then he may assume any month he wishes,[116] and if one makes a vow that he will fast a month's duration, then he may fast any month he wishes [at any time of his life].

In relation to [paying] *zakāh*, *ṣadaqat al-fiṭr*, and *ʿushr* (tenth), the known opinion is that one does not become negligent (*mufarriṭ*) by delaying, because if the *niṣāb* perishes, the obligation [to pay the due also] is omitted; one who violates an oath, if his wealth is lost and he has become poor (*faqīr*), may expiate by fasting.

Upon this basis, it is not permitted to make up for missed prayers (*qaḍāʾ*) during times repugnant [for prayer], since it became obligatory time-independent, it became obligatory perfect, and therefore the person does not depart responsibility by its imperfect performance.[117] Thus, it is permitted to perform the *ʿaṣr* [prayer] during the redness [of the sun at the onset of sunset] as (*adāʾ*)[118] performance but not [the *ʿaṣr* prayer] by delayed performance (*qaḍāʾ*).[119]

---

115 Ash-Shaybānī, Muhammad ibn al-Ḥasan (131 AH/749 CE – 189 AH/805 CE), *Al-Jāmiʿ al-Kabīr*.

116 At any time of his life.

117 The Ḥanafī jurists (Allah have mercy on them) have classified time, especially of prayer, into perfect (*kāmil*) and imperfect (*nāqiṣ*), and therefore, they permit the *ʿaṣr* prayer of that particular day to be performed when the sun is setting, albeit it is imperfect, but they hold as invalid the missed *ʿaṣr* prayer of any other day that is performed by way of *qaḍāʾ* (delayed performance) during the setting of the sun. Thus, the time being perfect (*kāmil*) or imperfect (*nāqiṣ*) does have legal implications.

118 This is the *ʿaṣr* prayer of that particular day.

119 This is the *ʿaṣr* prayer that was missed on any other day and must be discharged by delayed performance (*qaḍāʾ*). The obligation of its performance

TERMINOLOGY

Muṭlaq: Time-Independent

Muqayyad: Time-Constricted

Ẓarf: Adverbial noun of time or place

Mi'yār: Gauge

Al-wājib al-muḍayyaq: Constricted incumbence

Nadhr: Vow

The Opinion of Imam Abū'l-Ḥasan al-Karkhī (Allah have mercy on him)

According to [Imam Abu'l-Ḥasan] al-Karkhī (Allah have mercy on him),[120] the outcome of the *amr muṭlaq* (time-independent imperative) is immediate obligation.[121]

Though there is a disagreement with him in the obligation [of its immediacy],[122] there is, however, no disagreement that haste in adhering [to it] is recommended.

The Division of Muqayyad by Time (Time-Constricted)

[*Muqayyad* to time is also known as *muwaqqat* (time-constricted).]

As for *muwaqqat* (time-constricted), there are two types:[123]

i. *ẓarf*

ii. *mi'yār*

Ẓarf (Container)

One type is when the time is a *ẓarf* (container) for [the performance of] the act, such that it is not conditional for the entire time to be spent for that action, like prayer (*ṣalāh*).[124]

---

does not lapse and it may be made up at any time after its due time had lapsed, preferably as soon as possible, and so any time restriction that may affect its complete performance must be avoided so as to accomplish the obligation perfectly. In a case such as this, delayed performance (*qaḍā'*) of *'aṣr* prayer during the time when the sun is setting is not permitted.

120 He is is 'Ubaidullāh ibn al-Ḥasan ibn Dallāl ibn Dalham al-Karkhī (260 AH / 873 CE – 340 AH / 951 CE). He is known by the name Abu'l-Ḥasan as well as al-Karkhī, the latter being more common, due to his place of birth in the western part of Baghdad, Iraq. He took his *fiqh* (practical Islāmic law) from Aḥmad ibn al-Ḥusayn Abū Sa'īd al-Barda'ī (d. 317 AH / 929 CE), who took it from Ismā'īl ibn Ḥammād, who took it from his own father, namely Ḥammād ibn Abū Ḥanīfah (d. 176 AH / 793 CE), who took it from his father, namely Abū Ḥanīfah an-Nu'mān ibn Thābit (80 AH / 699 CE – 148 AH / 765 CE) (Allah have mercy on them), etc. and so this academic and spiritual lineage reaches the Beloved Messenger of Allah ﷺ. The following gems of Islamic scholarship learnt their *fiqh* from him: Abū Bakr ar-Rāzī al-Jaṣṣāṣ (d. 370 AH / 980 CE), Abū 'Abdullāh ad-Dāmighānī, Abū 'Alī ash-Shāshī (344 AH / 955 CE), Abu'l-Qāsim 'Alī ibn Muḥammad at-Tannūkhī, Aḥmad aṭ-Ṭabarī, Abū 'Abdullāh al-Jurjānī, Abū Zakariyyā ad-Darīr al-Baṣrī, and many others. Imam al-Karkhī (Allah have mercy on him) is the author of the earliest existing book on legal maxims (*al-qawā'id al-fiqhiyyah*).

121 This means that the incumbent act must be performed immediately and without delay.

122 The disagreement in the immediacy of an obliged act subject to time restriction to be performed immediately is upheld by the majority of the jurists as well as by Imam Abu'l-Ḥasan al-Karkhī from the Ḥanafī jurists (Allah have mercy on them). However, the majority of the Ḥanafī jurists (Allah have mercy on them) are of the view that immediacy in time-restricted acts is not a must, and that such acts may be delayed until the last portion of the valid time, such that the act performed during the last portion of the time is reckoned as duly executed.

123 The Shāfi'ī, Mālikī and Ḥanbalī jurists (Allah have mercy on them) have divided *muwaqqat* (i.e. *muqayyad*) into three types: i. *muwassa'* (extensive), ii. *muḍayyaq* (constricted) and iii. *dhu shabahayn* (resembling both).

124 *Ẓarf* in this case is not a standard for the performance of the act but for the act to be performed within it. As an example, *ẓuhr* prayer is obliged when its time begins, but the entire time of *ẓuhr* is not spent performing *ẓuhr* prayer;

NOTES

The Rulings of Ẓarf

Of the rulings of this type [*ẓarf*] is that the incumbency of performing an act during it [i.e. this particular time] does not negate the incumbency of performing another act during it that is of the same genus, such that if one was to make a vow that he will pray such-and-such units within the time of *ẓuhr*, it shall be binding upon him.[125]

From its rulings is that the incumbency of prayer during it [i.e. this particular time] does not negate the soundness of any other prayer within it, such that if one preoccupied himself throughout the entire time of *ẓuhr* with [the performance of] something other than *ẓuhr*, it is possible.

Of its rulings is that the *ma'mūr bihī* (the act that is enjoined) cannot be discharged without a specified intention, since something other than it [= the *ma'mūr bihī*] is legally permitted during that time, it would not be specified by its act [alone] even though the time may be constricted, and that is because the consideration of the intention is according to consideration of crowdedness and the crowdedness remains with constrictedness of the time.[126]

Miʿyār (Gauge)

The second type is that for which time is the *miʿyār* (gauge).[127]

EXAMPLE

That is like fasting (*ṣawm*); it is calculated by time, which [in this case] is the day.

The Ruling of Miʿyār and Its Types

[*Miʿyār* is divided into two types:

i. *al-wājib al-muḍayyaq al-muʿayyan* (specified constricted incumbence), and
ii. *al-wājib al-muḍayyaq ghayr al-muʿayyan* (non-specified constricted incumbence)]

---

one may delay the performance of *ẓuhr* prayer until the final stages of the due time or he may perform it at its beginning time. However, once someone has performed the *ẓuhr* prayer, they are not required to perform it repeatedly in order to fill that time.

125 When someone vows to perform a certain number of units of optional prayer, he shall be obliged to perform the *ẓuhr* prayer – which is obligatory – and also the units he has vowed to pray, because the vow has rendered the units of optional prayer incumbent.

126 This means that one may perform supererogatory prayers during the time of *ẓuhr*, etc.

127 When time is the *miʿyār* (standard), the obligation of the due act extends or constricts with the time, such that the entire time is filled with the performance of that act, such as fasting the entire day, irrespective of its duration. The Shāfiʿī jurists (Allah have mercy on them) term this type *muḍayyaq* (constricted).

NOTES

Al-Wājib al-Muḍayyaq al-Muʿayyan (Specified Constricted Incumbence)

Of the rulings [of *miʿyār*] is that when the Sharīʿah specifies a time for it then nothing else [of its genus] is incumbent to be performed during that time and nor is the performance of any other [act of its genus] permitted within it, such that if the healthy resident individual was to adopt abstinence [from eating, drinking and sexual intercourse] during [the month of] Ramaḍān for any other incumbent [fast], [the fast of] Ramaḍān takes effect and not what he intended.[128]

If crowdedness is impelled during the [due] time, the stipulation for specifying [the fasts] is omitted because it [was there] to end the crowdedness.[129]

However, the principal intention is not omitted[130] because [mere] abstinence (*imsāk*) does not amount to fasting (*ṣawm*) unless with intention. And thus, in the Sharīʿah, fasting (*ṣawm*) is abstinence from eating, drinking and sexual intercourse during the day with intention.[131]

Al-Wājib al-Muḍayyaq Ghayr al-Muʿayyan (Non-Specified Constricted Incumbence)

If the Sharīʿah does not specify a time for it [= the *ma'mūr bihī*] then time would not be specified for it if the person specified it, such that if the person specified some days in order to discharge [the fasts of] Ramaḍān by delay (*qaḍā'*), they would not be [legally] specified for that delayed performance (*qaḍā'*), and so the fasts for expiation (*kaffārah*) and supererogatory fasts are permitted therein, and the Ramaḍān fasts discharged by delay (*qaḍā'*) are [also] permitted during those days as well as in other days.[132]

---

128 The author has intentionally mentioned the 'healthy resident' individual, because the fasts of Ramadan are obligatory on such persons. However, according to the Ḥanafī jurists, because the fasts of Ramadan are not obligatory on someone who is sick or a traveller, such individuals may fast during the month of Ramadan other than the obligatory fasts, such as fasts to be made up by way of delayed performance (*qaḍā'*), expiation or other supererogatory fasts, because the sick and the travellers have the option of whether or not to fast in Ramadan, and hence, the obligatory fasts of Ramadan are not enjoined on them. However, Imam Abū Yūsuf (Allah have mercy on him) stated that the dispensation given to the sick or travelling persons was in order to remove hardship and discomfort from them and to offer them ease and comfort, and so their fasting will not differentiate between the sick and healthy, and the travelling and resident individual, in which case their fasting shall be reckoned as the fast of Ramadan.

129 The confluence in this case is the obligatory fasting of Ramadan, during which time supererogatory fasts are void, and so, anyone intending to fast on a supererogatory basis during the month of Ramadan will have their fasts overridden by the obligatory fasts of Ramadan.

130 This is in response to the question of whether the principal intention during Ramadan for its fasting is needed or not, based on the fact that the fasts of Ramadan are obligatory and that no other fasts can take their place.

131 The legal fast in accordance with the Sharīʿah is: 1. abstinence from: i. eating, ii. drinking, and iii. sexual intercourse, 2. during the day, 3. with intention. (al-Qudūrī, *Mukhtaṣar*, p.107).

132 One specifying certain days for the making up of missed obligatory fasts of Ramadan does not legally obligate them on him, and he may assume other

NOTES

Of the rulings of this type is that the specification of the intention is conditional due to the existence of the conflux.[133]

It is permitted for the person to oblige something on himself that may or may not be time-constricted (*muwaqqat*), but he has no right to alter the legal ruling.[134]

EXAMPLE

Its example occurs when someone makes a vow (*nadhr*) that he will fast a specific day, then that [particular day] becomes binding upon him, but if he fasted that day for the delayed performance (*qaḍā'*) of Ramadan or a fast for the expiation (*kaffārah*) of violating his oath (*yamīn*), it is [also] permitted, because the Sharīʿah has rendered the delayed performance unconstricted by time [to any day], and so it is not possible for the person to alter it by restricting it to any other day.

---

fasts during those particular days. Moreover, he may perform by delay (*qaḍā'*) the obligatory fasts missed in Ramadan during those days as well as on other days that he has not specified. This principle is based on the verse of the Qur'an:

فَمَن كَانَ مِنكُم مَّرِيضًا أَوْ عَلَىٰ سَفَرٍ فَعِدَّةٌ مِّنْ أَيَّامٍ أُخَرَ

'As for him who is sick among you, or on a journey, then [make up] a number of other days.' (Qur'an, 2:184).

In this verse, the delayed performance (*qaḍā'*) of the missed fasts from Ramadan is unrestricted by time, and so if anyone was to fix certain days for that delayed performance (*qaḍā'*), he would be shifting from unrestricted time to qualified time (*muqayyad*), which a person is lawfully incapable of doing as it is void for him according to the Sharīʿah.

133 It is conditional for one making up the missed fasts of Ramadan by delayed performance (*qaḍā'*) to form his intention as thus, and not a simple intention to make up for missed fasts and nor to perform obligatory fasts. The reason is that the conflux is present here, which in this case is the openness and non-specification of the time, in which one may fast for expiation, observe supererogatory fasts as well as delayed (*qaḍā'*) fasts. It is by reason to remove this confluence that the intention is formed specifying the missed obligatory fasts of Ramadan, the fasts for expiation or the supererogatory fasts, as the case may be.

134 This is the response to the following objection: 'If someone specifies some days in order to make up for the missed obligatory fasts (*qaḍā'*) of Ramadan, his such specifying is not legally valid, and this seems incorrect, because if he specifies something for himself whether that is time-restricted or not, it becomes incumbent on him to perform it. Therefore, if he is allowed to oblige something upon himself that was not incumbent on him (such as supererogatory fasts), then why is he not allowed to oblige something upon himself that was incumbent on him (such as the missed obligatory fasts of Ramadan)?'

The author responds by saying: 'One is permitted to oblige something upon himself that was not once incumbent on him, but he is not permitted to alter the ruling of the Sharīʿah. If he was to specify days for the delayed performance (*qaḍā'*) of the missed fasts of Ramadan, he would be rendering *muqayyad* what is legally *muṭlaq* because Verse 2:184 of the Qur'an has declared such delayed performance (*qaḍā'*) to be *muṭlaq* (unrestricted) – restricting what is unrestricted is against the Sharīʿah. On the contrary, obliging something on oneself that is not incumbent is not tantamount to altering the ruling of the Sharīʿah, and so one is legally permitted to specify it.'

Exception

It does not necessitate, according to this [principle], if he performs a supererogatory fast instead, hence the vow (*nadhr*) will occur and not what he had intended because the supererogatory [worship] is the right of the person, and he has an absolute right to omit it or fulfil it, so it is permitted that he influences his action regarding that which is his right but not regarding that which is the right of the Sharīʿah.

On the account of this meaning, our teachers[135] said: If the couple mutually stipulate in the *khulʿ* (divorce at the instance of the wife) that there shall be no maintenance (*nafaqah*) for the woman and no lodging, the maintenance is omitted[136] but not the lodging,[137] such that the husband does not have the capacity to evict her from the house where she spends her *ʿiddah* (waiting period before she can remarry).

That is because the lodging [provided to her as the] house where she spends her *ʿiddah* is a right of the Sharīʿah, and so therefore the person does not have the [legal] capacity to eliminate it, as opposed to maintenance (*nafaqah*).

POINTS TO NOTE

- The specific has other forms: The Unrestricted (مطلق), The Restricted (مقيد), The Imperative (امر), Proscriptive (نهي).

QUESTIONS

1. What are the two types of *ma'mūr bihī*?
2. What does the *amr* mean linguistically?
3. What is the ruling when the time to perform an action is within a *ẓarf*?
4. What is the ruling when the time to perform an action is within a *miʿyār*?

❖

135 The Ḥanafī jurists (Allah have mercy on them).

136 The woman may waive the maintenance (*nafaqah*) due to her as it is her independent right.

137 The lodging cannot be eliminated or waived as a right for this right belongs absolutely to the Sharīʿah.

2.13: MA'MŪR BI-HĪ BEING ḤASAN

The command [to do] (*amr*) something refers to the *ma'mūr bihī* (the act commanded) being *ḥasan* (good) provided the one issuing the command is someone wise, because the command is for elucidation that the *ma'mūr bihī* is something that ought to exist, and so therefore [the command] requires it to be *ḥasan*.

Its Types

Then, with regards to the *ma'mūr bihī* being *ḥasan*, there are two types:

i. *ḥasan bi-nafsi-hī* (*ḥasan per se*), and

ii. *ḥasan li-ghayri-hī* (*ḥasan per quod*).

Ḥasan Bi-Nafsi-hī (Ḥasan Per Se)

Ḥasan bi-nafsi-hī (*ḥasan per se*) is like the belief in Allah ﷻ, being grateful to the Absolute Benefactor – Allah ﷻ, [adopting] the truth, justice, prayer, and other such pure worship.

The Ruling of Ḥasan Bi-Nafsi-hī (Ḥasan Per Se)

The ruling of this type is that when its performance becomes incumbent on the person, it does not lapse without [due] performance, this [ruling] is for that which is not eliminable, such as the belief in Allah ﷻ.

As for that which is eliminable, it lapses by [due] performance, or due to elimination by the one who issued the command.

EXAMPLE

Upon this [principle] we said that, when the time for prayer becomes due at the earliest time, the incumbency lapses by [its due] performance, or because of the inhibition of insanity (*junūn*), menstruation (*ḥayḍ*) and postnatal bleeding (*nifās*) – at the latest time, on the assumption that the Sharīʿah had eliminated it from [the legally responsible person (*mukallaf*)] at the occurrence of these inhibitions. However, [this incumbency] shall not elapse due to the restriction of the time,[138] absence of water[139] or [absence of] clothing,[140] etc.

Ḥasan Li-Ghayrihī (Ḥasan Per Quod)

The second type is that which is *ḥasan* by virtue of an extrinsic circumstance (*wāsiṭah*)[141] [(i.e. *ḥasan li-ghayri-hī* (*ḥasan per quod*)].

---

138 Restriction of time does not eliminate the obligation to pray. Someone who misses prayer due to the lapse of time out of laziness is sinful, but if he misses it despite trying his utmost to perform it on time, he is not sinful.

139 Someone who does not find water may pray after performing *tayammum* (dry substitute wudu).

140 Whoever does not find garments, he prays naked whilst seated and indicating the bowing and the prostration. (Al-Qudūrī, *Mukhtaṣar*, p.32).

141 The extrinsic circumstance (*wāsiṭah*) is the cause for the action to be *ḥasan*, i.e. its means, and hence *ḥasan per quod*.

TERMINOLOGY

Ḥadd: Corporal punishments

Qiṣāṣ: Legally supervised retaliation

Jihād: Military campaign

Ḥasan: Good

Junūn: Insanity

EXAMPLE

That is like hurrying to [the masjid for] the *jumuʿah* [prayer] and performing *wuḍū'* (wudu) for prayer (*ṣalāh*) – hurrying is *ḥasan* because it is extrinsically conducive to the performance of *jumuʿah* [prayer], and *wuḍū'* (wudu) is *ḥasan* by extrinsic circumstance due to it being the key to prayer (*ṣalāh*).

The Ruling of Ḥasan Li-Ghayri-hī (Ḥasan Per Quod)

The ruling of this type [i.e. *ḥasan li-ghayri-hī* (*ḥasan* per quod)] is that it lapses by the lapsing of that extrinsic circumstance, such that the hurrying is not incumbent upon someone on whom the *jumuʿah* [prayer] is not due,[142] and *wuḍū'* (wudu) is not incumbent upon someone on whom prayer (*ṣalāh*) is not due.[143] However, if he hurries to [the masjid for] the *jumuʿah* [prayer], and then he is taken by coercion to another place prior to the *iqāmah*[144] of the *jumuʿah* [prayer being called], it is incumbent upon him to hurry a second time, but if he is someone in religious seclusion (*iʿtikāf*) in a congregational [masjid], the [incumbency of the] hurrying elapses from him.

Similarly, if he performs wudu (*wuḍū'*) and then invalidates [it] prior to performing prayer (*ṣalāh*), it is incumbent upon him to perform wudu (*wuḍū'*) a second time. If he is in [the state of] wudu (*wuḍū'*) when the [performance of] prayer is incumbent, it is not incumbent on him to renew [his] wudu (*wuḍū'*).

Ḥadd Punishments, Qiṣāṣ and Jihād

In proximity to this type [i.e. *ḥasan li-ghayri-hī* (*ḥasan per quod*)] are *ḥadd* (punishments), *qiṣāṣ* (legally supervised retaliation) and *jihād* (military campaign).

The *ḥadd* (punishment) is *ḥasan* because of the circumstance of deterring of [committing] offences.[145] *Jihād* is *ḥasan* because of the circumstance of repelling the evil of the disbelievers and an elevating the word of truth.[146] If we were to assume that this extrinsic circumstance did not exist, then that *ma'mūr bihī* would also not exist, because the *ḥadd* (punishment) would not be incumbent if there was no crime; if disbelief was not conducive to war, then *jihād* would not be incumbent for it.

---

142 An example of someone who is not obliged to perform the *jumuʿah* prayer is a traveller and an ill person, etc.

143 An example of someone who is not obliged to perform prayer (*ṣalāh*) is a woman experiencing menstrual bleeding, and a minor, etc.

144 The call for the commencement of prayer congregation.

145 Punishments are never something noble *per se* which is why they are not *ḥasan bi-nafsi-hī* (*ḥasan per se*), but because they deter people from committing crimes, they are extrinsically noble, i.e. noble *per quod*, or *ḥasan li-ghayri-hī* (*ḥasan per quod*).

146 *Jihād*, or any military campaign, is never something noble *per se* which is why it is not *ḥasan bi-nafsi-hī*, but because it repels the disbelievers from attacking the Muslims and spreading mischief, it is extrinsically noble, i.e. noble *per quod*, or *ḥasan li-ghayri-hī*.

QUESTIONS

1. What are the two types of *ma'mūr bihī* being *ḥasan*?
2. Is the incumbency of the prayer omitted due to the absence of water? Why, or why not?
3. Does the one issuing the command have to be wise for it to be *ḥasan*?

❖

2.14: ADĀ' (DUE PERFORMANCE) AND QAḌĀ' (DELAYED PERFORMANCE)

The incumbent (*wājib*) [act caused] by the ruling of the one giving the command is of two types:

i. *adā'* (due performance), and
ii. *qaḍā'* (delayed performance).

Adā' (Due Performance)

Adā' (due performance) is an expression for the delivery of the required due (*ʿayn al-wājib*) to one rightful to it.

Qaḍā' (Delayed Performance)

Qaḍā' (delayed performance) is an expression for the delivery of the like of the due (*mithl al-wājib*) to one rightful to it.

Division of Adā' (Due Performance)

Thereafter, *adā'* (due performance) is of two types:

i. *kāmil* (perfect), and
ii. *qāṣir* (imperfect).

Adā' Kāmil (Perfect Due Performance)

[*Adā'*] *kāmil* (perfect due performance)[147] is like the due performance of prayer (*ṣalāh*) in its time with congregation, circumambulation [of the Kaʿbah] in *wuḍū'*, submitting the object of sale (*mabīʿ*) in a sound state to the purchaser as the contract demands, or the usurper submitting the misappropriated item as [it was in the state that] he had usurped it.

The Ruling of Adā' Kāmil (Perfect Due Performance)

The ruling of this type [i.e. *adā' kāmil* (perfect due performance)] is that one is decreed to be free of its responsibility.[148]

---

147 *Adā' kāmil* (complete due performance) is also known as *adā' maḥḍ* (simple due performance).

148 The legal effect of *adā' kāmil* (perfect due performance) is that the legally responsible person (*mukallaf*) becomes free of the responsibility after having performed it in a perfect manner.

TERMINOLOGY

Adā': Due performance

Qaḍā': Delayed performance

Adā' Kāmil: Perfect due performance

Adā' Qāṣir: Imperfect due performance

Ghaṣb: Misappropriation

Wadīʿah: Deposit

It is on this [principle] that we say: If the usurper sells the misappropriated [item] to the [rightful] owner, or he pawns it with him or gifts it to him and [thereby] submits it to him, he becomes free from responsibility, and that [submission] is [deemed] the fulfilment of his right, but whatever he had expressly mentioned – sale or gift – stands void.[149]

If he misappropriates some food and feeds it to its [rightful] owner who is unaware of it being his own food, or he misappropriates some clothing and dresses its [rightful] owner in it who is unaware of it being his own clothing, that is [also] a fulfilment of his right.

If the purchaser in a corrupt sale lends the object of sale to the seller or pawns it with him [= the seller] or he [= the purchaser] leases it out to him [= the seller] or sells it [back] to him or gifts it to him and [thereby] submits it to him, that [submission] is [deemed] the fulfilment of his right, but whatever he had expressly mentioned – sale or gift, etc. – stands void.[150]

Adā' Qāṣir (Imperfect Due Performance)

As for *adā' qāṣir* (imperfect due performance), it is the submission of the due with a deficiency in its quality, for example: [performing] prayer (*ṣalah*) without balancing [its] rudimentary aspects[151], circumambulating [the Kaʿbah] in a state of ritual impurity, returning an object of sale that is now connected to a debt or to a crime, returning a misappropriated slave, the killing of whom is permitted due to a murder [he has committed] or he is connected to a debt or a crime the cause of which occurred with the usurper, the payment of inferior [currency] in the place of genuine [currency] when the creditor is not aware of that.

The Ruling of Adā' Qāṣir (Imperfect Due Performance)

The ruling of this type is that if it is possible for the deficiency to be made up with something similar (*mithl*) [to it], then it shall be made up with it, otherwise the ruling of the deficiency elapses – unless it is a sin.

Upon this [principle], if one omits the balancing of the rudimentary aspects in the category of prayer, then it is not possible to make up for it with something equivalent [to it] since there is nothing equivalent to it with the person, therefore, it elapses.

---

149 If A, the usurper, sells the usurped item to the rightful owner, B, A exonerates himself thereby, but the sale is legally void. The legal position is the same if A pawns the usurped item with B, and gifts it to him or submits it to him in whatever other manner.

150 In a vitiated sale, when the object of the sale is returned to the seller, it is akin to it being returned at the due rescission of the vitiated sale. Hence, the purchaser is said to have returned the object of sale, in which case he has fulfilled his obligation and thereby absolved himself of his responsibility. If the words sale, gift and the like thereof have been mentioned, they shall stand void.

151 The rudimentary aspects of prayer are the standing, the bowing, the prostrating, the sitting postures, etc. and balancing is achieved when someone performs them comfortably and without haste, and he or she settles in them well before moving into the next posture.

If one omitted prayer (*ṣalāh*) during the days of *Tashrīq*[152] and then he performed it by late discharge (*qaḍā'*) in days other than the days of *Tashrīq*, he does not say the *takbīr*[153] [of *Tashrīq*], because he has no right[154] to say the *takbīr* [of *Tashrīq*] audibly, legally [in the Sharīʿah].

We said regarding the omission of reciting Sūrat al-Fātiḥah, *al-Qunūt*, the *tashahhud* and the [six extra] *takbīrs* of the two *ʿĪd* [prayers], that they [can be] repaired by the [prostrations of] forgetfulness (*sujūd as-sahw*).

If one made the obligatory circumambulation [of the Kaʿbah] in a state of impurity, he makes that up with *dam* (atonement by sacrificing an animal) – that is [considered] equivalent to it in the Sharīʿah.

Upon this [principle], if one [= the debtor] pays inferior [currency] in the place of good [currency], that subsequently perishes whilst with the holder [= the creditor], he will have nothing against the debtor – according to Imam Abū Ḥanīfah (Allah have mercy on him) [and Imam Muhammad (Allah have mercy on him)] because there is no equivalent for the attribute of goodness on its own that would allow it to be made up with the equivalent [item].[155]

If one [= usurper/seller] submitted a slave, the killing of whom is permitted [due to] a crime [he committed] while [he was] with the usurper, or while [he was] with the seller after the sale, if he dies whilst he is with the owner or with the purchaser prior to being handed over [to the heirs of the slain], he [= the owner/purchaser] is bound [to pay] the price and the usurper is free [of liability] on account of having made the original payment. If he is killed because of that crime, the death is attributed to its first reason (*sabab*), and it becomes as if no due payment (*adā'*) was made at all – according to Imam Abū Ḥanīfah (Allah have mercy on him).

If the misappropriated slave-woman is returned [and she is] pregnant due to an act [that took place when she was] with the usurper, and then she died with the [rightful] owner when giving birth to the child, the usurper is not free of liability (*ḍamān*) – according to Imam Abū Ḥanīfah (Allah have mercy on him).

The Primary in Adā' (Due Performance)

The primary in this category is *adā'* (due performance), whether it is *kāmil* (perfect) or *nāqiṣ* (imperfect), and *qaḍā'* (delayed performance) is resorted to when the *adā'* (due performance) is unfeasible.

---

152 These are the eleventh, twelfth and thirteenth days of the month of Dhu'l-Ḥijjah.

153 The *takbīr* follows immediately after the obligatory prayers. It is to say: *'Allahu akbar, Allahu akbar, lā ilāha illa'llāhu wa'llāhu akbar, Allahu akbar, wa li'llāhi'l-ḥamd* – Allah is greater, Allah is greater, there is no god but Allah, Allah is greater, Allah is greater, and to Allah is all praise.'

154 It is incumbent to pronounce the *takbīr at-tashrīq* audibly after the obligatory prayers from the *fajr* prayer on the Day of ʿArafah (ninth of Dhu'l-Ḥijjah) until after the *ʿaṣr* prayer on the thirteenth of Dhu'l-Ḥijjah.

155 Attributes of items do not take a share of the payment of the item; also, when it comes to usurious items such as gold and silver, there is no difference between good quality and inferior quality.

It is due to this [principle] that the property (*māl*) is specified in the deposit (*wadʿīah*), the agency (*wakālah*) and misappropriation (*ghaṣb*), but if the deposit holder (*mūdaʿ*), the agent, or the usurper decide to retain the item and hand over something similar to it, they are not permitted to do that.

If one sells something and submits it, and then a blemish becomes apparent in it, the purchaser has the option between either retaining it or leaving it.[156]

Imam ash-Shāfiʿī's Inferences

On account of the primary [option] being *adā'* (due performance), Imam ash-Shāfiʿī (Allah have mercy on him) says: It is due on the usurper to return the misappropriated material item even if it may have altered while in the possession of the usurper, [and it is] a gross alteration,[157] and [the payment of] *arsh* (compensation) is [also] incumbent [on him] due to the loss.

Upon this [principle], if one usurps wheat and grinds it, a beam and builds a structure with it, a goat or sheep and slaughters it and roasts it, grapes and juices them, wheat and cultivates it and a plant grows [from it], all that [altered misappropriated property] is an ownership for the [rightful] owner – according to him [= Imam ash-Shāfiʿī (Allah have mercy on him)].

Ḥanafī Opinion

We[158] said: All of that is for the usurper, and the return of its value is due upon him.

If one usurps some silver and coins it into dirhams, or a [gold] nugget and renders it into dinars, or a goat or sheep and he slaughters it, the right of the [rightful] owner does not cease – according to *ẓāhir ar-riwāyah*.[159, 160]

---

156 When the purchaser becomes aware of a blemish in the goods, he has the choice: if he wants, he may take it by paying the complete payment, or if he wants, he may reject it, and return it to the seller for a refund. (Al-Qudūrī, *Mukhtaṣar*, p.166.)

157 A gross alteration (*taghayyur fāḥish*) occurs when the major part of its beneficial use is lost. In such a case, the usurper may not return the item, but retain it and replace it with a suitable substitute for the rightful owner. (Al-Qudūrī, *Mukhtaṣar*, p.331.)

158 The Ḥanafī jurists (Allah have mercy on them).

159 There are namely three types of expression used by the Ḥanafī scholars when referring to the rulings in the Ḥanafī school:

i. *Ẓāhir ar-riwāyah*: This is an expression used by Ḥanafī jurists referring to their legal standings as mentioned in the following books: *al-Jāmi' al-Kabīr*, *al-Jāmi' aṣ-Ṣaghīr*, *as-Siyar al-Kabīr*, *as-Siyar aṣ-Ṣaghīr*, *al-Mabsūṭ* and *az-Ziyādāt*.

ii. *Nawādir*: Similar to the above but referring to the legal rulings of the Ḥanafī jurists that are mentioned in books other than those mentioned above in *zāhir ar-riwāyah*.

iii. *Nawāzil*: These are the issues that are not mentioned in any of the above-stated books. Later scholars deduced rulings based on the issues that were already discussed in the above-stated books.

160 According to *ẓāhir ar-riwāyah*, the ownership of the rightful owner does not cease in cases such as these because the tangible item has not suffered a gross alteration.

Likewise, if one usurps some cotton and he yarns it, or [it was] yarn and he weaves it [into cloth], the right of the [rightful] owner does not cease – according to *ẓāhir ar-riwāyah*.[161]

Various subtopics branch out from this [principle], which is why he [= Imam ash-Shāfiʿī (Allah have mercy on him)] said: If the usurped slave appears after the [rightful] owner had received his due compensation from the usurper, the slave is [still] the property of the [rightful] owner,[162] and it is incumbent on the [rightful] owner to return what he had received as the value of the slave [to the usurper].

POINTS TO NOTE

- There is also a third type known as *adā' yushbih al-qaḍā'* (due performance that resembles delayed performance), and it is such when Mr. A, marries Mrs. B and he determines dowry for her as slave C, who belongs to Mr. D. Mr. A then purchases the slave, C, and delivers him to his wife, Mrs. B. In accordance with the terms of the marriage contract, this delivery is *adā'* (duly performed) but it is *shabīh bi'l-qaḍā'* or *adā' yushbih al-qaḍā'* (duly performed resembling performance by delay) because the ownership of the slave, C, changed. Or, if Mr. E begins his prayer (*ṣalāh*) behind an Imam, but then he invalidates his *wuḍū'* during prayer but he leaves to perform fresh *wuḍū'* after the Imam completes prayer.

QUESTIONS

1. What are the two types of incumbent (*wājib*) by the ruling of the one giving the command?
2. What is the ruling of *adā' kāmil* (perfect due performance)?
3. What is the ruling of *adā' qāṣir* (imperfect due performance)?
4. How does a person make up obligatory circumambulation [of the Kaʿbah] performed in a state of impurity?

---

161 In these cases, the objective of the item has been reached, and thus, the ownership of the rightful owner has not ceased.

162 The rightful owner is the victim of the usurpation.

2.15: DIVISION OF QAḌĀ' (DELAYED PERFORMANCE)

As for *qaḍā'* (delayed performance), it is of two types:

i. *kāmil* (perfect), and
ii. *qāṣir* (imperfect).

Qaḍā' Kāmil (Perfect Delayed Performance)

Of it, [*qaḍā'*] *kāmil* (perfect delayed performance) is to submit the equivalent of what is due (*mithl al-wājib*) in substance as well as in spirit.

EXAMPLE

[It is] like one misappropriates a *qafīz* (a volumetric measure) of wheat which he then destroys – he is liable for one *qafīz* of wheat; what is due on him must be equivalent to the original [= perished *qafīz* of wheat], in substance and in spirit.[163]

Likewise, is the command regarding all of the fungibles (*mithliyyāt*).[164]

Qaḍā' Qāṣir (Imperfect Delayed Performance)

As for [*qaḍā'*] *qāṣir* (imperfect delayed performance), it is that which is not equivalent to the due (*wājib*) in substance, but it is equivalent in spirit.

EXAMPLE

[It is] like someone who misappropriated a goat or sheep which then perished, he is liable to [compensate] its value, and its value is something equivalent to the goat or sheep in terms of spirit but not in terms of substance.

The Primary in Qaḍā' (Delayed Performance)

The primary (*aṣl*) in *qaḍā'* (delayed performance) is *kāmil* (perfect).[165]

Upon this [principle], Imam Abū Ḥanīfah (Allah have mercy on him) said: When someone misappropriates a fungible item which then perishes while in his possession, and it has ceased from existing with people, he is liable for its value [that was] on the day of the dispute, because the incapacity to submit the complete equivalent (*mithl kāmil*) only appears at the dispute, but as for prior to the dispute it cannot, because of the conceivability of acquiring its equivalent from every perspective.

---

163 The wheat must be like for like in quantity and in quality.

164 *Mithliyyāt* are all fungible items that are quantified by weighing, counting or measuring. Those items that are valued otherwise are known as *qīmiyyāt*.

165 *Qaḍā' qāṣir* will be resorted to if *qaḍā' kāmil* cannot be achieved.

That Which Has No Equivalent

As for that which has no equivalent, in substance as well as in spirit, it is not possible to fulfil the *qaḍā'* (delayed performance) for it with something equivalent. Due to this, we said usufructs are not compensated due to being wasted, because making compensation obligatory with something equivalent is unfeasible and making compensation obligatory with tangible property is likewise, because tangible property is not equivalent to usufruct, not in substance nor in spirit.

EXAMPLE

[That is] like when one usurps a slave and he takes service from him for a month, or a house wherein he lives for a month, and then he returns the usurped item to the [rightful] owner, it is not incumbent on him to compensate for the usufruct [he acquired], contrary to [the opinion of] Imam ash-Shāfiʿī (Allah have mercy on him).[166] Thus, the sin upon him remains as a [legal] command and his penalty transfers to the Hereafter.

Inferences

Due to this meaning, we[167] said:

i. usufruct of sexual pleasure via false testimony for divorce is not compensated,[168]
ii. for killing someone else's wife,[169]
iii. for sexual intercourse such that if one has sexual intercourse with someone else's wife, he does not compensate the husband whatsoever.[170]

Proviso

Unless the Sharīʿah mentions something equivalent [to be paid as compensation] despite there being nothing equivalent to it in substance nor in spirit, and so in that case it is equivalent to it, legally; this obliges its performance with the legal equivalent.

TERMINOLOGY

Qaḍā' kāmil: Perfect delayed performance

Qaḍā' qāṣir: Imperfect delayed performance

Diyah: Compensatory payment

Wakālah: Agency

---

166 Imam ash-Shāfiʿī (Allah have mercy on him) deems benefits to be compensable but Imam Abū Ḥanīfah (Allah have mercy on him) does not.

167 The Ḥanafī jurists (Allah have mercy on them).

168 This is if two men bear witness that Mr. A has divorced his wife after consummation of marriage, and the judge decrees upon that, instructing the husband to pay the *mahr* and causing a separation between the spouses. Later, the two men retract their testimony. According to the Ḥanafīs, they are not liable to compensate the husband for the loss of sexual pleasure.

169 When someone kills someone else's wife, he shall not compensate the husband for the loss of usufruct of sexual pleasure, though he will be liable to *qiṣāṣ*.

170 If someone has unlawful sexual intercourse with someone else's wife, he is not liable to compensate her husband for that, though he will be culpable for committing unlawful sexual intercourse (*zinā'*).

NOTES

EXAMPLE

Its illustration is [according to] what we said:

i. the redemption (*fidyah*) for the decrepit old person[171] is an equivalent to fasting (*ṣawm*), and

ii. the *diyah* (compensatory payment) for unintentional killing is an equivalent to the life [that was taken] even though there is no similarity between the two (i.e. the money with fasting and compensatory payment with another life).[172]

QUESTIONS

1. What are the two types of *qaḍā'* (delayed performance)?
2. What is the outcome of *qaḍā' kāmil* (perfect delayed performance)?
3. What is the outcome of *qaḍā' qāṣir* (imperfect delayed performance)?
4. Give an example of *qaḍā' kāmil* (perfect delayed performance).

❖

2.16: NAHY (THE PROSCRIPTION)

Division of Nahy

Nahy (proscription) is of two types:

i. [*Nahy* (proscription) of *ḥissī* actions (i.e. moral proscriptions), and]

ii. [*Nahy* (proscription) of *shar'ī* (Islamic legal) actions (i.e. legal proscriptions)].

Nahy (Proscription) of Physical Actions

Nahy (proscription) of *ḥissī* (physical) actions.

EXAMPLE

[It is] like unlawful sexual intercourse (*zinā'*), consumption of wine, lying, and cruelty.

Nahy (Proscription) of Islamic Legal Actions

Nahy (proscription) of Islamic legal (*shar'ī*) actions.

---

171 The decrepit old person (*shaykh fānī*) is someone who is too weak or too ill to fast, due to old age or a particular perpetual illness, and they have no hope to recover and make up for the fast. Their only choice is to pay redemption (*fidyah*) for each fast they miss.

172 These two are examples of when the Sharī'ah has mentioned legal equivalents to something that has no equivalent in theory or in practice. Hence, it is obligatory to apply the legal equivalent.

EXAMPLE

[It is] like the proscription of fasting on the Day of Sacrifice (*yawm an-naḥr*),[173] praying during the times repugnant [for prayer] and to sell one dirham for two.

The Ruling of Nahy (Proscription) of Actions Perceivable by the Senses

The ruling of the first type is that the proscribed action is precisely for what the proscription has appeared. Thus, the act itself will be *qabīḥ bi-nafsi-hī* (repulsive *per se*) and it will not be lawful whatsoever.

The Ruling of Nahy (Proscription) of Islamic Legal Actions

The ruling of the second type is that the proscribed action is other than that to which the proscription is attributed. Thus, the act itself is *ḥasan bi-nafsi-hī* (good *per se*) but *qabīḥ li-ghayri-hī* (repulsive *per quod*). The one who undertakes such an act shall be pursuing something *ḥarām li-ghayri-hī* (unlawful *per quod*) and not *ḥarām li-nafsi-hī* (unlawful *per se*).

Upon this [principle] (i.e. a legal action being *ḥasan bi-nafsihī* but *qabīḥ li-ghayrihī*), our Companions[174] have said: Proscription of legal actions entails their affirmation.

The intended meaning of this is that the action after the proscription remains as legal as it originally was,[175] and that is because if it did not remain legal, the person would be incapable of achieving what is legally prescribed, in which case it would be a proscription for someone who is incapable [of performing it] – which from the Lawgiver (i.e. Allah ﷻ) is impossible.[176]

Difference between the Two Types of Proscription

With this [principle], the distinction of the *ḥissī* actions is made, because if they were *qabīḥ bi-nafsi-hī* (repulsive *per se*) then it would not contribute to the [ruling of] proscription for someone who is incapable [of performing it] for with this description the person would not be incapable of performing a *ḥissī* action.

Inferences of the Primary Laws of Performance after Prohibition

From this is deduced the ruling of the vitiated sale, vitiated lease, a specific vow (*nadhr*) to fast the Day of Sacrifice (*yawm an-naḥr*), and all legal actions, with the proscription mentioned against them.[177]

TERMINOLOGY

Nahy: Proscription

Nafaqah: Maintenance

Maḥram: Unmarriageable relatives

Ḥissī: Perceptible to the senses

Shar'ī: Islamic legal

NOTES

173 This is the tenth of Dhu'l-Ḥijjah.

174 The Ḥanafī jurists (Allah have mercy on them).

175 The action, though legal and valid in origin, has been declared illegal and invalid in practice.

176 The Lawgiver ﷻ has proscribed something that was previously legally possible and practical. Had it not been previously legally possible and practical, the Lawgiver ﷻ would not have issued a prohibition, for that would have been unreasonable and futile.

177 Primarily, all of these examples are practical and valid due to either the

Therefore, we[178] said: The vitiated sale would grant ownership at the moment of taking possession on account of it being a sale, but it is incumbent to rescind it on account of it being *ḥarām li-ghayri-hī* (unlawful *per quod*).

This is contrary to marrying a polytheistic woman, the wife (and also ex-wife) of one's father, the woman who is in her waiting period (*ʿiddah*) from another husband, the wife of another man, marriage to women who are *maḥram* (unmarriageable relatives) and marriage without witnesses.

That is because marriage gives rise to the legality of [certain] actions, whereas *nahy* (proscription) gives rise to the unlawfulness of [those] actions. An amalgamation of the two is impossible and so therefore the *nahy* (proscription) is taken in the meaning of *nafy* (negation).

As for the sale, it gives rise to the establishment of ownership, and *nahy* (proscription) gives rise to the unlawfulness of disposal [of actions]. An amalgamation of the two is possible – the ownership is established and its usage is unlawful. Is it not that if one fermented juice into wine when [that juice was] in the ownership of a Muslim, it remains the ownership of the Muslim though usage of it is unlawful?

Upon this [principle], our companions said: If one makes a specific vow (*nadhr*) to fast the Day of Sacrifice (*yawm an-naḥr*) and the Days of Tashrīq, his specific vow (*nadhr*) is valid because it is a specific vow (*nadhr*) of a legally permissible fast.

Likewise, if one makes a specific vow (*nadhr*) to perform payers during times repugnant [for prayer], it is valid because it is a specific vow (*nadhr*) of a legally permissible form of worship, for the reason we have mentioned that *nahy* (proscription) necessitates the remaining of performing the action as legal.

Because of this, we said: When one begins supererogatory prayers during these times [i.e. the times repugnant for prayer], it is binding upon him due to his initiation of it, and perpetrating the prohibited is not binding for the obligation of completion, because if he bears patience so that the prayer becomes permissible by the rising of the sun [after dawn], its setting [after dusk] or its declining [from the meridian at noon], it shall be possible for him to complete it without repugnance.

With this, [is made] the distinction of fasting on [the Day of Sacrifice (*yawm an-naḥr*) and] the Day of *ʿĪd*, because if one commences it, it is not binding upon him to complete – according to Imam Abū Ḥanīfah and Imam Muhammad (Allah have mercy on them). That is because completing [the fast] is not free from perpetrating the unlawful.

Of this type is sexual intercourse with a menstruating woman; *nahy* (proscription) to approach her is on account of the harm, as Allah ﷻ says:

---

mutual acceptance between the parties to the contractual transactions, or due to the intention of the doer. However, they are all legally invalid because of the proscriptive measures placed by the Lawgiver ﷻ preventing their execution.

178 Ḥanafīs.

وَيَسْـَٔلُونَكَ عَنِ ٱلْمَحِيضِ ۖ قُلْ هُوَ أَذًى فَٱعْتَزِلُوا۟ ٱلنِّسَآءَ فِى ٱلْمَحِيضِ ۖ

وَلَا تَقْرَبُوهُنَّ حَتَّىٰ

'They ask you (O Beloved Messenger Muhammad ﷺ) about menstruation. Say: it is harm, so stay away from women during menstruation, and do not approach them.' Qur'an, 2:222

Inferences

Therefore, we said: Certain rulings are based upon this sexual intercourse [during menstruation]:

i. *iḥṣān* (chastity) of the one who has sexual intercourse is established by it,

ii. the woman becomes lawful for the first husband,

iii. the ruling of [the payment of] *mahr* is established by it, as well as,

iv. *ʿiddah* (waiting period), and

v. *nafaqah* (maintenance).

If the woman prevents [her husband] from making possible [the act of sexual intercourse after that] for the sake of acquiring the mahr, she is someone who is violating marital duties – according to the two [= Imam Abū Yūsuf and Imam Muhammad (Allah have mercy on them)], and therefore she is not entitled to maintenance.[179]

Unlawfulness of Action and Regulation of Rulings

The unlawfulness of the act does not contravene the regulation of the rulings [on it], such as divorcing the menstruating woman, making *wuḍū'* with usurped water, hunting with a usurped bow, slaughtering with a usurped knife, praying (*ṣalāh*) on misappropriated land, transacting [a sale, etc.] during the *adhān* (call to prayer) – the ruling is regulated on these actions even though they are in the category of prohibition.[180]

Inferences

And on account of this principle, we said regarding the saying of Allah ﷻ:

وَلَا تَقْبَلُوا۟ لَهُمْ شَهَـٰدَةً أَبَدًا ۚ

'And do not accept a testimony from them, ever.' Qur'an, 24:4

The morally corrupt (*fāsiq*) is of those from whom testimony is accepted (*ahl ash-shahādah*),[181] therefore, marriage (*nikāḥ*) may be

179 According to Imam Abū Ḥanīfah (Allah have mercy on him), she is still entitled to maintenance.

180 These examples are of those acts that are prohibited, but once they are concluded, the ruling upon them stands as a valid act, and the offender may be sinful for failing to comply with the process laid down by the Sharīʿah.

181 These qualities for someone to be accepted as a witness are that he/she must be: Muslim, sane, mature and free, and not having been guilty of unsubstantiated accusations of sexual impropriety.

NOTES

concluded with the testimony of those who are morally corrupt, because the *nahy* (proscription) of accepting the witnessing without any witnessing is absurd. However, their testimony is not accepted merely due to a corruption in fulfilling it and not because there is no witnessing to begin with.

Upon this [principle], imprecation (*liʿān*) is not obliged on them because it is the fulfilment of the testimony, but there is no testimony with moral corruption.

QUESTIONS

1. What are the two types of proscription?
2. Name three rulings that are based upon sexual intercourse during menstruation.
3. What happens if one makes a specific vow (*nadhr*) to perform prayers during times repugnant for prayer?
4. What is the ruling of proscription of actions perceivable by the senses?
5. Why can marriage be concluded with the testimony of those who are morally corrupt?

❖

2.17: DEDUCTION OF TEXTUAL INFERENCES

Know that, in order to identify the textual inference, there are various methods:

[i. when the *ḥaqīqah* overrides the *majāz*,

ii. when *takhṣīṣ* is not the best option, and

iii. when acting upon the amalgamation of two [or more] meanings is the best option.]

Ḥaqīqah Overrides Majāz

Of them, one occurs when the word denotes *ḥaqīqah* in one meaning and *majāz* in another, then the *ḥaqīqah* is the best option.

EXAMPLE

Its example is what our Scholars [= the Ḥanafī jurists (Allah have mercy on them)] have said: The female child born out of unlawful sexual intercourse (*zinā'*), her marriage (*nikāḥ*) is unlawful to the man who committed the unlawful sexual intercourse.[182]

Imam ash-Shāfiʿī (Allah have mercy on him) said: It [= the marriage] is lawful for him.[183]

---

182 The female child is the illegitimate daughter of the man who committed unlawful sexual intercourse.

183 According to Imam ash-Shāfiʿī, lineage is a sacred blessing of Allah ﷻ that cannot be acquired by unlawful means, and so in this case, she is not his real daughter. However, she may or may not be treated as his legal daughter. The

The correct view is what we [= the Ḥanafī jurists] have said, [and that is] because she is his daughter in *ḥaqīqah*, and so she enters the saying:

حُرِّمَتْ عَلَيْكُمْ أُمَّهَـٰتُكُمْ وَبَنَاتُكُمْ

'Unlawful to you are your mothers and your daughters... ' Qur'an, 4:23

Inferences from this Rule

Various rulings branch out from this [principle] according to the two [respective] schools [= the Ḥanafī and the Shafi'ī], regarding:

i. the lawfulness of sexual intercourse,
ii. the incumbency to [pay] the *mahr*,
iii. the obligation to [pay] maintenance,
iv. the passage of inheritance, and
v. the legal power of prevention from leaving [the home] and emerging [in public].[184]

Takhṣīṣ is Not Preferable

From those methods, is one of two possible meanings; when it necessitates *takhṣīṣ* in the text and the other does not, then to take the position that does not oblige *takhṣīṣ* is the best option.

EXAMPLE

Its example is in the saying of Allah ﷻ:

أَوْ لَـٰمَسْتُمُ ٱلنِّسَآءَ

'... or you touched [i.e. had sexual intercourse with] women... '
Qur'an, 4:43

If the word مُلَامَسَة (touching) is taken to mean sexual intercourse, then the text can be acted upon in all its existing forms, but if it is taken to mean touching with the hand, then the text would be *makhṣūṣ* (restricted to specific meanings) in many of its forms, for surely touching female unmarriageable relatives and the very young female child is not something that violates *wuḍū'* (wudu) – according to the most sound of the two opinions from Imam ash-Shāfi'ī (Allah have mercy on him).

Inferences from this Rule

Various rulings branch out from this [principle] according to the two schools [= Ḥanafī and Shāfi'ī], regarding:

i. the permissibility of prayer,
ii. touching the printed copy [of the Qur'an],

Ḥanafīs disagree and say that she is his real daughter.

184 These are rights a husband has over his wife and vice versa, which would not exist according to the Ḥanafī school because such a marriage is void.

TERMINOLOGY

Tashdīd: Gemination
Takhfīf: Non-gemination
Yawm an-naḥr: Day of Sacrifice

NOTES

iii. entering the masjid,

iv. validity of leading prayer,

v. obligation of performing *tayammum* in the absence of water, and

vi. remembering the touching during prayer.

Amalgamation of Multiple Meanings is Preferable

Of those methods, is when the text [of the Qur'an] is recited in two ways, or it [= ḥadīth] is narrated in two ways, then acting upon it in a manner whereby both ways will be acted upon [simultaneously] will be the best option.

EXAMPLE

Its example is in the saying of Allah ﷻ:

وَأَرْجُلَكُمْ

'... *and your feet* ...' Qur'an, 5:6

It is read with a ' َ (*naṣb* – in the accusative state)',[185] conjunctive to the washed parts, and it is also read with a ' ِ (*jarr*– in the genitive state)', conjunctive to the wiped part.[186]

Thus, the reading with a ' ِ (*jarr*)' is taken to mean the state of wearing *khuffs* (leather socks), and the reading with a ' َ (*naṣb*)' is taken to mean the state of not wearing *khuffs*.

On account of this meaning, some have said: The permissibility of wiping [over *khuffs*] is established by the Book.

Likewise, is the saying of Allah ﷻ:

حَتَّىٰ يَطْهُرْنَ

'... *until they have become pure.*' Qur'an, 2:222

It [= the word يَطْهُرْنَ] has been read with a *tashdīd* (gemination, as يَطَّهَّرْنَ) and also with *takhfīf* (non-gemination, as in يَطْهُرْنَ).

It can be acted upon with the reading of *takhfīf* (non-gemination) in terms of when her days [of menstruation] are ten, and the reading of *tashdīd* (gemination) in the meaning of when her days [of menstruation] are less than ten.

Upon this [principle], our Companions [= the Ḥanafī jurists (Allah have mercy on them)] have said: When the menstrual bleeding ceases in under ten days, sexual intercourse of the menstruating woman is not permitted until she takes a bath, because complete

185 Over the last letter of the Arabic word for 'feet'.

186 There is a contradiction here between both ways of reading the same word. Thus, there will also be a difference in their rulings, such that reading the Arabic word for 'feet' with a ' َ (*naṣb*)' would link it to the washed parts and thus render their obligation to be washed, whereas reading it with a ' ِ (*jarr*)' would link it to the wiped part and thus render their obligation to be wiped but not washed.

purity is established with bathing.[187] If her bleeding ceases at ten days, sexual intercourse with her is permitted before bathing, because unrestricted purity is established by the cessation of bleeding.[188]

Because of this, we [= the Ḥanafī jurists] said:

1. If the menstrual bleeding ceases at ten days during the end time for prayer (*ṣalāh*), the obligation [to perform the prayer] of that time is binding upon her, even though not enough time remains for her to take a bath.
2. However, if her bleeding ceases in less than ten days during the end time for prayer (*ṣalāh*):
   i. if enough time remains that she may take a bath and say the *taḥrīmah* (consecratory *takbīr*)[189] for prayer (*ṣalāh*), the obligation [to perform the prayer] of that time is binding upon her,
   ii. otherwise, it is not.

Methods of Weak Adherences

We then mention the methods of weak adherences, so that it may be a warning against the areas of deficiency in this category.

1. Of them is the adherence to what has been reported from the Prophet ﷺ, that:

أَنَّهُ قَاءَ فَلَمْ يَتَوَضَّأْ

'He ﷺ vomited but did not perform wuḍū'.'[190]

to establish that vomiting does not invalidate *wuḍū'*[191] – is weak.[192]

This is because the report indicates that vomiting does not oblige the [performance of] *wuḍū'* immediately – and in this there is no disagreement; the disagreement lies only in it [= vomiting] being a nullifier [of wudu].

2. Likewise, the adherence to the saying of Allah ﷻ:

حُرِّمَتْ عَلَيْكُمُ ٱلْمَيْتَةُ

'Forbidden to you is carrion... .' Qur'an, 5:3

---

187 According to the Ḥanafī scholars, the menstrual period of bleeding lasts between three to ten days. The Shāfi'ī scholars deem the menstrual period of bleeding to last between one and fifteen days. The minimum period of purity between two periods of menstrual bleeding is fifteen days with no maximum, according to both schools.

188 The menstrual cycle consists of a period of bleeding and a period of purity from bleeding. When menstrual bleeding ends, the period of purity has begun, and vice versa.

189 *Taḥrīmah*: The initial saying of *'Allahu Akbar'* whilst raising both hands to the ears, indicating the formal entry into the prayer.

190 No such ḥadīth exists according to Ibn al-Humam, Ibn Hajar and others (see Fath al-Qadir and Al-Dirayah).

191 The Shāfi'ī scholars do not decree vomiting to invalidate *wuḍū'*.

192 The Ḥanafī scholars hold a mouthful of vomit to be an invalidating cause for *wuḍū'*.

to establish the [ritual] spoiling of water with the death of a fly [in it] – is weak.[193]

This is because the *scripture* establishes the unlawfulness of carrion – there is no disagreement in this; the disagreement lies only in the water being spoiled.

3. Likewise, the adherence to the saying of the Prophet ﷺ [to Asmā' the daughter of Abū Bakr (Allah be pleased with them)]:

حُتِّيهِ ثُمَّ اقْرُصِيهِ ثُمَّ اغْسِلِيهِ بِالْمَاءِ

'Scratch it, then rub it, and then wash it with water.'

to establish that vinegar does not remove filth – is weak.[194]

That is because the report entails the obligation of washing the blood with water, and so this is restricted [i.e. to washing with water] to when the blood is present at that [particular] location – there is no disagreement in this; the disagreement lies in the purity of that location after the removal of the blood with vinegar.

4. Likewise, the adherence to the saying of the Prophet ﷺ:

فِي أَرْبَعِينَ شَاةً شَاةٌ

'In forty goats or sheep is one goat or sheep.'

to establish the impermissibility of paying the monetary value – is weak.[195]

That is because it [= the ḥadīth] demands the incumbency of a goat or sheep – there is no disagreement in this; the disagreement lies in the extinguishing of the obligation with the payment of its due value.

5. Likewise, the adherence to the saying of Allah ﷻ:

وَأَتِمُّوا۟ ٱلْحَجَّ وَٱلْعُمْرَةَ لِلَّهِ ۚ

'And complete the Ḥajj and the umrah for Allah.' Qur'an, 2:196

to establish the obligation of umrah initially – is weak[196] because the *scripture* demands the incumbency of *completion* [of umrah] which can only happen after it has begun – there is no disagreement in this; the disagreement lies in it [= the umrah] being incumbent to begin with.

---

193 A dead fly does not spoil the water, according to Ḥanafī scholars.

194 Imam ash-Shāfiʿī (Allah have mercy on him) ruled that blood can only be washed off clothing with water whereas the Ḥanafī jurists (Allah have mercy on them) decreed that vinegar also removes impurities like blood, etc.

195 Imam ash-Shāfiʿī (Allah have mercy on him) is of the view that *zakāh* payment for forty goats or sheep is one goat or sheep without the option of monetary equivalent, but the Ḥanafī jurists (Allah have mercy on them) rule the option of paying the one goat or sheep, or its equivalent, in monetary terms.

196 Imam ash-Shāfiʿī (Allah have mercy on him) rules the performance of umrah to be obligatory, just like the Ḥajj, but the Ḥanafī jurists (Allah have mercy on them) do not believe the umrah to be obligatory but sunnah, whereas the performance of Ḥajj is obligatory. The latter take this verse to mean the completion of umrah to be incumbent after one begins it.

6. Likewise, the adherence to the saying of the Prophet ﷺ:

لَا تَبِيْعُوا الدِّرْهَمَ بِالدِّرْهَمَيْنِ وَلَا الصَّاعَ بِصَّاعَيْنِ

'Do not sell one dirham for two dirhams, and nor one ṣāʿ (of measured product) for two ṣāʿs.'

to establish that the vitiated sale does not give the benefit of ownership – is weak.

That is because the [ḥadīth] scripture entails the unlawfulness of the invalid sale – there is no disagreement in this; the disagreement lies only in the establishment of the ownership or not.

7. Likewise, the adherence to the saying of the Prophet ﷺ:

أَلَا لَا تَصُوْمُوْا فِيْ هٰذِهِ الْأَيَّامِ فَإِنَّهَا أَيَّامُ أَكْلٍ وشُرْبٍ وَبِعَالٍ

'Behold! Do not fast on these days, for they are the days of eating, drinking and rejoicing with one's family.'

to establish that making specific vows to fast on the Day of Sacrifice (*yawm an-naḥr*) is not valid – is weak.[197]

That is because the [ḥadīth] scripture entails the unlawfulness of the action – there is no disagreement in that it is unlawful; the disagreement lies only in the benefit of the legal rulings while it itself is unlawful. The unlawfulness of the act does not contradict the accruing of the legal rulings upon it, for surely:

i. if the father has a child with the slave-woman of his son, it [= the act] is unlawful [even though] the ownership for the father is established by it,

ii. if one slaughters a sheep or goat with a usurped knife, it [= the act] is unlawful, but the slaughtered [sheep or goat] is lawful (*ḥalāl*),

iii. if one washes impure clothing with usurped water, it [= the act] is unlawful, but the clothing will be purified with it, and

iv. if one has sexual intercourse with his wife during menstruation, it [= the act] is unlawful, but the *iḥṣān*[198] of the one who has sexual intercourse is established, as well as the lawfulness [of the woman] for the first husband.

197 Imam ash-Shāfiʿī (Allah have mercy on him) does not allow fasting for specific vows during the days of the two ʿĪds and the eleventh, twelfth and thirteenth of Dhu'l-Ḥijjah; but the Ḥanafī jurists (Allah have mercy on them) deem it valid, albeit if the performer is sinful, it would have been better for him to delay such fasts of specific vows until after the prohibited days had passed.

198 *Iḥṣān* for the punishment of stoning is established by being: i. free, ii. adult, iii. sane, iv. Muslim, v. having married a woman in a valid marriage, and vi. having had sexual intercourse with her when both had the characteristics of *iḥṣān*. (Al-Qudūrī, *Mukhtaṣar*, p.541.)

NOTES

QUESTIONS

1. When a word denotes *ḥaqīqah* in one meaning and *majāz* in another, how do we resolve it?
2. When it necessitates *takhṣīṣ* in the text and the other does not, then to take the position that does not oblige *takhṣīṣ* is the best option. Give an example of this.
3. Give an example of a method of weak adherences.
4. What does amalgamation mean?

❖

2.18: MEANINGFUL PARTICLES

[This] part [is] on the discussion of meaningful particles.

و (wāw)

و (wāw) for Unrestricted Conjunction

و (*wāw*) is [used] for unrestricted conjunction.[199]

And it is said: Indeed, Imam ash-Shāfiʿī (Allah have mercy on him) has rendered it for sequence. Upon this [principle], he has rendered incumbent the sequence in the category of *wuḍū'* (wudu).

Our scholars [= the Ḥanafī jurists (Allah have mercy on them)] said: When one [= husband] says to his wife, 'إِنْ كَلَّمْتِ زَيْدًا وَ عَمْرًوا فَأَنْتِ طَالِقٌ (If you speak to Zayd *and* ʿAmr, you are divorced),' and she then spoke to ʿAmr and thereafter to Zayd, she will be divorced, because the meaning of sequence or association is not stipulated in it.[200]

If one said [to his wife], 'إِنْ دَخَلْتِ هٰذِهِ الدَّارَ وَ هٰذِهِ الدَّارَ فَأَنْتِ طَالِقٌ (If you enter this building *and* this building, you are divorced),' and she then entered the second [building] and thereafter she entered the first [building], she will be divorced.[201] Imam Muhammad (Allah have mercy on him) said: If one said, 'إِنْ دَخَلْتِ الدَّارَ وَ أَنْتِ طَالِقٌ (If you enter the building, *and* you are divorced),' she will be divorced immediately. If it [= the statement] necessitated sequence, then the divorce would accrue upon entry,[202] and that would be a conditional statement (*taʿlīq*) and not executionary (*tanjīz*).

---

199 و (*wāw*) is used for conjunction, concomitance (when the second conjunct is in the accusative case), and also simultaneous or relative order. (Lane, Edward William, *Arabic-English Lexicon*. London: Williams and Norgate, 1863. p.2913).

200 If the sequence was a stipulation, then the divorce would not take effect in the issue mentioned here but only if she spoke to Zayd and ʿAmr according to the sequence mentioned in the condition. Likewise, if association was stipulated, then the divorce would only be effective if she spoke to both of them simultaneously.

201 This proves that the particle و (*wāw*) relates to conjunction (*jamʿ*) and not sequence when used in an unrestricted sense.

202 This proves that the particle و (*wāw*) does not relate to sequence, otherwise the divorce would only take effect after her entry into the building.

و (wāw) for Describing the Ḥāl (Circumstantial Phrase)

Sometimes, the و (*wāw*) is [used] for describing the circumstantial phrase (*ḥāl*),[203] and therefore it combines the *ḥāl* and the noun denoted with the circumstantial phrase (*dhu'l-ḥāl*), in which case it conveys the meaning of condition (*sharṭ*).[204]

EXAMPLE

Its example is what Imam Muhammad (Allah have mercy on him) has stated regarding the *ma'dhūn* (authorised) [slave]: When one [= the master] says to his slave, 'أَدِّ إِلَيَّ أَلْفًا وَ أَنْتَ حُرٌّ (Pay me a thousand [dirhams] *and* you are free,)'[205] the payment is the condition (*sharṭ*) for the freedom.

In *as-Siyar al-Kabīr*,[206] Imam Muhammad (Allah have mercy on him) said: When the head of state says to disbelievers, 'إِفْتَحُوا الْبَابَ وَ أَنْتُمْ آمِنُوْنَ (Open the gate *and* you are in security),[207] they shall not be in security without opening [it].

Likewise, when one [= Muslim] says to a disbeliever [seeking security in Muslim lands], 'إِنْزِلْ وَ أَنْتَ آمِنٌ (Alight *and* you are in protection),'[208] he shall not be in protection without alighting.

Also, و (*wāw*) is taken for [describing] the circumstantial phrase metaphorically, and so the word ought to bear that [meaning] together with the presence of an indication establishing it, as there is in the saying of the master to his slave, 'أَدِّ إِلَيَّ أَلْفًا وَ أَنْتَ حُرٌّ (Pay me a thousand [dirhams] *and* you are free).' The freedom is ascertained at the moment of payment, and the indication is [also] present for that, because the master cannot oblige any property on his slave as long as bondage exists with him, and so therefore the statement conditional to it [= the freedom of the slave] is valid and it is taken in that [meaning].[209]

---

203 The state here refers to the condition, circumstances, or case in which the *dhu'l-ḥāl* is described, such as 'I saw him reading,' in which case 'him' is the object, and the *dhu'l-ḥāl*, that is described by the word 'reading', is its *ḥāl*. In other words, one means to say, 'I saw him *in a state that he was* reading.'

204 The meaning of و (*wāw*) in the *ḥaqīqah* is to convey the meaning of conjunction, and it may be used to convey the meaning of circumstantial denotation when taken in the *majāz*. As such, when it appears denoting *ḥāl* for the *dhu'l-ḥāl*, it carries the meaning of condition/protasis (*sharṭ*) because the *ḥāl* is bound to the *dhu'l-ḥāl* just like the *jazā'* (apodosis) is bound to the protasis (*sharṭ*).

205 This is akin to the master saying, 'Pay me a thousand [dirhams] and you are free,' or 'If you pay me a thousand [dirhams], you will be free.'

206 *As-Siyar al-Kabīr*, which forms part of the *ẓāhir ar-riwāyah* (manifest rulings), was authored by Imam Muhammad ash-Shaybānī (131 AH/749 CE – 189 AH/805 CE).

207 This is like the Imam saying, 'Open the gate and you shall be in security,' or 'If you open the gate, you shall be in security.'

208 This is like him saying, 'Dismount and you shall be in protection,' or 'If you dismount, you shall be protected.'

209 The و (*wāw*) used in this statement, as mentioned before, is to denote the circumstances, which in turn renders the statement conditional. In other words, the master is saying to his slave, 'If you pay me a thousand [dirhams], you will be free.' However, if the و (*wāw*) was not taken to denote the circumstances, then the sentence prior to it would not be the *sharṭ* but a distinct sentence *per*

If one said [to his wife]: 'أَنْتِ طَالِقٌ وَ أَنْتِ مَرِيْضَةٌ أَوْ مُصَلِّيَةٌ (You are divorced *and* you are ill/praying),'[210] she is divorced immediately.[211] If he intended it as a conditional statement, then his intention is valid according to what is between him and Allah ﷻ,[212] because even though the words may bear the meaning of *ḥāl*, the manifest meaning is contrary to it, and when that [= which is contrary to the manifest meaning] is supported with his intention, it [= meaning of *ḥāl*] is established.[213]

Example When و (wāw) Does Not Describe Ḥāl

If one said: 'خُذْ هٰذِهِ الْأَلْفَ مُضَارَبَةً وَاعْمَلْ بِهَا فِي الْبَزِّ (Take this thousand [dirhams] as *muḍārabah*[214] and trade with it in cloth),' the trade shall not remain confined to cloth, but the *muḍārabah* shall be of a general nature, because trading in cloth is not sufficient to be the *ḥāl* so as to take the thousand [dirhams] as *muḍārabah*. Therefore, it [= the *muḍārabah*] shall not be restricted by it [= trading in cloth] from the very onset of the statement.[215]

Inference

Upon this [principle], Imam Abū Ḥanīfah (Allah have mercy on him) said: 'When [a wife] says to her husband, 'طَلِّقْنِيْ وَ لَكَ أَلْفٌ (Divorce me and for you are a thousand [dirhams]),' and [subsequently] he divorces her, there is nothing due upon her to him, because her saying, 'وَ لَكَ أَلْفٌ (and for you are a thousand [dirhams]),' does not give the meaning of the *ḥāl* that obligates the thousand [dirhams] on her,

---

se where the master is asking the slave to pay a thousand dirhams when such payment by the latter is impossible, with him being in bondage and complete ownership of the master.

210 This is akin to him saying, 'You are divorced. And you are ill,' or 'You are divorced. And you are praying.'

211 In this case, there is nothing to indicate that what he meant was for *ḥāl* or for conjunction, and so the apparent meaning is taken into account. Moreover, both portions of the statement, i.e. that which is prior to the و (*wāw*) and that which follows it, are separable for being distinct informative sentences (*jumlah khabariyyah*), and hence there is no correlation between them – they are independent of one another and not *sharṭ* and *jazā'* for each other.

212 If he claims that what he intended by his words was for *ḥāl*, such as 'You are divorced *if* you are ill,' or 'You are divorced *if* you are praying,' then that is accepted, and his affair is left between him and Allah ﷻ.

213 The manifest meaning of such words stands, unless he professes an intention contrary to them, because the *ḥaqīqah* is initially sought, and the *majāz* is only resorted to when the *ḥaqīqah* is impossible to reach. In a case as such, the *ḥaqīqah* is the manifest meaning of the words because it is attainable, and so we need not incline to the *majāz*. However, the speaker expresses his intention that his و (*wāw*) in the statement was for *ḥāl* and not for conjunction (*'aṭf*) – a probability that we accept.

214 *Muḍārabah* is a trade contract in which the capital provider shares the profits with the trader but the former alone bears the losses. It is also known as *qirāḍ*, silent or dormant partnership, and speculative partnership.

215 In this case, the conditional statement is too remote for it to constitute the *ḥāl* of the *dhu'l-ḥāl*, and so there is no valid restriction here. The و (*wāw*) is taken in the meaning of the conjunctive و (*wāw*) and not the و (*wāw*) of *ḥāl* due to its manifest meaning and lack of indication for *ḥāl*. Moreover, the *jazā'* and the *ḥāl*, if any, in this case is the portion prior to the و (*wāw*) and the *sharṭ* and the *dhu'l-ḥāl*, if it were, is the latter portion. In a statement as such, the *ḥāl* only follows the *dhu'l-ḥāl* and does not come prior to it, and so this renders both portions independent sentences.

whereas her saying 'طَلِّقْنِي (Divorce me),' does itself give meaning on its own, so its implementation is not abandoned without evidence.[216]

[This is] contrary to one's saying [to a porter], 'اِحْمِلْ هذا الْمَتَاعَ وَ لَكَ دِرْهَمٌ (Carry this luggage *and* for you is a dirham)', because the indication of hiring (*ijārah*) prevents the effect of the real [meaning] of the words.[217]

ف (fā')

ف (fā') for Immediate Succession

ف (*fā'*) is [used] for immediate succession with conjunction (*ta'qīb ma'a'l-waṣl*),[218] and therefore, it is used as the *jazā'* (apodosis)[219] because it follows the *sharṭ* (protasis).[220]

EXAMPLE

Our Companions [= the Ḥanafī jurists (Allah have mercy on them)] said: When someone says [to another], بِعْتُ مِنْكَ هذا الْعَبْدَ بِأَلْفٍ (I have sold this slave to you for a thousand [dirhams]), and the other replies, 'فَهُوَ حُرٌّ (Then he is free),' it is an acceptance of the sale out of expediency, and the manumission from him [= the purchaser] is established immediately after the sale,[221] as opposed to if he [= the purchaser] says, 'وَ هُوَ حُرٌّ (And he is free),' or, 'هُوَ حُرٌّ (He is free),' for that shall be a rejection of the sale.

Also, when someone says to the tailor, 'أُنْظُرْ إِلَى هَذَا الثَّوْبِ، أَ يَكْفِينِي قَمِيصًا ؟ (Take a look at this cloth. Will it suffice me for a shirt?),' and he [= the tailor] looks [at it] and says, 'نَعَمْ (Yes),' and then the owner of

---

216 In this case, the و (*wāw*) used is for conjunction and not for *ḥāl*, and therefore, the latter portion of the statement is not conditional to the former, and thus void. The divorce, when issued, takes immediate effect without the obligation for the woman to pay anything. Imam Abū Yūsuf and Imam Muhammad (Allah have mercy on them), however, oppose Imam Abū Ḥanīfah (Allah have mercy on him) here, stating that the و (*wāw*) is for *ḥāl* and thus the divorcée is obliged to pay the one thousand dirhams. Imam Abū Yūsuf and Imam Muhammad (Allah have mercy on them) are of the opinion that the divorce shall take effect after the wife pays the thousand dirhams because according to them the و (*wāw*) is for the *ḥāl* and not for conjunction.

217 The porter is an employee who is paid for transporting goods from one place to another. Hence, the words used in his case indicate that the speaker intends to hire the porter for the transportation of his goods, and thus the و (*wāw*) is for the *ḥāl* and not for conjunction, rendering the latter portion of the statement conditional to the former. Thus, when the porter complies with the request, he is entitled to the payment of one dirham.

218 Immediate Succession (or proximate sequence) (*ta'qīb ma'a'l-waṣl*) occurs when a statement is mentioned immediately after another statement and in conjunction to it, referring to an immediate chronological connection between the two. For example, 'Mr. A entered, and then Mr. B,' tells us that both Mr. A and Mr. B entered, and that Mr. A entered prior to Mr. B, but the time difference between the two entering was nominal.

219 In a conditional statement, the main (consequent) clause is known as the *jazā'*, or apodosis in Greek.

220 In a conditional statement, the conditional clause is known as the *sharṭ*, or protasis in Greek.

221 This is similar to the purchaser of the slave saying, 'If you have sold this slave to me for a thousand [dirhams], then he is free.'

NOTES

the cloth says, 'فَاقْطَعْهُ (Then cut it),' and so he cuts it. If then it is not sufficient, the tailor is liable because he [= the owner] gave him the order to cut immediately after [its declaration of] being sufficient.[222]

[This is] contrary to if he had said: 'اِقْطَعْهُ (Cut it),' or, 'وَاقْطَعْهُ (And cut it),' and so he cuts it. Thus, the tailor is not liable.[223] If one said: 'بِعْتُ مِنْكَ هَذَا الثَّوْبَ بِعَشَرَةٍ فَاقْطَعْهُ (I sold this cloth to you for ten [dirhams], so cut it),' and so he cuts it and he does not say anything, the sale is complete.[224]

If one [= husband] says, 'إِنْ دَخَلْتِ هَذِهِ الدَّارَ فَهَذِهِ الدَّارَ فَأَنْتِ طَالِقٌ (If you enter this building, then this building, you are divorced),' the condition is the entry into the second [building] immediately after entry into the first, in an uninterrupted connection to it,[225] such that if she enters the second [building] first, or afterwards but after a while, divorce does not take effect.[226]

ف (fā') for ʿIllah (Effective Cause)

Sometimes, the 'ف (*fā'*)' is [used] to explain the *ʿillah* (effective cause).

EXAMPLE

Its example occurs when one [= master] says to his slave, 'أَدِّ إِلَيَّ أَلْفًا فَأَنْتَ حُرٌّ (Pay me a thousand [dirhams] for you are free),' the slave is free [immediately] even though he pays nothing.[227]

If [a Muslim] says to a disbeliever [seeking security in Muslim lands], 'إِنْزِلْ فَأَنْتَ آمِنٌ (Alight, for you are protected),' he is protected even if he does not alight.[228]

In *al-Jāmiʿ* [*al-Kabīr*], as when one says [to his agent], 'أَمْرُ إِمْرَأَتِي بِيَدِكَ فَطَلِّقْهَا (The affair of my wife is in your hands, so divorce her),'

---

222 This is as if the owner of the cloth said to the tailor, 'If it suffices me as a shirt then cut it.'

223 The command here is not connected to any prior statement, and so there is no immediate succession here. The command is thus an independent statement, and it does not hold the tailor liable should his informative statement be incorrect.

224 The cutting indicates the acceptance of the sale.

225 If the condition is fulfilled according to the statement, then the consequence takes effect. In this case, entry into Building A followed by immediate entry into Building B results in divorce, and therefore, such an act would cause divorce to take effect.

226 It is due to the particle ف (*fā'*) conveying the meaning of immediate succession and conjunction (*taʿqīb maʿa'l-waṣl*) that the stated order of events as well as the connection must occur for the condition to be fulfilled. This necessitates two requirements: i. order as mentioned, and ii. uninterrupted connection. Absence of either requirement voids the conditional statement.

227 In this case, the ف (*fā'*) is in the meaning of the *ʿillah* (effective cause), rendering the statement, 'Pay me a thousand dirhams because you are free.' The liberation is the *ʿillah* (effective cause) and the payment is the effect and the ruling – the *ʿillah* (effective cause) precedes the ruling, causing the slave to go free at the culmination of the master's statement. The slave stands manumitted and the payment of a thousand dirhams is a debt on him due to be paid to the manumitting master.

228 In this case, the ف (*fā'*) is not for conjunction but to explain the *ʿillah* (effective cause), and hence, it is as if the Muslim is saying, 'Dismount, because you are protected.' The disbeliever is protected, whether he dismounts or not.

and he [= the agent] divorces her in that [very] session, she is divorced one irrevocable divorcement, but the second divorce is not delegated [to the agent] other than the first, and so it is as if he [= the husband] said, 'طَلِّقْهَا بِسَبَبِ أَنَّ أَمْرَهَا بِيَدِكَ (Divorce her due to the reason that her affair is in your hands).'

If he said, 'طَلِّقْهَا ، فَجَعَلْتُ أَمْرَهَا بِيَدِكَ (Divorce her, *for* I have placed her affair in your hands),' and he [= the agent] divorces her in that [very] session, she is divorced one revocable divorcement.

If he said, 'طَلِّقْهَا ، وَجَعَلْتُ أَمْرَهَا بِيَدِكَ (Divorce her, *and* I have placed her affair in your hands),' and he [= the agent] divorces her in that [very] session, she is divorced two divorcements.[229]

Likewise, if he said, 'طَلِّقْهَا وَأَبِنْهَا (Divorce her *and* divorce her irrevocably),' or 'أَبِنْهَا وَطَلِّقْهَا (Divorce her irrevocably *and* divorce her),' and he [= the agent] divorces her in that [very] session, two divorcements take effect.[230]

Upon this [principle], our Companions [= the Ḥanafī jurists (Allah have mercy on them)] have said: 'When a married slave-woman is manumitted, the option [of whether to continue the marriage or not] for her is established, irrespective of whether her husband is a slave or a freeman, because of the saying of the Prophet ﷺ to Barīrah [رضي الله تعالى عنها] when she was manumitted:

مَلَكْتِ بُضْعَكِ فَاخْتَارِيْ

'You own your vagina, so decide [for yourself].'[231]

He ﷺ established the option due to the *sabab* of her owning her [own] vagina through manumission. This meaning does not differ between the husband being a slave or a freeman.[232]

229 In this case, two divorcements have occurred due to the و (*wāw*) appearing in conjunction; the first portion of the statement 'طَلِّقْهَا (Divorce her)' obliges one divorce, and the latter portion 'وَجَعَلْتُ أَمْرَهَا بِيَدِكَ (and I have placed her affair in your hands)', obliges another divorce. Hence, this statement calls for two irrevocable divorces when the agent pronounces, 'طَلَّقْتُهَا (I have divorced her).'

(The first portion declares the first divorce revocable because explicit words have been pronounced, and the latter portion declares the second divorce irrevocable because implicit words have been used. A combination of revocable and irrevocable divorces renders both the divorcements irrevocable.)

230 In this case, the conjunctive و (*wāw*) indicates the husband's delegation of two divorcements to his agent. Therefore, two irrevocable divorcements take effect. (One portion declares one divorce revocable because explicit words (i.e. طَلِّقْهَا) have been pronounced, and the other portion declares the other divorce irrevocable because implicit words (i.e. أَبِنْهَا) have been used. A combination of revocable and irrevocable divorces renders both the divorcements irrevocable.)

Please see last note for further details on the remainder of this issue.

231 Dāraquṭnī, Kitāb an-Nikāḥ; Ibn Sa'd, *Ṭabaqāt*; Bukhārī, *al-Jāmi' aṣ-Ṣaḥīḥ*, Kitāb an-Nikāḥ; Muslim, Kitāb al-'Itq; Abū Dāwūd, Kitāb aṭ-Ṭalāq; ad-Dārimī.

232 According to the Shāfi'ī jurists (Allah have mercy on them), she is free to choose if her husband is a slave but she has no choice if her husband is a freeman.

NOTES

Inferences

From this [ف (*fā'*) in the ḥadīth] is deduced the issue regarding divorce concerning women.[233] Indeed, the vagina of the married slave-woman is the property of the husband which does not lapse from his ownership by her being manumitted, and thus *ḍarūrah* (compulsive necessity) calls for the suggestion that the [husband's] ownership [of her] by her being manumitted increases, such that his ownership in the excess is established.[234] This becomes a *sabab* for the option being established for her,[235] and the increase in the ownership of the vagina by her manumission is in the meaning of 'the issue regarding divorce issued concerning women.' Therefore, the ruling of the ownership of three [divorcements] depends on the manumission of the wife and not the manumission of the husband – as in the school of Imam ash-Shāfi'ī (Allah have mercy on him).[236]

ثُمَّ (thumma)

ثُمَّ (*thumma*) is [used] for delayed succession.[237]

However, according to Imam Abū Ḥanīfah (Allah have mercy on him), it conveys a delayed succession in the word as well as in the ruling, but according to the two [= Imam Abū Yūsuf and Imam Muhammad (Allah have mercy on them)], it only conveys a delayed succession in the ruling.

---

233 The ف (*fā'*) in the ḥadīth has led to jurists debating over whether or not women are legally permitted to issue divorce.

234 The ownership of the husband increases by the legal maximum number of divorcements going from two to three.

235 It is due to the increase in the number of divorcements that the husband now has, owing to the increase in his ownership of her that she is legally entitled to diminish that excess in ownership, such that the option of nullification of marriage has been awarded to her.

236 Imam ash-Shāfi'ī (Allah have mercy on him) is of the view that the ownership of divorce is with men in accordance with their circumstances in terms of being free or in bondage, and the duration of the *'iddah* (waiting period) is specific to women according to their circumstances regarding being free and in bondage. He uses the following ḥadīth as evidence: الطَّلَاقُ بِالرِّجَالِ وَ الْعِدَّةُ بِالنِّسَاءِ (Divorce is by men and *'iddah* (waiting period) is by women). In other words, the circumstances of men being free or not is taken into account when calculating the number of divorcements they may issue (i.e. two for the slave and three for the freeman), and thus, women are not entitled to such. The Ḥanafī jurists (Allah have mercy on them) do not rely upon this ḥadīth and consider it to be possibly abrogated, whereas the Noble Companions (Allah be pleased with them) would resolve an issue like this by analogy and opinion rather than using this particular ḥadīth. If we were to accept this ḥadīth, we would only take it to mean 'Only men have the right to issue divorce, and only women have the right to await the *'iddah*,' for it does not mention the number of the divorcements. Moreover, the ḥadīth طَلَاقُ الْأَمَةِ اثْنَتَانِ وَ عِدَّتُهَا حَيْضَتَانِ (The divorce of the slave-woman is two and her *'iddah* is two periods of menstruation), relates that the maximum number of divorcements that a husband may issue to his wife who is a slave-woman is two, and her *'iddah* is a maximum of two periods of menstruation.

237 ثُمَّ (*thumma*) is a particle, or a conjunction, denoting order and delay between the word that is conjoined – the second conjunct (appearing after ثُمَّ (*thumma*)), and the word that is conjoined to it – the first conjunct (appearing before ثُمَّ (*thumma*)). Such delay is generally in accordance with the order, such as 'A entered, and then B, and then C, etc.' Here, the word 'then' is used for conjunction with a delayed succession.

Its explanation is in that which one [= husband] says to a woman [= his wife] whose marriage has not been consummated: 'إِنْ دَخَلْتِ الدَّارَ فَأَنْتِ طَالِقٌ ثُمَّ طَالِقٌ ثُمَّ طَالِقٌ (If you enter the building, you are divorced, *then* divorced and *then* divorced).' According to him [= Imam Abū Ḥanīfah (Allah have mercy on him)], the first [divorce] shall be attached to the entry [into the building], whereas the second occurs immediately and the third is void (*laghw*).[238] According to the two [= Imam Abū Yūsuf and Imam Muhammad (Allah have mercy on them)], all of them shall be attached to the entry [into the building] and the sequence is manifest upon entry in which case only one [divorce] occurs.[239]

If he said: 'أَنْتِ طَالِقٌ ثُمَّ طَالِقٌ ثُمَّ طَالِقٌ إِنْ دَخَلْتِ الدَّارَ' (You are divorced, *then* divorced and *then* divorced, if you enter the building),' according to Imam Abū Ḥanīfah (Allah have mercy on him), the first [divorce] takes place immediately, whereas the second and the third are void,[240] but according to the two [= Imam Abū Yūsuf and Imam Muhammad (Allah have mercy on them)], the first [divorce] takes effect upon entry [into the building], as we have [already] stated.[241]

If the woman [= his wife] is one whose marriage has been consummated, if he [= the divorcing husband] prefixes the condition, the first [divorce] shall be attached to the entry [into the building] whereas the other two [divorces] take effect immediately – according to Imam Abū Ḥanīfah (Allah have mercy on him),[242]

---

238 According to Imam Abū Ḥanīfah (Allah have mercy on him), the first divorce remains dependent on her entering the building; if she enters, she is divorced, otherwise not. The second divorce was mentioned after the word ثُمَّ (*thumma*), and since this word conveys a delayed succession, it is as if the husband has initiated a new sentence issuing a divorce; his wife is thus irrevocably divorced immediately. The third divorce is void because the divorcée is one whose marriage was not consummated with sexual intercourse and she was divorced (i.e. the second divorce in the statement), such that her divorce is irrevocable, not obliging *'iddah* (waiting period). Thus, the divorcée cannot be issued another divorce once her *'iddah* has lapsed, whereas in this case, there is no *'iddah* at all; the third divorce is null and void.

239 According to Imam Abū Yūsuf and Imam Muhammad (Allah have mercy on them), all three divorcements are dependent on her entering the building; the first, followed by the second, and then the third. However, being a woman whose marriage was not consummated with sexual intercourse, the first divorce issued to her results in an irrevocable divorce not obliging *'iddah* (waiting period). Thus, the second and third divorcements cannot be effective when she is not married nor in her *'iddah*. This results in only one effective divorce.

240 Imam Abū Ḥanīfah (Allah have mercy on him) takes the word ثُمَّ (*thumma*) to convey a delay in speech, and hence, he deems the second and third divorcements void, regardless of any condition attached to them. In his edict, the second and also the third divorcements were issued with sequential delay, as if they were fresh statements of divorce. The divorcée is a woman whose marriage was not consummated with sexual intercourse, and therefore the first divorce issued to her is irrevocable and not obliging *'iddah* (waiting period) – subsequent divorcements are void.

241 Imam Abū Yūsuf and Imam Muhammad (Allah have mercy on them) maintain their verdict for this statement with the same explanation as they have for the previous statement – all three divorcements are sequentially dependent on her entering the building, but the first divorce takes effect as one irrevocable divorce not obliging *'iddah* (waiting period).

242 According to Imam Abū Ḥanīfah (Allah have mercy on him), if the husband divorces his wife, whose marriage was consummated with sexual intercourse, with the following statement: 'إِنْ دَخَلْتِ الدَّارَ فَأَنْتِ طَالِقٌ ثُمَّ طَالِقٌ ثُمَّ طَالِقٌ' (If you

but if he suffixes the condition, the [first] two [divorces] take effect immediately whereas the third [divorce] shall be attached to the entry.[243] According to the two [= Imam Abū Yūsuf and Imam Muhammad (Allah have mercy on them)], all of them [i.e. divorces] shall be attached to the entry [into the building] in either case.[244]

بَلْ (bal)

بَلْ (*bal*) is [used] for amending a mistake by replacing the second in the place of the first.[245]

EXAMPLE

When someone [= husband] says to a woman [= his wife] whose marriage has not been consummated: 'أَنْتِ طَالِقٌ وَاحِدَةٌ لَا بَلْ ثِنْتَيْنِ (You are divorced once, no *but* twice),' only one [divorce] takes effect, because his saying 'لَا بَلْ ثِنْتَيْنِ (no *but* twice),' is a retraction of the first by placing the second in the place of the first. Such a retraction is not valid,[246] and hence, [only] one [divorce] takes effect. Hence, their remains no room for his saying, 'ثِنْتَيْنِ (twice).'

However, if she [= his wife] was one whose marriage had been consummated, then three [divorces] take effect.[247]

This is contrary to that when one says: 'لِفُلَانٍ عَلَيَّ أَلْفٌ ، لَا بَلْ أَلْفَانِ (I owe so-and-so a thousand [dirhams]. No *but*, two thousand),' such that

---

enter the building, you are divorced, then divorced and then divorced),' the first divorce is dependent on her entering the building, but the second and third divorcements take effect immediately. The second divorce takes effect with *'iddah* (waiting period) and the third divorce is effective during *'iddah* (waiting period). The word ثُمَّ (*thumma*) separates and disconnects the second and third divorcements from the condition attached to the first divorce.

243 Subsequent to the last note, if the husband divorces his wife, whose marriage was consummated with sexual intercourse, with the following statement: 'أَنْتِ طَالِقٌ ثُمَّ طَالِقٌ ثُمَّ طَالِقٌ إِنْ دَخَلْتِ الدَّارَ (You are divorced, then divorced and then divorced, if you enter the building),' the first two divorcements are effective immediately, according to our explanation given in the last note, and the third divorce takes effect upon her entering the building, provided she enters it during her *'iddah* (waiting period). Otherwise, the lapsing of her *'iddah* (waiting period) from the first two divorcements voids any subsequent divorce, regardless of condition.

244 According to Imam Abū Yūsuf and Imam Muhammad (Allah have mercy on them), all three divorcements are dependent on the wife entering the building, irrespective of whether the stipulation was prefixed or suffixed to the statement of divorce. Thus, when she enters the building, all three divorces take effect.

245 بَلْ (*bal*) is a particle of digression or denotes emendation wherever it occurs, in the case of a negation or an affirmation. (Lane, Edward William, *Arabic-English Lexicon*. London: Williams and Norgate, 1863. p.243).

246 Retraction of divorce is only valid during *'iddah* (waiting period). A woman whose marriage was not consummated does not bear *'iddah* (waiting period) and so the first divorce takes effect, in which case the husband's retraction and issuing two divorces is not valid.

247 In this case, three divorces take effect due to the following: the first divorce is irrevocable (*ṭalāq bā'in*), and it is issued with his initial statement. During *'iddah* (waiting period), she may be issued other divorcements, totalling three, and so the words 'ثِنْتَيْنِ (twice),' denote two further divorcements after the first divorce. This totals three divorces.

three thousand are not obliged – according to us.[248] Imam Zufar (Allah have mercy on him)[249] said: 'Three thousand are obliged,'[250] because [according to us,] the essence of the word [بَلْ (*bal*)] is to amend the mistake by establishing the second in the place of the first, and nullification of the first is not valid for it,[251] in which case it is incumbent to render the second valid with the continuance of the first. That is in the manner of adding the thousand to the first thousand.

This is contrary to one's saying: 'أَنْتِ طَالِقٌ وَاحِدَةً لَا بَلْ ثِنْتَيْنِ (You are divorced once, no *but*, twice),' because this is a performative (*inshā'*) [statement] whereas that is an informative (*ikhbār*) [statement], and the mistake occurs in the *ikhbār* rather than the *inshā'*. Thus, it is possible to rectify the wording by emending the mistake in the confession but not in divorce, such that if the divorce was to occur by way of *ikhbār*, that one says, 'كُنْتُ طَلَّقْتُكِ أَمْسِ وَاحِدَةً لَا بَلْ ثِنْتَيْنِ (Yesterday, I had divorced you once, *but* no, twice),' two [divorces] take effect, as we have [already] stated.[252]

لَكِنَّ (lākinna/lākin)

لَكِنَّ (*lākinna/lākin*) is [used] for emendation after the negation,[253] and thus it entails the affirmation of what comes after it. As for the negation of what precedes it, it is established with its [own] proof.[254] The conjunction of this word [= لَكِنَّ (*lākinna/lākin*)] is only ascertained

TERMINOLOGY

Laghw: Void
Jazā': Apodosis
Ta'līq: Conditional statement
Ikhbār: Informative statement
Mabī': Object of sale

---

248 According to the majority of the Ḥanafī jurists (Allah have mercy on them), echoing the edict of the *madhhab*, one's retraction of a subsequent confession using the word بَلْ (*bal*) is permitted.

249 He is Imam Zufar ibn Hudhayl (d. 158 AH/774 CE), one of the senior Imams in the Ḥanafī legal school.

250 Imam Zufar (Allah have mercy on him) takes the issue of confession akin to the issue of divorce.

251 A confession stands and it is not voidable, based on the ḥadīth: المَرْءُ يُؤْخَذُ بِإِقْرَارِهِ (A man is liable for his confession).

252 The difference between performative (*inshā'*) and informative (*ikhbār*) statements is that the former issue commands, and thus the speaker cannot be accused of lying when he or she issues it; the command stands irrespective of what was said, and the emendation is of no consequence. The speaker of the latter can be labelled truthful or a liar for what he or she says, as it is a statement giving information, and so the statement may be emended, if necessary, with the word بَلْ (*bal*) as conjunction between the first conjunct – the initial incorrect statement, and the second conjunct – the emended statement replacing the first.

253 لَكِنَّ (*lākinna*) is used for denial of expectation, i.e. it emends the presumption formed in the former part of the sentence – its first conjunct, by replacing it with the latter part – its second conjunct. It presents a contrastive relationship between both the conjuncts.

254 The difference between بَلْ (*bal*) and لَكِنَّ (*lākinna* and *lākin*) is: i. the former appears after positive and negative statements, whereas the latter only appears after negative statements, provided both conjuncts (i.e. first and second) appear as individual words. If the first and the second conjuncts are complete sentences and the first is a positive statement and the second is negative, then لَكِنَّ (*lākinna* and *lākin*) may appear between the two, and thus it appears after a positive statement. ii. لَكِنَّ (*lākinna* and *lākin*) only establishes the positivity of its second conjunct and leaves the negativity of its first conjunct to prove itself using the particle of negation. On the contrary, بَلْ (*bal*) itself proves the positivity of its second conjunction and also establishes the negativity of its first conjunction.

when the statement [= sentence] is in harmony;[255] if the statement is in harmony, then the negation attaches to the affirmation that follows it, otherwise it is a fresh sentence (*musta'nif*).

EXAMPLE

Its example is that which Imam Muhammad (Allah have mercy on him) has mentioned in *al-Jāmiʿ* [*al-Kabīr*], when one says: 'لِفُلَانٍ عَلَيَّ أَلْفٌ قَرْضٌ (I owe so-and-so a thousand [dirhams] as a debt),' and then that so-and-so [= the creditor] responds, 'لَا وَلَكِنَّهُ غَصْبٌ (No, *but* it was usurped),' the money [= the thousand dirhams] is binding upon him [= the debtor], because the statement is in harmony, and it is apparent that the negation is in the *sabab* and not in the property *per se*.[256]

Likewise if one says: 'لِفُلَانٍ عَلَيَّ أَلْفٌ مِنْ ثَمَنِ هَذِهِ الْجَارِيَةِ (I owe so-and-so a thousand [dirhams] for the price of this slave-woman),' and then that so-and-so replies, 'لَا، الْجَارِيَةُ جَارِيَتُكَ، وَلَكِنَّ لِي عَلَيْكَ أَلْفٌ (No. The slave-woman is yours, *but* you owe me a thousand [dirhams]),' the property [= the thousand dirhams] is binding upon him [= the confessor], for it is apparent that the negation is in the *sabab* and not in the property itself.

If one possesses a slave and says: 'هَذَا لِفُلَانٍ (He belongs to so-and-so),' and then that so-and-so replies, 'مَا كَانَ لِيْ قَطُّ وَ لَكِنَّهُ لِفُلَانٍ آخَرَ (He was never mine, *but rather* he belongs to another so-and-so),' thus, if the statement is connected, the slave belongs to the one in whose favour the second confession is made (*muqarr lahū*) because the negation attaches to the affirmation;[257] but if it [= the statement] is disconnected, the slave belongs to the first confessor, and so the saying of the one in whose favour the confession is made is a refutation of the [first] confession.[258]

If a slave-woman marries herself for a hundred dirhams [as mahr] without the permission of her master, and the master says: 'لَا أُجِيْزُ الْعَقْدَ بِمِائَةِ دِرْهَمٍ، وَ لَكِنْ أُجِيْزُهُ بِمِائَةٍ وَ خَمْسِيْنَ (I do not permit the contract [of marriage] for a hundred dirhams, *but* I do permit it for a hundred and fifty [dirhams]),' the contract [of marriage] is void because the statement is inharmonious; negation of permission and its affirmation

255 A statement is said to be harmonious when there is nothing to separate its various constituents, and when the subjects of the negative and the affirmative conjuncts are not the same.

256 In a case such as this, the confessor is declaring his debt to the creditor of one thousand dirhams, albeit the nature of the debt, i.e. the *sabab*, is different in the view of either party – the creditor deems it a general debt of borrowed moneys whereas the creditor claims it to have been wrongfully taken from him. The confessor still owes the stated amount.

257 If A possesses a slave, X, and he says, 'This slave belongs to B,' and then B says, 'It is not mine, but it belongs to C,' – if B had uttered his statement in a unified manner, then it is treated as his confession in favour of C, and hence, X belongs to C. The statement made by B is harmonious.

258 In contrast to the last note, if B uttered his statement without connection between the first and the second conjunctions, i.e. he says, 'It is not mine,' and then he becomes silent for a while before saying, 'But it belongs to C,' his statement cancels the confession made by A as its refutation. In this case, X belongs to A. This is an example of an inharmonious statement, rendering it a fresh sentence (*musta'nif*).

are incongruous. Thus, his saying, ' لَكِنْ أُجِيْزُهُ (... *but* I do permit it),' is his affirmation after the rejection of the contract [of marriage].[259]

Likewise, if he said: 'لَا أُجِيْزُهُ، وَ لَكِن أُجِيْزُهُ إِنْ زِدْتَنِي خَمْسِيْنَ عَلَى الْمِائَة (I do not permit it, *but* I shall permit it if you add to it for me fifty [dirhams] to the one hundred [dirhams]),' it shall be a rescission of the marriage [contract] due to there being no possibility of explanation (*bayān*) – because harmony is one of its conditions, and there is no harmony [here].

أَوْ[260] (aw)

أَوْ (*aw*) is [used] to include one of the two that are mentioned.[261]

EXAMPLE

Thus, if one says: 'هذَا حُرٌّ أَوْ هذَا (He is free *or* he)', it remains in the status of him saying, 'أَحَدُهُمَا حُرٌّ (One of the two is free),' inasmuch that he has the capacity to explain [= as to which of the two is free.]

If one says: 'وَكَّلْتُ بِبَيْعِ هذَا الْعَبْدِ هذَا أَوْ هذَا (I have delegated the sale of this slave to this [person] *or* this [person]),' [only] one of two [persons] will be the agent whereas selling [the slave] is permitted for either of the two. So if either of the two sells [him] and then the slave returns to the ownership of the principal [i.e. the master], it is not [permitted] for the other [agent] to sell him.

If one [= husband] says to three of his wives: 'هذِه طَالِقٌ أَوْ هذِه وَ هذِه (She is divorced, *or* she, and [i.e. including] she),' [only] one of the first two is divorced, and the third is divorced immediately due to her conjunction with the divorcée among the [first] two.[262] The choice of the husband in explaining the divorcée among the [first] two is in the status of that as if he had said, 'إِحْداكُمَا طَالِقٌ وَ هذِه (One of you two is divorced, plus her).'

Opinion of Imam Zufar (Allah have mercy on him)

Upon this [principle], Imam Zufar (Allah have mercy on him) says: When one says, 'لَا أُكَلِّمُ هذَا أَوْ هذَا وَ هذَا (I shall not speak to him *or* him and him),' it is in the status of him saying, 'لَا أُكَلِّمُ أَحَدَ هذَيْنِ وَ هذَا (I shall not speak to either of these two, plus him).' He does not violate his oath provided he does not speak to either one of the first two, and

---

259 In this case, the master affirms the marriage after rejecting it; the subjects of the negative and the affirmative conjuncts are the same – the contract of marriage – and this does not harmonise the statement. His latter portion (second conjunct) 'وَ لَكِن أُجِيْزُهُ بِمِائَةٍ وَّ خَمْسِيْنَ (... but I permit it for a hundred and fifty [dirhams]),' is rendered a fresh sentence (*musta'nif*) disconnected from his first conjunct. It is a rejection of the marriage by the master and thus voids his second conjunct.

260 In this example, the first conjunct and the second conjunct lack mutual harmony, and so the first conjunct is effective with the second conjunct having no consequence at all. For further explanation, see previous note. Furthermore, a lack of conjunctive influence does not allow the second conjunct to act as an explanation (*bayān*) for the first conjunct, thus rendering them separate and distinct sentences.

261 The English equivalent of أَوْ (*aw*) is 'or', and is used for an exclusion of choices.

262 If Mr. A indicates to his three wives; B, C and D, and he issues a divorce saying, 'B is divorced, or C, and D,' either B or C is divorced together with D.

NOTES

the third. According to us [= the majority of the Ḥanafī jurists (Allah have mercy on them)],[263] he violates his oath if he speaks to the first one [alone], and if he speaks to [only] one of the latter two he does not violate his oath provided he does not speak to them both [together].[264]

If one says: 'بِعْ هذَا الْعَبْدَ أَوْ هذَا (Sell this slave *or* this),' he [= the agent] may sell either of the two [slaves], whichever of the two he so wishes.[265]

If he [= the husband] adds [the particle] أَوْ (*aw*) to the mahr, that he will marry her for this *or* for that, *mahr al-mithl* (mahr a woman of her standing would receive) shall be decreed [for her] – according to Imam Abū Ḥanīfah (Allah have mercy on him), because the word encompasses one of the two, and the primary obligation is *mahr al-mithl*, and so that which is similar to it is preferred.[266]

Inferences

Upon this [principle] we said: '*Tashahhud* is not an integral of prayer,' because of the saying of the Prophet ﷺ:

إِذَا قُلْتَ هذَا أَوْ فَعَلْتَ هذَا فَقَدْ تَمَّتْ صَلٰوتُكَ

'When you say this or do this, your prayer has completed.'[267]

---

263 The majority of the Ḥanafī jurists in this case are Imam Abū Ḥanīfah, Imam Abū Yūsuf and Imam Muhammad (Allah have mercy on them).

264 According to the majority of the Hanafī jurists (Allah have mercy on them), to the exclusion of Imam Zufar (Allah have mercy on him), he violates his oath if he speaks to only the first of them, or if he speaks to the latter two together. However, his speaking to only one of the latter two does not cause a breach of his oath. They base their evidence on the conjunctive particle و (*wāw*) being used to include both of the latter two conjuncts who are mentioned in non-specific terms (*ghayr muʿayyan*), i.e. common terms (*nakirah*), and also in the negative (*manfī*), rendering them individually general when both are combined by the و (*wāw*). The first object of the oath is also general (i.e. non-specific), and this separates him from being part of the other two, whereas the other two partake in the oath in conjunction with one another. (Their example is as if the oath-taker said, 'I swear not to speak to A, or B + C together.')

Imam Zufar (Allah have mercy on him), on the contrary, explains his opinion by proposing only one of the first two as objects of the oath, and the third being an individual object. This renders one of the first two to be in the non-specific and negative sense and not the other, and thus opposing the rule that 'the negated common noun provides a general meaning'. (His example is as if the oath-taker said, 'I swear not to speak to A or B, and C.')

265 This is a performative (*inshā'iyyah*) statement with the conjunctive particle أَوْ (*aw*) – it serves to provide a choice in performative statements.

266 The primary obligation of payment in marriage is that of *mahr al-mithl* and not *mahr*, and the former is resorted to in the absence of an appropriate amount or a known amount of *mahr*. In case such occurs when the groom promises to pay one of two amounts mentioned, the obligated amount shall be decreed to be that which is closer to the *mahr al-mithl*. This is according to Imam Abū Ḥanīfah (Allah have mercy on him) and it is the preferred verdict of the Ḥanafīs. Imam Abū Yūsuf (Allah have mercy on him) and Imam Muhammad (Allah have mercy on him), however, are of the opinion that the groom has the choice of paying either amount, irrespective of the *mahr al-mithl*.

267 Abū Dāwūd, *As-Sunan*, Kitāb aṣ-Ṣalāh, Bāb at-Tashahhud; At-Tirmidhī, Bāb Mā Jā'a fī Waṣf aṣ-Ṣalāh; An-Nasa'ī; Ad-Dārimī, etc.

He ﷺ [conditionally] attached the completion [of the prayer] to one of the two,[268] and thus both of them are not conditional for it. The final sitting is conditional [in prayer], according to the agreement [of the Ḥanafī and the Shāfiʿī jurists (Allah have mercy on them)], and hence the recitation of *tashahhud* is not a condition.[269]

أَوْ (*aw*) in Negation

Thereafter, this word [i.e. the particle أَوْ (*aw*)] used in a negative location necessitates the negation of both that are mentioned, such that if someone says: 'لَا أُكَلِّمُ هذَا أَوْ هذَا (I shall not speak to this [person] *or* this [person]),' he violates his oath if he speaks to either of the two.[270]

أَوْ (*aw*) in Affirmation

For affirmation, it [= أَوْ (*aw*)] encompasses one of the two with the element of being provided with choice, such as the people's saying: 'خُذْ هذَا أَوْ ذلِكَ (Take this *or* that).'[271]

أَوْ (*aw*) in General Permissibility

Of the necessities of being provided with choice is general permissibility.[272]

Allah ﷻ says:

فَكَفَّٰرَتُهُۥٓ إِطْعَامُ عَشَرَةِ مَسَٰكِينَ مِنْ أَوْسَطِ مَا تُطْعِمُونَ أَهْلِيكُمْ أَوْ كِسْوَتُهُمْ أَوْ تَحْرِيرُ رَقَبَةٍ ۖ

'... and its expiation is to feed ten destitute persons out of the average of what you feed your families with, or their clothing, or to manumit a slave.'
Qur'an, 5:89

أَوْ (*aw*) in the Meaning of حَتّٰى (*ḥattā*)

It [= أَوْ (*aw*)] is sometimes [used] in the meaning of حَتّٰى (*ḥattā*).[273]

---

268 When someone pronounces the words of the *tashahhud* or he sits for the duration of the *tashahhud*, his prayer becomes complete. Thus, one of the two is obligatory (*farḍ*) and the other is incumbent (*wājib*); both of them cannot be obligatory (*farḍ*) or incumbent (*wājib*).

269 According to the Ḥanafī jurists (Allah have mercy on them), pronouncing the words of the *tashahhud* is incumbent (*wājib*) whereas sitting the duration of the final *tashahhud* is obligatory (*farḍ*), in agreement with what the Shāfiʿī jurists (Allah have mercy on them) hold. Hence, the pronunciation of the words of the *tashahhud* is not conditional for prayer.

270 When the particle أَوْ (*aw*) comes between two common nouns in the negative sense, both of them are rendered general, i.e. non-specific.

271 When the particle أَوْ (*aw*) appears between two common nouns in the affirmative sense, only one of the two shall be taken as the intended object, which is dependent on the choice of the speaker. This is subject to the sentence or statement being performative (*inshā'iyyah*) and not informative (*ikhbāriyyah*).

272 When a choice of many is presented, there must exist a general and unrestricted permissibility to adopt any one of them.

273 The particle أَوْ (*aw*) is originally used for conjunction. However, when the conjunction cannot be appropriately applied, the *majāz* comes into effect and renders it a metaphorical حَتّٰى (*ḥattā*) [see p.88 حَتّٰى (*ḥattā*)]. This is an example of *ḥaqīqah mutaʿadhdhirah*, in which case the *majāz* is resorted to [see p.20].

NOTES

Allah ﷻ says:

لَّيْسَ لَكَ مِنَ ٱلْأَمْرِ شَىْءٌ أَوْ يَتُوبَ عَلَيْهِمْ أَوْ يُعَذِّبَهُمْ

'You have nothing in the affair or He turns to them [in mercy].'
Qur'an, 3:128

It is said: It means, 'حَتّى يَتُوْبَ عَلَيْهِم (*until/unless* He turns to them [in mercy]).'[274]

Our Companions [= the Ḥanafī jurists (Allah have mercy on them)] said: If one says, 'لَا أَدْخُلُ هذِهِ الدَّارَ أَوْ أَدْخُلَ هذِهِ الدَّارَ (I shall not enter this building, *or* I shall enter this building),' [the particle أَوْ (*aw*)] would be in the meaning of حَتّى (*ḥattā*), such that if he enters the former first he violates his oath, but if he enters the latter first he becomes free of his oath.

EXAMPLE

An example of this is if one says to another, 'لَا أُفَارِقُكَ أَوْ تَقْضِي دَيْنِي (I will not leave you *or* you repay my debt),' [the particle أَوْ (*aw*)] would be in the meaning of 'حَتّى تَقْضِي دَيْنِي (... *until/unless* you repay my debt)'.

QUESTIONS

1. Name one of the things ف (*fā'*) is used for, with an example.
2. What is ثُمَّ (*thumma*) used for?
3. Name one of the things و (*wāw*) is used for with an example.
4. What is بَلْ (*bal*) used for?
5. What is لكِنَّ (*lākinna/lākin*) used for?
6. Name one of the things أَوْ (*aw*) is used for, with an example.

❖

حَتّى (ḥattā)

حتى (*ḥattā*) is [used] for [the end of] the extent, like إِلَى (*ilā*).[275]

Thus, when its preceding [word or statement] is extendable and its succeeding [word or statement] enables an extent for it, the word [i.e. حَتّى (*ḥattā*)] will execute its literal meaning.[276]

---

274 The words يَتُوْبَ عَلَيْهِمْ are verbs in the future tense, and so they cannot be in conjunction to the verb لَيْسَ for it is in the past tense, and nor to the word شَيْءٌ for it is a noun. Due to the case of *ḥaqīqah muta'adhdhirah*, the *majāz* is resorted to, in which case the conjunctive particle أَوْ (*aw*) is taken in the meaning of حَتّى (*ḥattā*).

275 حَتّى (*ḥattā*) is a particle used in three senses: i. denoting the end of an extent, and this is its predominant meaning, denoting a motive, cause, and used as an exceptive particle, ii. used as a preposition in the accusative case, similar to إِلَى (*ilā*), and iii. used as a preposition in the genitive case, as an exceptive particle similar to إِلَّا (*illā*). There are many other uses of this word, but details have been purposefully omitted.

276 It is imperative for the preceding word or statement (i.e. first conjunct) of the particle حَتّى (*ḥattā*) to have the capacity to extend its meaning or have

EXAMPLE

Its example is that which Imam Muhammad (Allah have mercy on him) said: When one [= master] says, 'عَبْدِيْ حُرٌّ إِنْ لَمْ أَضْرِبْكَ حَتّىٰ يَشْفَعَ فُلَانٌ، أَوْ حَتّىٰ تَصِيْحَ، أَوْ تَشْتَكِيَ بَيْنَ يَدَيَّ، أَوْ حَتّىٰ يَدْخُلَ اللَّيْلُ. (My slave is free if I do not beat you *until* so-and-so intercedes, or *until* you scream, or *until* you protest to me, or *until* the night begins),' the word [حَتّىٰ (*ḥattā*)] will execute its literal meaning, because repetitive beating carries extension [of meaning], and the intercession of such-and-such a person, and the likes thereof [i.e. the other examples] suffice for the extent of the beating. Thus, if he was to cease the beating prior to the extent [being reached], he violates his oath.[277]

If one [= creditor] vows not to leave his debtor *until* he repays him his debt, and then he leaves him prior to the furnishing of the debt, he violates his oath.[278]

Diversion from the Literal Meaning

When executing the literal meaning is impossible due to an impediment, like custom (*'urf*), such as when one vows to beat another *until* he [= the latter] dies or *until* he kills him [= the latter], it shall [be deemed to] carry [the meaning of] severe beating in accordance with custom.[279]

Diverting to Jazā' (Apodosis)

If the first [portion][280] is not extendable and the latter [portion][281] lacks the capacity to [reach] the extent, provided the first [portion] is suitable as a *sabab* (reason) and the latter [portion] as a *jazā'* (apodosis), it is taken as the *jazā'*.[282]

---

it extended, and also for the succeeding word or statement (i.e. the second conjunct) to take that meaning to its extent.

277 In this example, the preceding statement of the particle حَتّىٰ (*ḥattā*) is extendable due to continuous beating, and the succeeding statement enables the beating to end with the intervention of a certain person's intercession, the victim's screaming or protesting, or the entry of the night. Any cessation of beating by the oath-taker's own accord and without any intervention of the aforementioned stipulations renders the oath violated.

278 As in the previous example, the preceding statement of the particle حَتّىٰ (*ḥattā*) is extendable by the succeeding statement – pursuing the debtor until he furnishes the debt.

279 In the event of the literal meaning being against that which may effectively be achieved, or against that which ought to be avoided, then it shall carry the meaning of that which is customarily understood, such as A saying to B, 'I am going to kill you!' This does not necessitate the actual or the effective meaning, which would be unlawful, in which case the customary meaning applies, 'I am going to beat you severely!' This is an example of *ḥaqīqah muta'adhdhirah*, in which case the *majāz* is resorted to [see p.20].

280 This first portion is the first conjunct, i.e. the word or statement that appears prior to the particle حَتّىٰ (*ḥattā*).

281 The second portion is the second conjunct, i.e. the word or statement that appears after the particle حَتّىٰ (*ḥattā*).

282 If the preceding word or statement (i.e. first conjunct) of the particle حَتّىٰ (*ḥattā*) lacks the capacity to extend its meaning or have it extended, and the succeeding word or statement (i.e. the second conjunct) also lacks the capacity to take that meaning to its extent, i.e. both or any one of the conditions are missing, then the succeeding statement is taken in the meaning of the *jazā'*, provided that the preceding statement can be used as the *sabab* (reason) and

EXAMPLE

Its example is that which Imam Muhammad (Allah have mercy on him) said: When one [= master] says to another, 'عَبْدِيْ حُرٌّ إِنْ لَمْ آتِكَ حَتَّى تُغَدِّيَنِيْ (My slave is free if I do not come to you, *unless* you feed me breakfast)', and then he [= the master] comes to him but he [= the latter] does not feed him breakfast, he [= the master] does not violate his oath. [And that is] because the breakfast is not suitable as an extent for the [master's] coming, but rather it is an inviting factor to increase visits, [rendering it] suitable as *jazā'*. Thus, it is carried [to mean] *jazā'*, and so it is in the meaning of 'لَامْ كَيْ (*lām bearing the meaning of kay* – 'so that')'. It thus becomes as if he [= the master] said, '... إِنْ لَمْ آتِكَ إِتْيَانًا جَزَاؤُهُ التَّغْدِيَةُ (if I do not come to you, a coming the remuneration of which is breakfast).'[283]

Diversion to Conjunction

If this is impossible [as well] due to the latter [portion] being unsuitable as *jazā'* for the former [portion], it is taken in the meaning of a simple conjunction.[284]

EXAMPLE

Its example is that which Imam Muhammad (Allah have mercy on him) said:[285] When one [= master] says [to another], 'عَبْدِيْ حُرٌّ إِنْ لَمْ آتِكَ حَتَّى أَتَغَدّٰى عِنْدَكَ الْيَوْمَ (My slave is free if I do not come to you *so that* I have breakfast with you today), or, '... إِنْ لَمْ تَأْتِنِيْ حَتَّى تَغَدّٰى عِنْدِيْ الْيَوْمَ (if you do not come to me *so that* you have breakfast with me today),' and so he [= the master] came but he did not have breakfast with him that day,[286] he violates his oath. And that is because each of the two actions was annexed to the same [person] [in a manner that] his [one] action cannot be suitable as a *jazā'* for his [other] action. Hence, it is carried in [the meaning of] a simple conjunction, and therefore the combination [of both actions] is a *sharṭ* (protasis) for the manumission [of the slave].[287]

---

the succeeding statement can be used as the *jazā'*. In such cases, the particle حَتّٰى (*ḥattā*) adopts the meaning of 'لَامْ كَيْ (*lām bearing the meaning of kay*)'.

283 The meaning of the initial statement, 'My slave is free if I do not come to you, *until* you feed me breakfast,' is not the apparent meaning, but rather, 'My slave is free if I do not come to you, *so that* you feed me breakfast.' The feeding of breakfast does not end the visits, but rather is a cause for inviting further visits, and hence, the preceding statement does not extend to the succeeding statement. This makes both the statements as *sharṭ* and *jazā'*, respectively, in which case if the *jazā'* is not fulfilled, it does not render the oath violated.

284 If the particle حَتّٰى (*ḥattā*) cannot be used in its original or real meaning, and none of the aforementioned diversions can be applied to it, then it is used as a simple particle of conjunction, like و (*wāw*) and ف (*fā'*).

285 In *az-Ziyādāt*.

286 ... or if the other person came to the master and had breakfast with him that day.

287 If one swears an oath to do two actions himself, or he annexes them to someone else, then both actions cannot be a *sharṭ* and a *jazā'* in relation to one another. In this example, the arrival of the master cannot be a *sharṭ* for his having breakfast with the other person – the would-be *jazā'* – and hence, the particle حَتّٰى (*ḥattā*) bears the meaning of a conjunction; both the actions must

إلى (ilā)

إِلَى (*ilā*) is [used] for the end of the extent.[288, 289]

Types of إلى (ilā)

Thereafter,

i. it sometimes conveys the meaning of the [continued] extension of the ruling (*ḥukm*), and

ii. it sometimes conveys the meaning of termination [of the ruling].[290]

إلى (ilā) Denoting Extension of the Ruling

If it conveys the meaning of [continued] extension, then the extent is not included in the ruling.[291]

إلى (ilā) Denoting Termination of the Ruling

If it conveys the meaning of termination, then it [= the extent] is included [in the meaning of the ruling].[292]

Example of Extension of the Ruling

An example of the first [type] is: 'اِشْتَرَيْتُ هٰذَا الْمَكَانَ إِلَى هٰذَا الْحَائِطِ (I bought this place *up to* this wall),' the wall is not included in the sale.[293]

---

be performed by the same person for the oath to be fulfilled, otherwise he violates it.

288 The 'غَايَة (*ghāyah*) extent' here denotes the utmost limit of space or time.

289 إِلَى (*ilā*) is a preposition or a particle governing a noun in the genitive case and denotes the end of an extent, or the space between two points or limits, or the end of an extent of place but does not extend beyond it. It also denotes the end of a space of time. (Lane, Edward William, *Arabic-English Lexicon*. London: Williams and Norgate, 1863. p.85.)

290 The statement preceding the particle إِلَى (*ilā*) is known as the 'مُغَيًّا، الْمُغَيّىٰ *mughayyā*' – the object to which the limit is set, and the statement that follows it is the *ghāyah* (extent). There are four opinions regarding whether or not the extent (*ghāyah*) enters the *mughayyā*: i. it unequivocally enters, ii. it unequivocally does not enter, iii. it enters subject to homogeneity of genus, and iv. it enters subject to certain factors. Only two occasions have been mentioned here, incorporating all four in a general format.

291 Extension of meaning takes place when both the statements lack homogeneity, or if the homogeneity is doubtful, and the particle إِلَى (*ilā*) is used to extend the meaning of the ruling from the preceding statement to the succeeding statement. This does not incorporate the extent (*ghāyah*) into what the *mughayyā* is ruled by.

292 Termination of the ruling takes place when both the statements are homogeneous, and thus the particle إِلَى (*ilā*) is used to include the extent (*ghāyah*) into the ruling of the *mughayyā*. This excludes from the ruling whatever falls prior to the *mughayyā* and beyond the extent (*ghāyah*).

293 In this example, the مَكَان (place) is unlimited for it is used as a general term for a small amount and also a large amount, and the حَائِط (wall) is the extent to which the object of purchase shall extend. The wall is not included in the purchase for it lacks homogeneity with the place, and only serves as the extent to which the purchase applies.

Example of Termination of the Ruling

An example of the second [type] is: 'بَاعَ بِشَرْطِ الْخِيَارِ إِلَى ثَلَاثَةِ أَيَّامٍ (He sold with the option stipulated for *up to* three days).'[294]

An example of this is when someone swears an oath, 'لَا أُكَلِّمُ فُلَانًا إِلَى شَهْرٍ (I will not talk to so-and-so for *up to* a month),' [the whole of] the month is included in the ruling. It conveys the benefit of termination here.[295]

Inferences

It is on this [principle] that we said: The elbow and the ankles are included in the ruling of washing [in *wuḍū'*], in the saying of Allah ﷻ:

وَأَيْدِيَكُمْ إِلَى ٱلْمَرَافِقِ

'... up to [and including] the elbows.' Qur'an, 5:6

[That is] because the word إِلَى (*ilā*) is for [used for] termination here, for had it not been there, the prescription [of washing] would have incorporated the whole arm.[296]

It is because of this [principle] that we said: The knee is [included] within the nakedness, because the word إِلَى (*ilā*), in the saying of the Prophet ﷺ:

عَوْرَةُ الرَّجُلِ مَا تَحْتَ السُّرَّةِ إِلَى الرُّكْبَةِ

'The nakedness of a man is [from] what is below the navel to the knees.'[297]

conveys the benefit of termination, and so the knee enters the ruling [of nakedness].[298]

Delayed Ruling

Sometimes, the word إِلَى (*ilā*) conveys the benefit of delaying the ruling to the extent.[299]

---

294 In this example, all three days are included in the option that is stipulated due to the presence of homogeneity of day one (the *mughayyā*) with days two and three (the extent (*ghāyah*)), in which case the sale does not exclude anything, i.e. the option stipulated in the contract of sale, except for it going beyond the three days.

295 In this example, the oath-taker swears not to speak to a particular individual, and that renders it binding forever. However, his mentioning the extent (*ghāyah*) of his oath to be of one month terminates the oath after the extent (*ghāyah*) has been reached.

296 The word يَدٌ (*yad* – arm) extends from the tips of the fingers to the shoulders. In *wuḍū'*, it would have been obligatory to wash the يَدٌ (*yad* – arm) up to and including the shoulder, unless otherwise stated. Now this ruling is restricted with the particle إِلَى (*ilā*) and the extent (*ghāyah*) that follows it, which is المَرَافِقُ (*marāfiq* – elbows), and since المَرَافِقُ (*marāfiq* – elbows) are included in the meaning of يَدٌ (*yad* – arm), the particle إِلَى (*ilā*), although includes them, excludes anything beyond them.

297 Ad-Dāraquṭnī, *Sunan*, Kitāb aṣ-Ṣalāh; Al-Ḥākim, *Al-Mustadrak ʿala'ṣ-Ṣaḥīḥayn*. The ḥadīth is weak and uses the word 'bayna' not 'taḥta'.

298 The meaning of the words 'مَا تَحْتَ السُّرَّةِ (What is below the navel)' extends to the toes, but the ruling is restricted by the words 'إِلَى الرُّكْبَةِ (to the knees)' as the extent (*ghāyah*), and thereby excluding whatever is beyond the knees but including them.

299 The particle إِلَى (*ilā*) may also be used for a delay in the ruling when time

EXAMPLE

It is because of this [principle] that we said: When one [= husband] says to his wife, 'أَنْتِ طَالِقٌ إِلَى شَهْرٍ (You are divorced *up to* a month),' and he made no [particular] intention, divorce does not take effect immediately – according to us [= the Ḥanafī jurists (Allah have mercy on them)], contrary to Imam Zufar (Allah have mercy on him),[300] because the mention of the month does not legally render suitable the extension of the ruling and nor the termination, whereas the divorce carries [the possibility of] delay with the conditional [attachment], and therefore it is applied to that.

عَلَى (ʿalā)

The word عَلَى (*ʿalā*) is [used] to render obligation.[301] It originally conveys the meaning of superiority and loftiness.[302]

EXAMPLE

It is because of this [principle] that if one said: 'لِفُلَانٍ عَلَيَّ أَلْفٌ (For so-and-so *upon* me are a thousand [dirhams]),' it is taken to mean debt, as opposed to if he had said, 'عِنْدِي (*with* me),' 'مَعِي (*with* me),' or 'قِبَلِي (*from* my *side*).'[303]

Upon this [principle], he [= Imam Muhammad (Allah have mercy on him)] said, in *as-Siyar al-Kabīr*, 'When the head of the [besieged enemy] fort says, 'آمِنُونِي عَلَى عَشَرَةٍ مِنْ أَهْلِ الْحِصْنِ (Give me asylum *over* ten of the fort),' and we do that, the ten are other than he, and he has the option of specifying [the ten].[304]

---

is the receptacle and not space. This is only subject to the former two occasions being impossible to apply.

300 According to the majority of the Ḥanafī jurists (Allah have mercy on them), divorce in this issue takes effect after the lapsing of one month, and thereby the statement, 'You are divorced up to a month,' gives the meaning, 'You are divorced after the lapsing of a month,' provided the divorcing husband does not intend to issue the divorce immediately. If such an interpretation was inapplicable to this statement of divorce, the divorce would take effect immediately and the latter portion of the statement, '... up to a month,' would be void.

Contrary to the majority Ḥanafī opinion, Imam Zufar (Allah have mercy on him) said that divorce takes effect immediately, irrespective of the husband's intention.

301 عَلَى (*ʿalā*) is a genitive preposition, or particle عَلَى (*ʿalā*), that when used between two statements, the preceding statement has a legally binding effect on the succeeding statement.

302 The primary meaning of the particle عَلَى (*ʿalā*) is to express elevation and superiority of the preceding statement or word over the succeeding statement or word.

303 The former statement would oblige a duty, and thus render it a debt, whereas the latter statements are not particles that may render a thing obliged due to the absence of the particle عَلَى (*ʿalā*). The latter statements are not obligations but expressions of what is entrusted with him.

304 When a belligerent enemy seeks asylum using the particle عَلَى (*ʿalā*) and it is thus granted to him, he has the option of choosing those to whom asylum is granted with him. This option of choosing is granted to him because of two reasons: i. he is the head of the belligerents, and ii. he used the particle عَلَى

But if he said, 'آمِنُونِي وَ عَشَرَةٌ (Give me asylum, *and* ten),' or 'فَعَشَرَةٌ (*thus* ten),' or 'ثُمَّ عَشَرَةٌ (*then* ten),' and we do that, it is likewise, but the option of specifying [the ten] is for the one granting the asylum.[305]

عَلَىٰ ('alā) in the Meaning of ب (bi)

Sometimes, it [= عَلَىٰ (*'alā*)] is [used] in the meaning of ب (*bi*) for *majāz*.[306]

EXAMPLE

[It is] such that if someone said: 'بِعْتُكَ هٰذَا عَلَى أَلْفٍ (I sold this to you *over* a thousand [dirhams]),' it shall be in the meaning of ب (*bi*) due to the existence of indication of mutual exchange.[307]

عَلَىٰ ('alā)' for Condition

Sometimes, it [= 'عَلَىٰ (*'alā*)] is [used] in the meaning of condition.[308]

EXAMPLE

Allah ﷻ says:

يَٰٓأَيُّهَا ٱلنَّبِيُّ إِذَا جَآءَكَ ٱلْمُؤْمِنَٰتُ يُبَايِعْنَكَ عَلَىٰٓ أَن لَّا يُشْرِكْنَ بِٱللَّهِ شَيْـًٔا

'They [i.e. the believing women] give you a pledge on [the condition] that they will not associate anything with Allah ﷻ.' Qur'an, 60:12

Because of this [principle], Imam Abū Ḥanīfah (Allah have mercy on him) said: 'When she [= the wife] says to her husband, 'طَلِّقْنِي ثَلَاثًا عَلَى أَلْفٍ (Divorce me thrice *over* a thousand [dirhams]),' and he divorces her [only] once, then the money is not incumbent [on her],[309] because the word [عَلَىٰ (*'alā*)] conveys the meaning of condition,[310]

(*'alā*), which obliges authority.

305 In contrast to the last issue, if the belligerent leader seeks asylum using the particle عَلَىٰ (*'alā*), and it is granted to him, he plus ten others may be granted asylum, but he has no choice in selecting those to whom asylum should be granted, and such right of choice vests with the authority granting the asylum.

306 The particle بَاء (*bā'*) is used for adhesion (*ilṣāq*). See p.98.

307 In this case, عَلَىٰ (*'alā*) is used as بَاء (*bā'*) for adhesion (*ilṣāq*), i.e. due to the association of the consideration of payment for the consideration of giving away the sold commodity.

308 When the primary meaning and application of the particle عَلَىٰ (*'alā*) is not possible, it is taken in the meaning of a stipulation. In such cases, the statement preceding the particle عَلَىٰ (*'alā*) and the statement succeeding it are like a *sharṭ* and *jazā'* to one another.

309 Imam Abū Yūsuf and Imam Muhammad (Allah have mercy on them) are of the opinion that if he divorces her once when the condition for three divorces was stipulated on the payment of one thousand dirhams, the wife is obliged to pay a third of the thousand dirhams to the husband; divorce in exchange for property is a financial contract wherein the considerations are equally divided for both parties. Imam Abū Ḥanīfah (Allah have mercy on him), however, concluded nil payment; the word عَلَىٰ (*'alā*), in this context, is used as a condition, the complete fulfilment of which is essential for the promise of payment to be due, as if the wife had meant to say, 'Divorce me all three divorcements and I will then pay you a thousand dirhams.'

310 As a condition, the meaning shall render thus, 'Divorce me thrice on the condition of a thousand dirhams.'

and hence, the 'thrice' will be a condition for the obligation [to pay] the property.

فِيْ (fī)

The word فِيْ (*fī*) is [used] for *ẓarf* (an adverbial noun for time or place).[311]

EXAMPLE

On account of this principle, our Companions [= the Ḥanafī jurists (Allah have mercy on them)] said: 'When someone says, 'غَصَبْتُ ثَوْبًا فِيْ مِنْدِيْلٍ (I usurped a garment *inside* a kerchief),' or '... تَمْرًا فِيْ قَوْصَرَةٍ (... dates *inside* a basket),' both of them will be binding upon him [to return] together.[312]

The Uses of فِيْ (fī)

Thereafter, this word [i.e. فِيْ (*fī*)] is used for time, place, and action (*ẓarf*).

فِيْ (fī)' for Time

As for when it is used for time, such as when one [= husband] says: 'أَنْتِ طَالِقٌ غَدًا'[313] (You are divorced tomorrow),' Imam Abū Yūsuf and Imam Muhammad (Allah have mercy on them) said, 'Its [= the particle فِيْ (*fī*)] omission or its expression are [both] the same in this regard, such that if he had said, 'أَنْتِ طَالِقٌ فِيْ غَدٍ (You are divorced *in* the morrow (*archaic*)),' it shall be in the status of his saying, 'أَنْتِ طَالِقٌ غَدًا (You are divorced tomorrow),' – divorce takes effect at the onset of dawn in both scenarios.

Imam Abū Ḥanīfah (Allah have mercy on him) took [the opinion] that when it [= the particle فِيْ (*fī*)] is omitted, divorce takes effect at the onset of dawn, but when it is expressed then its intended [meaning] is the occurrence of divorce in any portion[314] of the next day in an unknown manner. Thus, if there is no presence of intention, the divorce takes effect in the first portion [of the next day] due to the absence of the conflux to it, but if he makes the intention of the last [portion] of the day, his intention is valid.

---

311 فِيْ (*fī*) is a particle governing the genitive case. It relates to a receptacle, and denotes inclusion, or inbeing, either in relation to place or in relation to time, either real or metaphorical. (Lane, Edward William, *Arabic-English Lexicon*. London: Williams and Norgate, 1863. p.2466.) It serves to render the word or statement succeeding it as a receptacle for the word or statement that precedes it.

312 According to the Ḥanafī jurists (Allah have mercy on them), this is as if he said, 'I usurped a garment and also the kerchief,' or 'I usurped the dates and also the basket.'

313 This is also used 'أَنْتِ طَالِقٌ فِيْ غَدٍ,' without the omission of فِيْ (*fī*).

314 Generally, the parts of a day are two: i. day and ii. night. Divided further, they become four: i. morning, ii. afternoon, iii. evening, and iv. night. These are divided again, thus making twelve portions: i. dawn, ii. twilight, iii. sunrise, iv. morning, v. noon, vi. afternoon, vii. evening, viii. sunset, ix. twilight, x. dusk, xi. night, xii. midnight. Further divisions of these parts portion the day into our modern timing system of: i. 24 hours, or ii. 1,440 minutes, or iii. 86,400 seconds, etc.

Example according to Imam Abū Ḥanīfah's statement

An example of this is in the saying of a man [= husband, to his wife], 'إِنْ صُمْتِ الشَّهْرَ فَأَنْتِ كَذَا (If you fast the month then you are like this [i.e. divorced]),' then that shall take effect upon [her] fasting the [complete] month.[315] If he said, 'إِنْ صُمْتِ فِي الشَّهْرِ فَأَنْتِ كَذَا (If you fast *within* the month then you are like this [i.e. divorced]),' that shall take effect upon [her] abstinence [i.e. fasting] for [even] a moment within the month.[316]

فِيْ (fī) for Place

As for [when فِيْ (*fī*) is used for] place, it is like one's [= the husband's] saying: 'أَنْتِ طَالِقٌ فِي الدَّارِ (You are divorced *in* the house),' or '... فِيْ مَكَّةَ (... *in* Makkah),' that shall be an unrestricted divorce in all places.[317]

On account of the meaning of *ẓarf* we [= the Hanafī jurists (Allah have mercy on them)] said: When one swears to do something and he annexes it [i.e. as a condition] to a time or a place, if that action is such that may be accomplished by the one performing it [i.e. the subject], the presence of that performer in that time or place is conditional.[318]

If the action is transitive [and connected] to a site (*maḥall*) [= object], then the presence of that site is conditional in that time or place, because the action is ascertained with its effect, and its effect is on the site.[319]

Imam Muhammad (Allah have mercy on him) in *al-Jāmiʿ al-Kabīr* said: 'When one says, 'إِنْ شَتَمْتُكَ فِي الْمَسْجِدِ فَكَذَا (If I abuse you *inside* the masjid, it shall be like this),' and then he abused him while inside the masjid and the victim of abuse is outside of it, he [= the one who made the oath, i.e. the abuser] violates his oath, but if the abuser is outside the masjid and the victim of abuse is inside of it, he [= the one who made the oath, i.e. the abuser] does not violate his oath.[320]

If one said: '... إِنْ ضَرَبْتُكَ (If I strike you...),' or 'إِنْ شَجَجْتُكَ فِي الْمَسْجِدِ فَكَذَا (If I give you a head wound *in* the masjid, it shall be like this),' it is

---

315 This wording refers to fasting for the entire month without missing a day.

316 This wording refers to fasting for any moment in the month.

317 If the husband said to his wife, 'You are divorced if you enter the house,' her entrance into the house would give effect to the divorce. If, however, the husband specified a place, such as the city of Makkah, or a particular house, but he did not add the condition of her entrance, then her divorce takes effect immediately irrespective of whichever place or building she may be in.

318 If someone vowed to perform a certain action at a certain time or in a certain place, and the act was such that it could be performed without the need for the object (*mafʿūl*), i.e. it was intransitive, then it is conditional for the person who ought to perform that act to be present at that particular time or in that particular location, as the case may be.

319 When the action is such that it needs an object, it is transitive, and without the object its effect is not achievable.

320 If A swears an oath that if he abuses B inside a particular building, he shall pay B a certain amount of money, and then A abuses B when A was inside that building but B was outside of it, the oath is breached. However, if A abuses B when he was outside of that particular building and B inside of it, the oath stands. In a case such as this, it is conditional for the one making the oath, in this case A, to be inside the building when abusing B, in order to violate the oath, irrespective of whether B is inside or outside of it.

conditional for the wounded, or the victim of the head wound [as the case may be,] to be inside the masjid but it is not conditional for the smiter or the awarder of the head wound to be inside it.

If one said: 'إِنْ قَتَلْتُكَ فِيْ يَوْمِ الْخَمِيْسِ فَكَذَا (If I kill you *in* the day of Thursday, it shall be like this),' and he injures him prior to Thursday but he dies on Thursday, he [= the one who made the oath] violates his oath.[321] However, if he injures him on Thursday and he dies on Friday, he [= the one who made the oath] does not violate his oath.

في (fī) for Action

If the word [في (fī)] enters upon an action, it conveys the meaning of condition.

Imam Muhammad (Allah have mercy on him) said: If one [= husband] says, 'أَنْتِ طَالِقٌ فِيْ دُخُوْلِكَ الدَّارَ (You are divorced *in* your entering the house),' it shall be in the meaning of condition, and so divorce does not take effect prior to entering the house.

If he says, 'أَنْتِ طَالِقٌ فِيْ حَيْضَتِكَ (You are divorced *in* your menstrual period),' if she is in her menstrual period she is divorced immediately; otherwise the divorce will be conditionally attached to the [subsequent] menstrual period.[322]

[It is stated] in the *al-Jāmiʿ al-Kabīr*, if one [= husband] says, 'أَنْتِ طَالِقٌ فِيْ مَجِيْئِ يَوْمٍ (You are divorced *in* the coming of the day),' she will not be divorced until *dawn occurs*.[323]

If he says, '... فِيْ مُضِيِّ يَوْمٍ (... *in* the passing of the day),' if that is [said] during the night, divorce takes effect at the sunset of the following day due to the existence of the condition.[324] If it is [said] during the day, she is divorced when that moment arrives the following day.[325]

[It is stated] in the *Ziyādāt*, if he [= the husband] says, 'أَنْتِ طَالِقٌ فِيْ مَشِيْئَةِ الله تَعَالَى (You are divorced *in* the wish of Allah ﷻ),' or '... فِيْ إِرَادَةِ الله تَعَالَى (... *in* the will of Allah ﷻ),' this will be in the meaning of condition, such that she will not be divorced.[326]

---

321 A vows that if he kills B on Thursday, his property Z goes to C. A injures B on Wednesday, but B dies on Thursday. Now A must transfer his property Z to C due to the breach of oath. In this case, the condition that was specified in the oath has been fulfilled, and that is the occurrence of the death of B on Thursday due to an act of A against B. If, however, A injures B on Thursday and B dies on Friday, A does not violate his oath.

322 If the husband attaches a condition to divorce and that condition is in a state of being fulfilled at the very moment the husband pronounces the conditional divorce, the divorce shall take effect immediately. If the condition is such that it will be fulfilled at some point in the future, then the divorce remains suspended pending the fulfilment of that condition.

323 When the husband attaches the condition of divorce to the onset of the day, the word 'day' shall refer to daylight and not darkness. In this case, the day is not the twenty-four hour period but the period between dawn and dusk. Hence, the word في (fī) is used in the form of a condition, i.e. 'You are divorced in the moment when the light of dawn breaks.'

324 At night, if the husband attaches the occurrence of divorce to the 'passing of the day', it shall refer to the light of day completely passing over, i.e. sunset.

325 During the day, if the husband attaches the occurrence of divorce to the 'passing of the day', it shall refer to the passing of twenty-four hours from the moment the conditional divorce was pronounced, as opposed to sunset in the previous case.

326 If the husband uses the word في (fī) in attaching the will of Allah ﷻ for

ب (bi)

The particle ب (*bi*) is [used] for adhesion in the literal composition, and that is why it is closely associated with payments. The substantiation of this [claim] is that the object of sale (*mabīʿ*) is the basis (*aṣl*) of the sale and the payment is the condition for it. It is because of this meaning that the perishing of the object of sale obliges the termination of the sale, but the perishing of the payment does not [oblige the termination of the sale].

The Successor Adheres to the Principal

When this is established, we say: Fundamentally, the successor[327] ought to be adhered to the principal (*aṣl*) [= which in this case is the basis], and not the principal (*aṣl*) being adhered to the successor.

In the category of sale, when the particle ب (*bi*) is prefixed to the exchange, it identifies that [= substitute] as a successor [that is] adhered to the principal [= essence of the sale], in which case it [= that which is adhered] is not the object of sale but the payment [such that it is permitted to substitute it prior to taking possession of it].[328]

EXAMPLE

Upon this [principle], we said: When someone says, 'بِعْتُ مِنْكَ هٰذَا الْعَبْدَ بِكُرٍّ مِنَ الْحِنْطَةِ (I sold this slave to you *for* a *kurr*[329] of wheat),' and he describes it [= the wheat], the slave will be the object of sale and the *kurr* will be the price, in which case it is permitted to have it substituted before taking possession [of it].[330]

---

the occurrence of the divorce, the word فِي (*fī*) will be taken to have been used in the conditional sense, i.e. 'If Allah ﷻ wishes,' or, 'If Allah ﷻ wills,' respectively. As the will of Allah ﷻ cannot be known, we must discount this condition and declare it void, in which case divorce will not take effect at all.

327 We find two considerations in a contract, one being from either party. In a contract of sale, these considerations are the object of sale and the payment. The object of sale is the essential consideration, for without it the sale would never have conceptualised, and hence, it is the basis. The payment, however, is the condition for the sale to be concluded effectively, and its existence depends on that of the object of sale, hence, it is the successor to the essence.

328 The basis is succeeded by whatever is adhered to it, such as one's saying, 'I will write with the pen.' The writing is the basis, and it is succeeded with 'the pen'. The word 'with' is employed for adhesion, and it cannot be employed but with the successor and not with the basis. Though the act of writing (being the basis) cannot be changed, the successor (or that which is adhered) can, such as, 'I will write with the pencil,' etc.

329 *Kurr* is a dry volumetric measure equal to sixty *qafīz*. The *qafīz* is a measure of about 40 litres.

330 A sells a shirt to B, saying, 'I sell this shirt to you for two pairs of shoes,' and he describes the shoes to him (i.e. the quality, the make, the size, the colour, etc.). The shirt in this case is the basis of the sale and the shoes are deemed its payment. If the basis changes, i.e. to a cloak, it would void the sale, but the changing of that which is adhered, i.e. the successor, which in this case is the shoes, is changeable without any adverse effect to the sale, provided it is changed prior to the seller taking hold of the shoes. Thus, if A changes the payment from two pairs of shoes to four hats, subject to the consent of B, it is permitted.

But if he says, 'بِعْتُ مِنْكَ كُرًّا مِنَ الْحِنْطَةِ (I sold this *kurr* of wheat to you),' and he describes it, [and then he says,] 'بِهَذَا الْعَبْدِ (for this slave),' the slave is the payment and the *kurr* [of wheat] is the object of sale;[331] this contract is of advance payment (*salam*), [which is] not valid unless delayed.

Our scholars [= the Ḥanafī jurists (Allah have mercy on them)] have said: If one [= master] says to his slave, 'إِنْ أَخْبَرْتَنِيْ بِقُدُوْمِ فُلَانٍ فَأَنْتَ حُرٌّ (If you inform me *of* the arrival of so-and-so, you are free),' this is in [the meaning of] the true report for it to be adhered to the arrival; if he gives a false report, he is not manumitted.[332]

However, if he [= the master] said, 'إِنْ أَخْبَرْتَنِيْ أَنَّ فُلَانًا قَدِمَ فَأَنْتَ حُرٌّ (If you inform me that so-and-so has arrived, you are free),' that is in [the meaning of] a general report; if he gives him a false report, he is [still] manumitted.[333]

If one [= husband] says to his wife, 'إِنْ خَرَجْتِ مِنَ الدَّارِ إِلَّا بِإِذْنِيْ فَأَنْتِ كَذَا (If you leave the house but *with* my permission, you are like this [i.e. divorced]),' she needs permission each time [she leaves the house], because what is excluded is the leaving [the house] adhered to the permission; if she leaves [the house] the second time without permission, she is divorced.[334]

If he [= the husband] says, 'إِنْ خَرَجْتِ مِنَ الدَّارِ إِلَّا أَنْ آذَنَ لَكِ... (If you leave the house but that I permit you ...),' that is in [the meaning of] permission [only] once, such that if she leaves [the house] a second time without permission [from her husband], she is not divorced.[335]

In the *Ziyādāt* [it says]: If he [= the husband] says, 'أَنْتِ طَالِقٌ بِمَشِيْئَةِ اللهِ تَعَالَى (You are divorced *with* the wish of Allah ﷻ),' or 'بِإِرَادَةِ اللهِ تَعَالَى ...

---

331 If A sells the shoes to B, saying, 'I sell these shoes to you,' and he describes them to him, followed by him saying, 'for this shirt,' the shoes are the object of sale, and the shirt is the payment. This renders the sale a contract of advance payment (*salam*); it obliges a delay in the mutual exchange of the goods, in which case the shoes, being the object of sale, will be handed over to the purchaser with delay.

332 In this statement, the master has made it conditional for the manumission of his slave that the latter reports to him of the arrival of a particular person. The condition here is the arrival, and anything else will not suffice.

333 In contrast to the last issue, the condition that the master has made here is the slave's mere reporting that a particular person has arrived, irrespective of whether that report is true or false; the slave wins his freedom by his mere report, even if he lies. The main reason for non-adhesion of true reporting to manumission is the absence of the particle ب (*bi*).

334 The husband has restricted his wife's movements, and he has forbidden her from leaving the house. However, she may leave the house with permission from her husband, otherwise his divorce comes into effect. The words that he has used in order for her to seek his permission to leave the house are such that she must seek his permission each time she intends to leave the house. The basis is that she is prohibited to leave the house at any time, but the subordinate, which in this case is the exclusion, has been identified as a successor to the basis, and it allows her to leave the house subject to its fulfilment. The letter ب (*bāʾ*) has applied adhesion to the restriction and excluded it from the general rule.

335 The condition that the husband has made in order to allow his wife to leave the house is to seek his permission, but the wording is such that a single permission shall fulfil all future conditions, i.e. she needs permission only once and not a second permission to leave the house a second or any subsequent time. Here again, the main reason for non-adhesion of exiting the house to divorce is the absence of the particle ب (*bi*).

(... *with* the will of Allah ﷻ),' or 'بِحُكْمِهِ (... *with* His command),' she will not be divorced.[336]

QUESTIONS

1. Name one of the things حَتّٰى (*ḥattā*) is used for with an example.
2. Name one of the things إِلٰى (*ilā*) is used for with an example.
3. Name one of the things عَلٰى (*'alā*) is used for with an example.
4. Name one of the things فِي (*fī*) is used for with an example.
5. Name one of the things بِ (*bi*) is used for with an example.

❖

2.19: BAYĀN (EXPLANATION)

Types of Bayān

Bayān is of seven types:

i. *bayān at-taqrīr* (determinative explanation)
ii. *bayān at-tafsīr* (interpretive explanation)
iii. *bayān at-taghyīr* (transformative explanation)
iv. *bayān aḍ-ḍarūrah* (compulsive explanation)
v. *bayān al-ḥāl* (circumstantial explanation)
vi. *bayān al-'aṭf* (conjunctive explanation)
vii. *bayān at-tabdīl* (abrogative explanation)

Bayān at-Taqrīr (Determinative Explanation)

As for the first [*bayān at-taqrīr* (determinative explanation)], it is when the meaning of the word is apparent, but it may denote another [meaning]. Hence, one explains that which is apparent and so the ruling of the apparent [meaning] is determined by his explanation of it.

EXAMPLE

Its example is that when one says: 'لِفُلَانٍ عَلَيَّ قَفِيْزُ حِنْطَةٍ بِقَفِيْزِ الْبَلَدِ (I owe so-and-so one *qafīz* of wheat according to the *qafīz* of this land),' or 'أَلْفٌ مِنْ نَقْدِ الْبَلَدِ ... (... one thousand from the currency of this land),' it shall be *bayān at-taqrīr*.

---

336 If the husband uses the particle بِ (*bi*) in adhering the will of Allah ﷻ for the occurrence of the divorce, the particle بِ (*bi*) will be taken to have been used in the conditional sense, i.e. 'If Allah ﷻ wishes,' 'If Allah ﷻ wills,' or, 'If it is His command,' respectively, and it is because the will of Allah ﷻ cannot be known that we must discount this condition and declare it void, in which case divorce will not take effect at all.

[And that is] because the unrestricted meaning is taken for the *qafīz* of the land, as well as its currency, with the [possible] denotation of a different intended meaning, and so when one explains it, he has determined it by his explanation of it.

Likewise, when one says: 'لِفُلَانٍ عِنْدِيْ أَلْفٌ وَدِيْعَةً (I have one thousand [dirhams] as a deposit (*wadīʿah*) of so-and-so with me),' the word 'عِنْدِيْ *ʿindī* (with me)' in its unrestricted sense gives the benefit of a trust (*amānah*), [but] with the possibility of a different intended meaning. Thus, when he said, 'وَدِيْعَة *wadīʿah* (deposit)', he determined the ruling of the apparent by his explanation of it.

Bayān at-Tafsīr (Interpretive Explanation)

As for *bayān at-tafsīr* (interpretive explanation), it is when the intended meaning of the word is not disclosed, one discloses it with his explanation of it.

EXAMPLE

Its example is when one says: 'لِفُلَانٍ عَلَيَّ شَيْءٌ (I owe so-and-so something),' and then he interprets that something to be clothing.

Or he says: 'عَلَيَّ عَشَرَةُ دَرَاهِمَ وَ نَيِّفٌ (I owe twenty plus dirhams),' and then he interprets the [meaning of] 'نَيِّفٌ *nayyif* (plus – 1 to 3)'.

Or he says: 'عَلَيَّ دَرَاهِمُ (I owe some dirhams),' and then he interprets them to be ten, for example.

The Ruling of Bayān at-Taqrīr and Bayān at-Tafsīr

The ruling of these two types of *bayān* is that it is valid [to explain them] connected or disconnected [= to the previous unexplained sentence].[337]

Bayān at-Taghyīr (Transformative Explanation)

As for *bayān at-taghyīr* (transformative explanation), it is when the [apparent] meaning of one's statement is changed by his explanation.

EXAMPLE

Its illustration is:

i. the conditional (*taʿlīq*),[338] and

ii. the exclusion (*istithnāʾ*).[339]

The jurists (Allah have mercy on them) have differed in both areas.

TERMINOLOGY

Istithnāʾ: Exclusion
Ajnabiyyah: Female non-relative
Mabtūtah: Irrevocably-divorced woman
Bayān at-taqrīr: Determinative explanation
Bayān at-tafsīr: Interpretive explanation
Bayān at-taghyīr: Transformative explanation
Bayān aḍ-ḍarūrah: Compulsive explanation
Bayān al-ḥāl: Circumstantial explanation
Bayān al-ʿaṭf: Conjunctive explanation
Bayān at-tabdīl: Abrogative explanation

337 *Bayān at-taqrīr* and *bayān at-tafsīr* can both be used in connection with the previous unexplained sentence and also independently of it.

338 An illustration of the *taʿlīq* (conditional) is when Mr. A stipulates to his wife Mrs. B that she will be divorced, if she enters the house of Mr. C. The entry of Mrs. B into the house of Mr. C is the condition.

339 An illustration of *istithnāʾ* (exclusion) is when Mr. A says to Mr. B, 'I owe you 100 dirhams less 10,' which denotes '90 dirhams'. In this case, 'less 10,' is the exclusion.

Conditional to an Attachment

Our Companions [= the Ḥanafī jurists (Allah have mercy on them)] have said: The thing stipulated with the condition is the *sabab* when [that] condition exists but not prior to it.[340]

Imam ash-Shāfiʿī (Allah have mercy on him) said: The conditional is immediately the *sabab*, except that the absence of the condition shall prevent its ruling [from taking effect].

Conclusion of Difference in Opinion

The conclusion of [this] disagreement is apparent in:

When one says to a female non-relative (*ajnabiyyah*), 'إِنْ تَزَوَّجْتُكِ فَأَنْتِ طَالِقٌ (If I marry you, you are divorced),' or he says to someone else's slave, 'إِنْ مَلَكْتُكَ فَأَنْتَ حُرٌّ (If I own you, you are free),' the conditional [statement] will be void with him [= Imam ash-Shāfiʿī (Allah have mercy on him)].

[That is] because the ruling of the conditional [statement] is that it is enacted at the beginning of the statement for it to be the effective cause (*ʿillah*). The divorce and the manumission, here, will not be enacted as the effective cause (*ʿillah*) because of the lack of their attribution to the due object.[341] Thus, the ruling of the conditional [statement] is void and therefore [the attachment of] the conditional statement is invalid.

According to us [= the Ḥanafī jurists (Allah have mercy on them)], this conditional [statement] is valid, such that if the man married her, the divorce would take effect. [That is] because his statement is enacted as the effective cause (*ʿillah*)[342] when the condition exists,[343] and the ownership is established when the condition exists, and therefore the conditional [statement] is valid.

Due to this meaning we [= the Hanafī jurists (Allah have mercy on them)] said: The stipulation of the validity of the conditional [statement] for its occurring in the case of non-ownership is that it must be attributed to the ownership or to the *sabab* of the ownership, such that if one said to a female non-relative 'إِنْ دَخَلْتِ الدَّارَ فَأَنْتِ طَالِقٌ (If you enter the building, you are divorced),' and then he marries her and the condition exists, divorce will not take effect.[344]

Likewise, according to him [= Imam ash-Shāfiʿī (Allah have mercy on him)], the [man's] ability to [marry] a freewoman prevents the permissibility of marrying a slave-woman.

That is because the Book has stipulated [the permissibility of] marrying a slave-woman [only] in the absence of the ability [to marry a freewoman].[345] Thus, when someone has this ability, the condition

---

340 According to the Ḥanafī Imams, the condition must be fulfilled for the stipulated act to take effect.

341 According to Imam ash-Shāfiʿī (Allah have mercy on him), a man cannot stipulate to divorce a female non-relative nor manumit someone else's slave in the cases mentioned here because the condition cannot be effective.

342 The reason (*ʿillah*) in this case is the divorce.

343 The condition in this case is the marriage.

344 That is because the husband did not attribute the divorce to the marriage; he only stipulated entry into the building.

345 وَمَن لَّمْ يَسْتَطِعْ مِنكُمْ طَوْلاً أَن يَنكِحَ ٱلْمُحْصَنَٰتِ ٱلْمُؤْمِنَٰتِ فَمِن مَّا مَلَكَتْ أَيْمَٰنُكُم مِّن

is [deemed to be] absent, and the absence of the condition prevents the ruling, and so it is not permitted.

Likewise, Imam ash-Shāfiʿī (Allah have mercy on him) said: There is no maintenance for the irrevocably-divorced woman (*mabtūtah*), unless she is pregnant. That is because the Book has attached spending [the maintenance] to pregnancy, due to the saying of Allah ﷻ:

وَإِن كُنَّ أُوْلَٰتِ حَمْلٍ فَأَنفِقُوا عَلَيْهِنَّ حَتَّىٰ يَضَعْنَ حَمْلَهُنَّ

'And if they [i.e. women] are pregnant, then spend on them until they give birth to their child.' Qur'an 65:6

So in the absence of pregnancy, the condition is [deemed to be] absent,[346] and the absence of the condition prevents the ruling[347] - according to him [= Imam ash-Shāfiʿī (Allah have mercy on him)].[348]

But according to us [= the Ḥanafī jurists (Allah have mercy on them)], as long as the absence of the condition does not prevent the ruling, it shall be permitted to establish the ruling with its [own] evidence, so it is permitted to marry a slave-woman, and [spending on her] maintenance is incumbent due to the general (*ʿāmm*) [commands].[349]

Of those [issues] that follow this type [i.e. conditional to an attachment] is the application of the ruling to the noun that is depicted (*mawṣūf*) due to a depiction (*ṣifah*). [In this case,] it is in the status of attaching the ruling to that depiction.

Upon this basis, Imam ash-Shāfiʿī (Allah have mercy on him) said: It is not permitted to marry the slave-woman from the People of the Book (*Ahl al-Kitāb*). That is because the scripture has applied the ruling upon the believing slave-woman, based upon the saying of Allah ﷻ:

يَنكِحَ ٱلْمُحْصَنَٰتِ ٱلْمُؤْمِنَٰتِ

'... from among your believing maidens... ' Qur'an 4:25

Therefore, it is restricted to the believing female, and so the ruling is prevented due to the absence of the depiction. Thus, it is not permitted to marry a slave-woman from the People of the Book.

Exclusion

From among the scenarios of *bayān at-taghyīr* is *istithnā'* (exclusion).

Our companions [= the Ḥanafī jurists] (Allah have mercy on them) have gone with the opinion that the *istithnā'* (exclusion) is

---

فَتَيَٰتِكُمُ ٱلْمُؤْمِنَٰتِ

'If one is unable to marry the free believing women, then [he may marry] the one you people own from among your believing women.' (Qur'an, 4:25).

346 The condition is the pregnancy.

347 The ruling in this case is the payment of maintenance.

348 According to Imam ash-Shāfiʿī (Allah have mercy on him), the absence of the condition will not obligate the rule.

349 The general commands include verses such as Sūrat al-Baqarah, Verse 233; Sūrat an-Nisā', Verse 3, etc. and numerous ḥadīths.

to speak about the remainder after the exclusion as if one had not spoken but [only] of the remainder.[350]

With him [= Imam ash-Shāfi'ī (Allah have mercy on him)], the initial statement enacts the effective cause (*'illah*) that obliges the totality, but the exception prevents it from being active, [as if] in the status of the absence of the condition in the category of the conditional [attachment].[351]

EXAMPLE

An example of this is in the saying of the Prophet ﷺ:

لَاتَبِيْعُوا الطَّعَامَ بِالطَّعَامِ إِلَّا سَوَاء بِسَوَاءٍ

'Do not sell food for food unless it is equal to each other.'[352]

According to Imam ash-Shāfi'ī (Allah have mercy on him), the initial statement enacts the reason for the unlawfulness of the sale of food for food, unequivocally. However, from this ruling the situation of equality is removed due to the exclusion, and so the remainder stays under the ruling of the initial [statement].[353]

And consequently, this renders one handful of food for two handfuls of food unlawful.

According to us [=the Ḥanafī jurists (Allah have mercy on them)], the sale of one handful does not come under [this] *naṣṣ*. [And that is] because the intended [meaning] of what is forbidden is restricted with the condition of selling when the person is able to establish parity and disparity in it by measure (*kayl*) – so that it does not contribute to the prohibition of someone who is incapable.[354]

---

350 An illustration of this is when A says, 'I am selling this item for 10 dirhams less 1.' This means that A intends to sell the item for 9 dirhams; '10 dirhams' is the initial statement and '1' is the exclusion. Thus, it is as though he had only said, 'I am selling this item for 9 dirhams.'

351 According to Imam ash-Shāfi'ī (Allah have mercy on him), our last illustration would oblige the 10 dirhams, but the exception would prevent the 10 dirhams being due and so the 9 dirhams would be decided upon. This is similar to the respective Imam's interpretation of the attachment of a condition, and that the absence of the condition prevents its ruling from taking effect.

352 There are many similar ḥadīths, for example, it is reported by 'Ubādah ibn ath-Thābit (Allah be pleased with him) that he heard the Messenger of Allah ﷺ say:

ينهى عن الذهب بالذهب، والفضة بالفضة، والبر بالبر، والشعير بالشعير، والتمر بالتمر، والملح بالملح، إلا سواء بسواء عيناً بعين

'Forbidding the sale of gold for gold, silver for silver, wheat for wheat, barley for barley, dates for dates, and salt for salt, unless they are like for like, same for the same.' Muslim, *al-Musnad aṣ-Ṣaḥīḥ*, Ch. Aṣ-Ṣarf wa Bay' adh-Dhahab bi'l-Waraq Naqdan, Ḥadīth 4061; etc.

353 According to Imam ash-Shāfi'ī (Allah have mercy on him), the initial statement is enforced without question, i.e. it is unlawful to sell or exchange food for food. However, he also says that the food being equal is an exception to this case, hence, the equality of food would render the sale or exchange valid otherwise unlawful.

354 This means that specific measuring instruments must be used honestly in order to ascertain parity of the exchange, and that handfuls are not specific measuring instruments though they may be used as such, and slight differences between each handful are likely.

And whatever does not enter the equal standard, it shall be outside the decree of the ḥadīth.[355]

Miscellaneous

From among the scenarios of *bayān at-taghyīr* is when one says: 'لِفُلَانٍ عَلَيَّ أَلْفٌ وَدِيْعَةٌ (I owe so-and-so one thousand [dirhams] as a deposit (*wadīʿah*)),' his saying 'عَلَيَّ *ʿalayya* (I owe/due upon me)' conveys [the meaning of] incumbency, but he has changed it to 'protection' by his saying 'وديعة *wadīʿah* (deposit)'.[356]

And one's saying: 'أَعْطَيْتَنِي (You gave to me...),'[357] or 'أَسْلَفْتَنِي أَلْفًا فَلَمْ أَقْبِضْهَا' (You prepaid[358] me one thousand [dirhams] but I did not take possession of them),' is from the category of *bayān at-taghyīr*.

Likewise, if one said: 'لِفُلَانٍ عَلَيَّ أَلْفٌ زُيُوفٌ (I owe so-and-so one thousand low-quality [monies].'[359]

The Ruling of Bayān at-Taghyīr

The ruling of *bayān at-taghyīr* is that it is valid if it is connected but invalid if it is disconnected [= to the previous unexplained sentence].[360]

After this, there are various issues in which the scholars have differed

i. that they are [either] from *bayān at-taghyīr* and so they are valid provided they are connected, or

ii. they are from *bayān at-tabdīl* and so they are not valid. An aspect of these will come in [the discussion on] *bayān at-tabdīl*.[361]

Bayān aḍ-Ḍarūrah (Compulsive Explanation)

EXAMPLE

As for *bayān aḍ-ḍarūrah* (compulsive explanation), its example is in the saying of Allah ﷻ:

---

355 In this case, the handful is not an equal standard, hence the Ḥanafī imams do not include it within the ruling of this ḥadīth.

356 'I owe one thousand ....' would generally refer to being in debt, but the word 'deposits' has clarified the vagueness in this statement, for a deposit *per se* is not something owned but provided with protection until it is returned to its rightful owner or depositor.

357 إعطاء *iʿṭā'* (to give), is used for the literal submission of something to someone, but it is metaphorically used for contract.

358 إسلاف *islāf* (prepayment), is used similarly to the last footnote.

359 In this case, one would owe 'one thousand' of the genuine currency by default (being *ḥaqīqah*), but the mention of the 'counterfeit currency (or monies)' (*majāz*) would render the statement *bayān at-taghyīr*.

360 *Bayān at-taghyīr* is only valid if it is connected to its primary statement, such as when the condition is mentioned with the primary sentence, such as one says, 'I will sell this item to you if you pay me in cash,' or if the exclusion is mentioned with its primary statement, such as one says, 'I will sell this item to you for 10 dirhams less 1.'

361 See p.108.

فَإِن لَّمْ يَكُن لَّهُۥ وَلَدٌ وَوَرِثَهُۥٓ أَبَوَاهُ فَلِأُمِّهِ ٱلثُّلُثُ ۚ

'... and [if only] his parents inherit him, then for his mother is one-third.'
Qur'an 4:11

It obliges sharing between the parents, [but] then it explains the share of the mother, which becomes an explanation for the share of the father.

Upon this [principle] we [= the Ḥanafī jurists (Allah have mercy on them)] said: If the two [partners] explained the share of the *muḍārib* (working partner in a contract of *muḍārabah*), but they remained silent regarding the share of the *rabb al-māl* (owner of the capital), the partnership is valid.

Likewise, if the two [partners] explained the share of the *rabb al-māl* but they remained silent regarding the share of the *muḍārib*, it shall be an explanation [of the share of the *muḍārib*].[362]

Upon this [principle] is the ruling of *muzāraʿah* (cropsharing).[363]

Likewise, if one bequeathed one thousand [dirhams] to so-and-so and so-and-so, and then he explained the share of either of the two, it is an explanation of the share of the other.

If one [husband] divorced one of his two wives, and then he had sexual intercourse with [any] one of the two, it is an explanation of the divorce to the other [wife].[364]

This is contrary to having sexual intercourse while issuing an unclear manumission [to slave-women][365] – according to Imam Abū Ḥanīfah (Allah have mercy on him). That is because the legitimacy of sexual intercourse with slave-women is established in two ways,[366] but ownership is not specified by the lawfulness of sexual intercourse.[367]

---

362 If both partners agree that the share of the *rabb al-māl* will be 50%, but they do not mention the share of the *muḍārib*, the share of the latter shall by default be 50%; the nature of the contract of *muḍārabah* calls for such adequate ratio of shares.

363 The determining of the share of either party to the contract, or partner in the partnership, will set aside the share of the other party or partner.

364 If Mr. A is married to two women, Mrs. B and Mrs. C, at the same time, and then he divorces one of the two without explaining which one, his sexual intercourse with Mrs. B would amount to an explanation that the divorce was intended for Mrs. C.

365 If a master frees one of two slave-women he owns, A and B, without explaining which one, his sexual intercourse with A will not result in the manumission of B. Imam Abū Yūsuf and Imam Muḥammad (Allah have mercy on them) are of the opinion that in this case the master's sexual intercourse with A is an explanation of his intention to manumit B, and consequently, it takes effect.

366 The two ways that establish the ownership of a slave-woman are marriage or sexual intercourse.

367 This issue discusses the ownership of slave-women legalising the master's sexual intercourse with them but not vice versa. Hence, the master's unspecified manumission of one of two slave-women followed by sexual intercourse with one of the two does not manumit the other, as it does not disclose the master's intention as clearly as it would in the case of a divorce.

Bayān al-Ḥāl (Circumstantial Explanation)

EXAMPLE

As for *bayān al-ḥāl* (circumstantial explanation), its example is in when the Lawgiver [= the Messenger of Allah ﷺ] sees something take place [in his presence] and he does not prohibit it, his silence is in the status of explaining that it is legal.

When the pre-emptor (*shafīʿ*) comes to know of the sale but he remains silent [about it], it is in the status of explaining that he consents to it.

When the virgin comes to know of [her] marriage by the guardian but she remains silent from rejecting [it], it is in the status of explaining [her] approval and permission.

When the master sees his slave selling and buying in the marketplace and he remains silent, it is in the status of authorising [that slave], and so he [= the slave] becomes one who is authorised (*ma'dhūn*) to execute transactions.

When the defendant refuses to take the oath in the session of the court, the refusal is in the status of acknowledging that the property is binding upon him [to pay] by way of confession – according to the two,[368] or by way of surrendering [it] – according to Imam Abū Ḥanīfah (Allah have mercy on him).

Outcome

The outcome is that silence at a place where explanation is needed is in the status of explanation [*per se*].

In this manner we said: Scholarly consensus (*ijmāʿ*) is concluded with enactment of the scripture by some and silence of the rest.

Bayān al-ʿAṭf (Conjunctive Explanation)

As for *bayān al-ʿaṭf* (conjunctive explanation), it is like when a measured or a weighed item is conjoined to an ambiguous sentence; it is an explanation for [that] ambiguous sentence.

EXAMPLE

Its example is when one said: 'لِفُلَانٍ عَلَيَّ مِائَةٌ وَ دِرْهَمٌ' (I owe so-and-so one hundred plus a dirham),' or '...مِائَةٌ وَ قَفِيْزُ حِنْطَةٍ (... one hundred plus a *qafīz* of wheat),' the conjunction will be in the status of the explanation that all of them are of the same genus.

Likewise, if one said: '...مِائَةٌ وَ ثَلَاثَةُ أَثْوَابٍ (... one hundred plus three garments),' or '...مِائَةٌ وَ ثَلَاثَةُ دَرَاهِمَ (... one hundred plus three dirhams),' or, '...مِائَةٌ وَ ثَلَاثَةُ أَعْبُدٍ (... one hundred plus three slaves),' it is an explanation that the hundred is of the same genus, in the [same] status of his saying, '... أَحَدٌ وَ عِشْرُوْنَ دِرْهَمًا (... twenty-one dirhams),' contrary to his saying, '... مِائَةٌ وَ ثَوْبٌ (... one hundred plus a garment),' or, '... مِائَةٌ وَ شَاةٌ (... one hundred plus a goat),' such that this is not an explanation

368 Imam Abū Yūsuf and Imam Muḥammad (Allah have mercy on them). Imam Abū Ḥanīfah (Allah have mercy on him) does not accept one's refusal to swear an oath to mean his acknowledgement.

of the hundred. This [principle] has been specified for the single conjunction when it is efficient to be a debt that is due such as a measured item or a weighed item.

Imam Abū Yūsuf (Allah have mercy on him) said: In '... مِائَةٌ وَ شَاةٌ (... one hundred plus a goat),' and '... مِائَةٌ وَ ثَوْبٌ (... one hundred plus a garment),' this is an explanation according to this principle.[369]

Bayān at-Tabdīl (Abrogative Explanation)

As for *bayān at-tabdīl* (abrogative explanation), it is abrogation, which is permitted by the Lawgiver [= Allah ﷻ] and not for the people.

Upon this [principle], it is invalid to exclude the entire ruling from the entire ruling for that would be an abrogation of the ruling [itself].

It is not permitted to retract the confession, divorce or manumission because it is an abrogation, and the slave (i.e. person) does not have that [right].

If one said: 'لِفُلَانٍ عَلَيَّ أَلْفٌ قَرْضٌ (I owe so-and-so one thousand [as] a loan),' or, '... ثَمَنُ الْمَبِيْعِ (... the price of sold goods),' and [then] he said: 'وَ هِيَ زُيُوْفٌ (They are low-quality [currency]),' it is *bayān at-taghyīr* – according to the two,[370] and so it is valid if connected.

But it is *bayān at-tabdīl* – according to Imam Abū Ḥanīfah (Allah have mercy on him), and so it is not valid even if it is connected.

If one said: 'لِفُلَانٍ عَلَيَّ أَلْفٌ مِنْ ثَمَنِ جَارِيَةٍ بَاعَنِيْهَا وَ لَمْ أَقْبِضْهَا (I owe so-and-so one thousand for the price of a slave-woman he sold to me but I did not take possession of her),' and there is no trace of her,'[371] it is *bayān at-tabdīl* – according to Imam Abū Ḥanīfah (Allah have mercy on him), because the confession that the payment is due [from him] is a confession of taking possession when the object of sale perishes, since if it perished prior to taking possession [of it], the sale will be rescinded and the payment will not remain due.

QUESTIONS

1. Explain *bayān aḍ-ḍarūrah* (compulsive explanation). Give an example.
2. What is *bayān at-taqrīr* (determinative explanation)?
3. What is the ruling of *bayān at-taqrīr* (determinative explanation)?
4. What is *bayān at-taghyīr* (transformative explanation)?
5. What is *bayān at-tafsīr* (interpretive explanation)?

---

369 According to Imam Abū Yūsuf (Allah have mercy on him), the primary statement is that the conjoined (*ma'ṭūf*) – the second conjunct, and to which it is conjoined (*ma'ṭūf 'alayhi*) – the first conjunct, are both the same, and that is because the conjunctive و (*wāw*) is for combining.

370 Imam Abū Yūsuf and Imam Muḥammad (Allah have mercy on them).

371 There is no indication as to which of the slave-women was the one he had bought.

UNIT **THREE**

THE SUNNAH OF **THE MESSENGER OF ALLAH** ﷺ

3.1: TYPES OF REPORT (KHABAR) OF THE MESSENGER OF ALLAH ﷺ

Report Being Equal to the Book of Allah ﷻ

The Report of the Messenger of Allah ﷺ is equal to the status of the Book in terms of certainty of knowledge and acting upon it.

Thus indeed, whoever has obeyed him [= the Messenger of Allah ﷺ] has [ultimately] obeyed Allah ﷻ.

As for the mention of whatever has passed regarding the discussion on *khāṣṣ*, *ʿāmm*, *mushtarak*, and *mujmal* in the Book, it is the same in the Sunnah, except that there may be doubt in terms of:

i. the report being established from the Messenger of Allah ﷺ, and

ii. its [continuous] connection to him ﷺ.

Types of Report

In this aspect, the report is rendered three types:

i. one type is that which is sound from the Messenger of Allah ﷺ and established with him ﷺ without a doubt [to its authenticity] – it is *mutawātir* (continuously mass-transmitted),

ii. another type is that which contains a kind of doubt – it is the *mash'hūr* (well-known), and

iii. another type is that which contains a probability as well as a doubt; it is the *āḥād* (solitary).

Mutawātir (Continuously Mass-Transmitted) Report

The *mutawātir* (continuously mass-transmitted) [report] is that which a large number of people have transmitted from a large number of people – [inasmuch that] their collaborating on a lie cannot be conceived due to their multitude, and in this manner, it reached you.

EXAMPLE

Its examples are the transmission of the Holy Qur'an, the number of units [in prayers (*ṣalāh*)], and the appointed shares in *zakāh* [etc.].

Mash'hūr (Well-Known) Report

The *mash'hūr* (well-known) [report] is the beginning[372] of which was like the *āḥād* (solitary) [reports], but thereafter it became well known in the second[373] and the third[374] generations, and the [Muslim] community (ummah) received it with acceptance. It thus became like the *mutawātir*, until it reached you.

---

372 This is the generation of the Companions (*Ṣaḥābah*, singular. *Ṣāḥābī*).

373 This is the generation of the Successors (*Tābiʿīs*).

374 This is the generation of 'Those Who Came After the Successors' (*Tābi aṭ-Ṭābiʿīn*).

EXAMPLE

This is like the ḥadīth on wiping over the *khuffs*, and stoning [as punishment] in the commission of unlawful sexual intercourse.

Difference Between the Legal Positions of Mutawātir and Mash'hūr

Thereafter, the *mutawātir* [report] conveys definite knowledge and rejecting it is disbelief, whereas the *mash'hūr* [report] conveys confident knowledge and rejecting it is an [evil] innovation (*bidʿah*). There is no difference among the scholars regarding the obligation to act on both [these types]. In fact, the discussion [of difference] takes place regarding *āḥād* [reports].

Khabar al-Āḥād (Solitary) Report

We [= the Hanafī jurists (Allah have mercy on them)] say: *Khabar al-āḥād* [solitary report] is that which one person has transmitted from one person, or one person from a large number of people, or a large number of people from one person. There is no reckoning the number as long as it [i.e. the number of narrators] does not reach the level of *mash'hūr*.

Legal Positions of Khabar al-Āḥād

It is that on which, with regards to legal commands, it is incumbent to act.

Proviso

[This is] subject to:

i. the narrator[s] being Muslim,

ii. their moral uprightness (*ʿadālah*),

iii. accurate retention (*ḍabṭ*),

iv. sanity (*ʿaql*), and

v. that it reaches you from the Messenger of Allah ﷺ with this condition [throughout].[375]

Kinds of Narrators

Originally [= in the first generation], there are two kinds of narrators:

[i. those who are known for their knowledge and *ijtihād*, and

ii. those who are known for their memory and moral uprightness.]

Narrators Known for their Knowledge and Ijtihād

[The first kind of narrators are those who are] known for [their] knowledge and *ijtihād*, such as the four caliphs (Allah be pleased

TERMINOLOGY

Khabar: Report

Mutawātir: Continuously mass-transmitted

Mash'hūr: Well-known

Āḥād/Khabar al-āḥād: Solitary

375 This condition refers to all the aforementioned conditions. This means that all the conditions, i.e. i. the narrator being Muslim, ii. their moral uprightness (*ʿadālah*), iii. accurate retention (*ḍabṭ*), and iv. sanity (*ʿaql*) must be present in every narrator in the chain of narration beginning from the Prophet Muhammad ﷺ until it reaches the final recipient.

with them),[376] ʿAbdullāh ibn Masʿūd (Allah be pleased with him), ʿAbdullāh ibn ʿAbbās (Allah be pleased with him), ʿAbdullāh ibn ʿUmar (Allah be pleased with him), Zayd ibn Thābit (Allah be pleased with him), Muʿādh ibn Jabal (Allah be pleased with him), and [others of] similar to them (Allah be pleased with them).

Thus, when their narration to you is sound from the Messenger of Allah ﷺ, acting upon their narration is superior to acting upon *qiyās* (analogical extrapolation).

Due to this [principle], Imam Muhammad (Allah have mercy on him):

- narrated the ḥadīth of the Bedouin who was visually impaired regarding the issue of laughing, and he abandoned *qiyās* for it;
- narrated the ḥadīth regarding making the women stand at the back [in prayer],[377] in the issue of *muḥādhāt* (being parallel), and he abandoned *qiyās* for it;
- narrated the ḥadīth about vomiting[378] from ʿĀʾishah (Allah be pleased with her) for which he abandoned *qiyās*; and,
- narrated the ḥadīth[379] about the prostration of forgetfulness (*sujūd as-sahw*) being after the salutation[380] from Ibn Masʿūd (Allah be pleased with him), and he abandoned *qiyās* for it.

Narrators Known for their Memory and Moral Uprightness

The second kind of narrators are those who are well known for [their] memory and moral uprightness (*ʿadālah*), but not [known] for performing *ijtihād* or issuing decrees (*fatwā*), such as Abū Hurayrah (Allah be pleased with him) and Anas ibn Mālik (Allah be pleased with him).

When the narration of those like these two is sound with you; if the report agrees with *qiyāṣ*, the incumbency of acting upon it is obvious, but if it opposes it then acting upon *qiyās* is superior.

EXAMPLE

Its example is that which Abū Hurayrah (Allah be pleased with him) reported:

الْوُضُوْءُ مِمَّا مَسَّتْهُ النَّارُ

'Wuḍū' is due from that which fire touches.'

Ibn ʿAbbās (Allah be pleased with him) asked him, 'What do you think that if you performed *wuḍū'* with warm water, would you perform *wuḍū'* [again] because of it?' He [= Abū Hurayrah (Allah be

376 They are the al-Khulafā' ar-Rāshidūn (the Rightly-Guided Caliphs), namely, Abū Bakr aṣ-Ṣiddīq, ʿUmar ibn al-Khaṭṭāb, ʿUthmān ibn ʿAffān and ʿAlī ibn Abū Ṭālib (Allah be pleased with them).

377 أَخِّرُوْهُنَّ مِنْ حَيْثُ أَخَّرَهُنَّ اللهُ 'Let them stand at the back as Allah ﷻ has let them stand at the back'.

378 That it invalidates *wuḍū'*.

379 Ibn Mājah, Kitāb aṣ-Ṣalāh, Bāb fī Man Sajada-hā baʿd as-salām.

380 Not prior to it.

pleased with him)] went quiet).[381] Ibn ʿAbbās (Allah be pleased with him) refuted him with *qiyās*, for if he[382] had a report, he would have narrated it.

On this [principle], our Companions [= the Ḥanafī jurists (Allah have mercy on them)] have disregarded the narration[383] of Abū Hurayrah (Allah be pleased with him) in the issue of the unmilked [animal][384] for *qiyās*.[385]

Conditions for Practising the Khabar al-Āḥād

On account of the variation in the states of the narrators,[386] we [= the Ḥanafī jurists (Allah have mercy on them)] said: The conditions for acting upon the *khabar al-āḥād* (solitary report) are:

i. that it does not oppose the Book,

ii. [that it does not oppose] the [*mutawātir* and] *mash'hūr* Sunnah, and

iii. that it does not oppose the *ẓāhir* [= observable (customary actions of the masses)].

The Prophet ﷺ said:

تَكْثُرُ لَكُمُ الْأَحَادِيْثُ بَعْدِي، فَإِذَا رُوِيَ لَكُمْ عَنِّيْ حَدِيْثٌ فَاعْرِضُوْهُ عَلَى كِتَابِ
اللهِ فَمَا وَافَقَ فَاقْبَلُوْهُ وَمَا خَالَفَ فَرُدُّوْهُ

'Reports will increase for you after me, so therefore, whenever a ḥadīth is reported to you from me, review it with the Book of Allah; whatever conforms to it, accept it and whatever opposes [it], reject it.'[387]

The affirmation of this[388] is in what was reported from ʿAlī ibn Abū Ṭālib (Allah be pleased with him) that he said: 'There were three types of narrators:

381 At-Tirmidhī, Kitāb aṭ-Ṭahārah, bāb mā jā'a fī al-wuḍū'i mimmā ghayyarat an-nār; Ibn Mājah – same; Abū Dāwūd – same.

382 This could be either Abū Hurayrah (Allah be pleased with him), that the statement regarding the performance of *wuḍū'* (wudu) after coming into contact with something that had been heated using fire, or it could mean Ibn ʿAbbās (Allah be pleased with him) that if he had any ḥadīth in favour of or in opposition to what Abū Hurayrah (Allah be pleased with him) had said, he would have narrated it and not relied on *qiyās*. The latter is the more likely scenario.

383 Al-Bukhārī narrated from Abū Hurayrah: 'The Prophet ﷺ said, "Don't keep camels and sheep unmilked for a long time, for whoever buys such an animal has the option to milk it and then either to keep it or return it to the owner along with one *Sa*ʿ of dates."'

384 Some people would leave their animals unmilked in order for the milk to gather in the udders of the she-camel, cow, buffalo, sheep, goat or any other such animal. This would deceive the purchaser into buying the animal, believing it produces milk in abundance.

385 Compensating one *ṣā*ʿ of dates against an undetermined amount of milk is against *qiyās*. This ḥadīth calls for the purchaser to compensate with one *ṣā*ʿ of dates, whereas *qiyās* obliges him to compensate with the same amount of milk or its equivalent payment.

386 These are the narrators of *akhbār āḥād* (solitary reports).

387 Al-Hindī, ʿAlī ibn Ḥusāmuddīn al-Muttaqī (888 AH/1472 CE – 975 AH/1567 CE), *Kanz al-ʿUmmāl fī Sunan al-Aqwāl wa'l-Afʿāl.*

388 This refers to the variation in the numbers of the narrators and also the

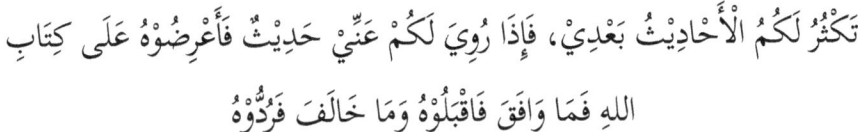

i. a sincere believing person who associated with the Messenger of Allah ﷺ and was aware of the meaning of his ﷺ statement;

ii. a Bedouin who came from any tribe and he heard only a portion of whatever he heard but he was not aware of the reality [of the meaning] of the statement of the Messenger of Allah ﷺ, and thus he returned to his tribe and reported [it] without [using] the wording of the Messenger of Allah ﷺ, and so the meaning changed while he thought that the meaning did not differ; and

iii. a hypocrite[389] whose hypocrisy was not known, who reported that which he did not hear and he fabricated [therein] – many people heard from him believing him to be a sincere believing person, and so they reported that [fabrication] from him which then became popular among the people.

Therefore, it is because of this purpose that it is incumbent to review the report with the Book and the [*mutawātir* and] *mash'hūr* Sunnah.

Reviewing the Khabar al-Āḥād with the Book

An illustration of reviewing it with the Book is in the ḥadīth of touching the penis, according to what has been narrated from him ﷺ:

مَنْ مَسَّ ذَكَرَهُ فَلْيَتَوَضَّأْ

'Any man who touches his penis ought to perform wuḍū'.'

Thus, we reviewed it with the Book and it emerged contrary to the saying of Allah ﷻ:

فِيهِ رِجَالٌ يُحِبُّونَ أَن يَتَطَهَّرُوا

'Therein are men who love to be well pure.' Qur'an 9:108

because they would perform *istinjā'* (cleansing of excretal passages) using stones followed by washing with water.

If touching the penis was a ritual impurity (*ḥadath*), then this [act of theirs] would have been an absolute [cause of] defilement and not purification.[390]

Likewise, is the saying of the Prophet ﷺ:

أَيُّمَا امْرَأَةٍ نَكَحَتْ نَفْسَهَا بِغَيْرِ إِذْنِ وَلِيِّهَا فَنِكَاحُهَا بَاطِلٌ، بَاطِلٌ، بَاطِلٌ

'Any woman who marries herself without the permission of her guardian, her marriage is void, void, void!'[391]

[This ḥadīth] emerged contrary to the saying of Allah ﷻ:

---

authentication of ḥadīths in the light of the Book of Allah ﷻ.

389 Hypocrite in this sense is one who is not Muslim yet professes to be one in order to deceive Muslims.

390 This is because washing is not possible without touching the area to be washed, although, this reason for revelation of the verse is questionable in and of itself.

391 Tirmidhi; Ibn Majah; Abu Dawud; Darimi; Hakim; Ahmad.

فَلَا تَعْضُلُوهُنَّ أَن يَنكِحْنَ أَزْوَٰجَهُنَّ

'... then do not prevent them [i.e. the women] from marrying their husbands...' Qur'an 2:232

for indeed, the Book proves the validity of marriage by them [= women].

Reviewing the Khabar al-Āḥād with the Mash'hūr Report

An example of reviewing [the *khabar al-āḥād* (solitary report)] with the *mash'hūr* (well-known) report is the narration of [issuing] the judicial decree with one [male] witness plus an oath.

It emerged contrary to the saying [= *mash'hūr* ḥadīth] of the Prophet ﷺ:

اَلْبَيِّنَةُ عَلَى الْمُدَّعِي وَالْيَمِيْنُ عَلَى مَنْ أَنْكَرَ

'The [burden of] proof lies upon the plaintiff, and the oath is taken from the one who denies [the accusation].'

Reviewing the Khabar al-Āḥād with the Ẓahir (Observable)

On account of this meaning, we said: The *khabar al-āḥād* (solitary report), when it emerges opposing the *ẓāhir* (observable), it [= the *khabar al-āḥād*] will not be acted upon.

Of the scenarios opposing the *ẓāhir* (observable) is the report not being well-known (*mash'hūr*), when its need was common during the first and second centuries [AH], and that is because they [= the Muslims of the first two centuries AH] cannot be suspected to have fallen short when adhering to the Sunnah.

Thus, when the report did not become well-known when there was the intense need [for it] and common urge [for it], it is an indication of its not being sound.

EXAMPLE

Its example is in the [legal] cases: When one person reports [to the husband] that his wife is unlawful for him due to the contingent [relationship of] suckling (*raḍā'*), it is permitted for him [= the husband] to rely upon his report and he may marry her sister.[392]

But if he reports that the contract [of marriage] was void due to the ruling of suckling then his report is not accepted.[393]

Likewise, when a woman is informed of the death of her husband or of his divorcing her while he is not present, it is permitted that she relies on his report, and that she marries someone else.[394]

---

392 Mr. A marries Miss B, a minor. Mr. C, a reliable person, then informs Mr. A that Miss B was breastfed by Mrs. D, the mother of Mr. A. In this case, the marriage between Mr. A and Miss B is prohibited due to their milk relationship (i.e. suckling). However, Mr. A may marry the sister of Miss B.

393 This goes against the *ẓāhir* (observable). The marriage was conducted in the presence of witnesses and many people are aware of it, hence, the report is abandoned.

394 There is no opposition to the *ẓāhir* (observable) in this case.

If the *qiblah* is doubtful to him [= the worshipper] and one person informs him of it, it is incumbent for him to act upon it.

If one finds water, the state of which he does not know [whether it is pure or impure], and then one person informs him of filth [having contaminated it], he does not perform *wuḍū'* with it but performs *tayammum*.

Authoritative Status of Khabar al-Āḥād

The *khabar al-āḥād* (solitary report) is an authoritative source (*ḥujjah*) in four circumstances:

i. [when there exists] purely the right of Allah ﷻ that does not lead to a punishment,

ii. [when there exists] purely the right of the slave (i.e. person) wherein is merely an obligation [against another],

iii. [when there exists] purely his right wherein there is no obligation [against another],

iv. [when there exists] purely his right wherein there is an obligation [against another] to an extent.

Khabar al-Āḥād Purely for the Right of Allah ﷻ

As for the first, the *khabar al-āḥād* is admissible for it, because indeed, the Messenger of Allah ﷺ accepted the testimony of the Bedouin for [sighting] the crescent of Ramadan.

Khabar al-Āḥād Purely for the Right of the Person that is an Obligation against Another

As for the second, quantum and moral uprightness are stipulated for it [= the *khabar al-āḥād*], and its example is disputes.[395]

Khabar al-Āḥād for the Right of the Person that is Not an Obligation against Another

As for the third, the *khabar al-āḥād* is admissible for it, whether [the narrator] is morally upright or morally corrupt, and its example is [general] dealings.[396]

Khabar al-Āḥād for the Right of the Person that is an Obligation against Another to an Extent

As for the fourth, quantum or moral uprightness are stipulated for it [= the *khabar al-āḥād*] – according to Imam Abū Ḥanīfah (Allah have mercy on him),[397] and its example is deposal and interdiction.[398]

---

395 Such as in sales, contracts, etc.

396 Such as agency, profit-sharing partnership (*muḍārabah*), partnerships, etc.

397 According to Imam Abū Yūsuf and Imam Muhammad (Allah have mercy on them), this is the same as iii, i.e. both the conditions of quantum and moral uprightness must be satisfied.

398 A, an honest man, tells B, who is an agent for C, that C has deposed him of his being agent for the latter. This is an example of one man of moral uprightness breaking the news. The quantum has been disregarded here. A similar example of such circumstances includes one where two men of ill repute break such news to C, in which case the quantum will have been fulfilled but not the stipulation of moral uprightness.

QUESTIONS

1. The *mash'hūr* (well-known) [report] is the beginning of which was like the *āḥād* (solitary) [reports], but thereafter it became well known in the first and the second generations, and the [Muslim] community (ummah) received it reluctantly. True or false?
2. Define the *mutawātir* (continuously mass-transmitted).
3. Give an example of the *mash'hūr* (well-known).
4. What are five conditions before it is incumbent to act upon *khabar al-āḥād?*
5. Why is it incumbent to review *khabar al-āḥād* with the Book and the *mash'hūr* Sunnah?

❖

NOTES

IJMĀʿ
(SCHOLARLY CONSENSUS)

4.1: LEGAL STATUS OF IJMĀʿ

The *ijmāʿ* (scholarly consensus) of this community (ummah),[399] in the branches of the religion,[400] after the Messenger of Allah ﷺ passed away,[401] is an authoritative source (*ḥujjah*),[402] obliging acting upon it, legally,[403] as an honour to this community (*ummah*).[404]

4.2: RANKS OF IJMĀʿ

Thereafter, there are four types [(or ranks)] of *ijmāʿ*:[405]

i. express *ijmāʿ* of the Noble Companions (Allah be pleased with them) upon the ruling of a new issue,[406] then

ii. their *ijmāʿ*, by expression of some [of them] and silence of others from rejection,[407] then

iii. *ijmāʿ* of those who came after them[408] in that which the saying of the predecessors[409] was not found, and then

iv. *ijmāʿ* upon any single saying of the predecessors.

---

399 *Ijmāʿ* must be made by competent distinguished jurists who are experts in the relative fields of knowledge and discipline. They must be from the community (ummah) of the Prophet Muhammad ﷺ, otherwise their agreement will not constitute *ijmāʿ*.

400 The branches of Islam are its subsidiary issues that lack clear guidance in the Book of Allah ﷻ and the Sunnah of the Messenger of Allah ﷺ. Hence, solutions to new problems are sought by qualified legal experts in light of the texts of the Book and the Sunnah, though not directly from these texts. Examples of such subsidiary issues include the legal status of *tarāwīḥ* prayer and the total number of its units, the second *adhān* for the *jumuʿah* prayer, certain issues in inheritance law such as the doctrine of *ʿawl* (Al-Qudūrī, 721), etc. Primary issues would include prayer, fasting, Ḥajj, etc. and issues attached to them that are discussed in the Book and the Sunnah.

401 During the physical life of the Messenger of Allah ﷺ, *ijmāʿ* was not needed, for if he ﷺ became a part of the *ijmāʿ* process, his opinion on its own would be the legal source and would outweigh all other suggestions.

402 *Ijmāʿ* is an authoritative source for legal guidance and implementation.

403 As an authoritative source of law, it is obligatory to act upon decisions made by *ijmāʿ*.

404 This community (ummah) of Prophet Muhammad ﷺ.

405 Initially, there are two kinds of *ijmā'*: i. narrative (*sanadī*), and ii. that which pertains to an agreement of the Schools of Law (*madhhabī*). This division is of narrative consensus (*ijmā' sanadī*), of which there are four ranks that are relative to the legal superiority of one another.

406 The Noble Companions (Allah be pleased with them) would decide matters on which the Book and the Sunnah were not clear, such as their *ijmāʿ* on the twenty units of *tarāwīḥ* prayer on each night during the thirty nights of the month of Ramadan.

407 If some Noble Companions (Allah be pleased with them) agreed on an issue and the others remained silent but they did not express any opposition to it, then that would also be a form of *ijmāʿ*.

408 The Noble Companions (Allah be pleased with them) are known as the *Ṣaḥābah* (sing. *Ṣaḥābī*), and those who came after them are the Successors, or *Tābiʿūn* (sing. *Tābiʿī*).

409 The 'predecessors' refers to the Noble Companions (Allah be pleased with them).

Legal Statuses of the Ranks of Ijmāʿ

i. As for the first, it is in the same rank as a verse from the Book of Allah ﷻ, then

ii. their *ijmāʿ*, by expression of some [of them] and silence of others; it is in the same rank as the *mutawātir* (continuously mass-transmitted) [report], then

iii. *ijmāʿ* of those who came after them is in the same rank as the *mash'hūr* (well-known) among the reports, then

iv. *ijmāʿ* of the later [generations] upon any single saying of the predecessors is in the same rank as the *ṣaḥīḥ* (sound) among the *āḥād* (solitary) [reports].

Authoritative Ijmāʿ

The authoritative in this category is the *ijmāʿ* of the *ahl ar-ra'y wa'l-ijtihād* (those who have discernment and exercise juristic reasoning). So, the saying of the common people, the Muslim scholastic theologian, and the ḥadīth expert, [all who] who lack the insight into the principles of Islamic law, is not authoritative.[410]

4.3: KINDS OF IJMĀʿ

Thereafter, *ijmāʿ* is of two kinds:[411]

i. compound (*murakkab*), and

ii. non-compound (*ghayr-murakkab*).

Compound Ijmāʿ

The compound [*ijmāʿ*] is when many opinions have gathered [in agreement] upon the ruling of a new issue with there being a disagreement in the effective cause (*ʿillah*).

EXAMPLE

Its example is the *ijmāʿ* upon the invalidation [of *wuḍū'* (wudu)] when vomiting and [when] touching a woman. As for with us [= the Ḥanafī jurists (Allah have mercy on them)], it is based on the vomiting[412] but with him [= Imam ash-Shāfiʿī (Allah have mercy on him)] it is based on touching [a woman].[413, 414]

TERMINOLOGY

Ijmāʿ: Scholarly consensus

Ḥujjah: Authoritative source

Murakkab: Compound

Qāḍī: Judge

Ṭawl al-ḥurrah: Capacity to marry a freewoman

Shubhah fi'ẓ-ẓann: Conceptual doubt

410 In-depth comprehension of the principles of Islamic Jurisprudence is fundamental for anyone to partake in *ijmāʿ*.

411 This division is of the consensus of the schools of law (*ijmā' madhdhabī*).

412 According to the Ḥanafīs, *wuḍū'* is nullified by vomiting a mouthful or more, but this is not the case with the Shāfiʿis.

413 According to the Shāfiʿīs, *wuḍū'* is nullified when a man and woman touch one another, but this is not the case with the Ḥanafīs.

414 In this case, as an example of compound *ijmāʿ*, *wuḍū'* is nullified according to the *ijmāʿ* between the Ḥanafīs as well as the Shāfiʿīs, but the effective cause (*ʿillah*) differs between both schools. If A vomits a mouthful and also touches a woman at the same time, his *wuḍū'* becomes invalid according to both schools, but the legal reason in both schools is different.

Thereafter, this type of *ijmāʿ* shall not remain an authoritative source (*ḥujjah*) after the appearance of invalidity in either of the two sources, such that:

i. if it is established that vomiting does not invalidate [*wuḍū'* (wudu)], then Imam Abū Ḥanīfah (Allah have mercy on him) will not decide that it [= *wuḍū'* (wudu)] is invalidated by it, and

ii. if it is established that touching does not invalidate [*wuḍū'* (wudu)], then Imam ash-Shāfiʿī (Allah have mercy on him) will not decide that it [= *wuḍū'* (wudu)] is invalidated by it,

[and that would be] due to the invalidity of the effective cause (*ʿillah*) upon which the ruling was based.

The invalidity is suspected on both sides; it is possible that Imam Abū Ḥanīfah (Allah have mercy on him) may have been correct in the issue of touching but mistaken in the issue of vomiting, and Imam ash-Shāfiʿī (Allah have mercy on him) may have been correct in the issue of vomiting but mistaken in the issue of touching.

This does not contribute to basing the existence of *ijmāʿ* on absurdity (*bāṭil*),[415] contrary to whatever [discussion] on *ijmāʿ* has passed.[416]

Consequently, it is permitted to remove this [type of] *ijmāʿ* due to the appearance of invalidity in that upon which it is based.

Thus, when the judge (*qāḍī*) decides in any [legal] case, and then it appears that the witnesses were [either] slaves, or they were false by their retracting [their testimony], his decree will be void even though that may not have appeared to be in the favour of the plaintiff.

On account of this meaning, the category of 'those whose hearts have been reconciled'[417] has been omitted from the eight categories [of *zakāh* recipients] due to the omission of the effective cause (*ʿillah*).

The share of the close relatives [of the Messenger of Allah ﷺ] has also lapsed, because of the ending of its effective cause (*ʿillah*).

Upon this [principle], when one washes filthy clothing with vinegar and the filth is removed, it will be ruled that its location is pure due to the omitting of its effective cause (*ʿillah*).

Upon this [principle], the difference between ritual impurity (*ḥadath*) and physical impurity (*khubth*) is established, because, surely, vinegar removes filth *from* its place. As for vinegar [*per se*], it does not avail in *purifying* the location, but that which does avail [of purifying] is the purifier, which is water.[418]

---

415 If the corruption (*fasād*) is certain on both sides, then the *ijmāʿ* shall be void.

416 Thereafter, this type of *ijmāʿ* shall not remain an authoritative source (*ḥujjah*) after the appearance of invalidity (*fasād*) in either of the two sources, contrary to whatever discussion on *ijmāʿ* has already passed in the previous division of *ijmā'*.

417 Qur'an, 9:60.

418 Physical purity can be achieved by using vinegar to wash away the filth, whereas ritual purity is only achieved with water, unless water is not available, in which case a suitable substitute may be used.

Non-Compound Ijmāʿ

[The non-compound *ijmāʿ* is when many opinions have agreed upon the ruling of a new issue with there being no disagreement in the effective cause (*ʿillah*).]

4.4: IJMĀʿ ʿADAM AL-QĀ'IL BI'L-FAṢL (CONSENSUS OF THE ABSENCE/REJECTION OF ONE HOLDING AN OPPOSING VIEW) AND ITS TYPES

Thereafter, there is another type of *ijmāʿ*, and it is *ʿadam al-qā'il bi'l-faṣl* (consensus of the absence/rejection of one holding an opposing view),[419] and it is of two kinds:

i. one of the two is that when the onset of the disagreement in both issues is the same, and
ii. the second is that when the onset [of the disagreement] is different.

Their Legal Ruling

i. The first is an authoritative source (*ḥujjah*), and
ii. the second is not an authoritative source (*ḥujjah*).

Example of Ijmāʿ ʿAdam al-Qā'il bi'l-Faṣl when the Source is the Same

An example of the first is in what the scholars have extracted from legal issues based upon the one [and the same] principal case (*aṣl*), and its example is when we established that the prohibition (*nahy*) from legal disposal proves their [legal] affirmation.

We said: It is valid to make a specific vow (*nadhr*) to fast the Day of Sacrifice (*yawm an-naḥr*), and also that a corrupt sale gives ownership – due to *ʿadam al-qā'il bi'l-faṣl* (consensus of the absence/rejection of one holding an opposing view).

If we said: Indeed, the conditional [attachment] (*taʿlīq*) is the *sabab* (reason) when the condition is present [and not prior to it], we would also say: The conditional attachment (*ta'līq*) of divorce or [of] manumission to ownership, and the *sabab* (reason) of ownership are both valid.[420]

Likewise, if we established that the application of the ruling to a noun that is depicted (*mawṣūf*) with an adjective (*ṣifah*) does not oblige the attachment (*taʿlīq*) of the ruling upon it, we would also say: The ability [to marry] the freewoman does not prevent the permissibility of marriage to a slave-woman, for it has been soundly transmitted from the predecessors that Imam ash-Shāfiʿī (Allah

---

419 This type of *ijmā'* is among the kinds of compound *ijmā'*.

420 If we take something to exist because of a particular reason (*sabab*) then we also have to accept the validity of stipulating ownership because of that reason, as well as the validity of the reason for ownership, when divorce of the wife or manumission of the slave takes place, i.e. divorce or manumission cannot take place unless the one issuing the same owns them.

have mercy on him) deduced the issue of '*ṭawl al-ḥurrah* (capacity to marry a freewoman)' from this principle.

If we established the permissibility of marriage to the believing slave-woman while having the ability [to marry a freewoman], it would [also] be permitted to marry a slave-woman from the People of the Book due to this principle.[421]

Upon this [principle] is the example that we have mentioned before.

Example of Ijmāʿ ʿAdam al-Qā'il bi'l-Faṣl when the Sources are Different

An example of the second is when we say that: Vomiting is a nullifier [of *wuḍū'*], then the corrupt sale will give ownership due to *ʿadam al-qā'il bi'l-faṣl*, or that intentional homicide obliges retaliation due to *ʿadam al-qā'il bi'l-faṣl*.[422]

Similar to this, vomiting does not nullify [*wuḍū'*], then touching [a woman] would nullify [it]. Thus, this is not an authoritative source (*ḥujjah*) because although the soundness of the novel case (*farʿ*) indicates the validity of its primary case (*aṣl*), it does not [however] merit the soundness of another primary case (*aṣl*) so that another issue could have been deduced from it.

The Obligations of the Mujtahid (The Independent Distinguished Jurist)

It is incumbent on the *mujtahid* (independent distinguished jurist) to seek the ruling for a new issue in the Book of Allah ﷻ, then in the Sunnah of the Messenger of Allah ﷺ – in explicit texts (*ṣarīḥ an-naṣṣ*) or indicative texts (*dalālat an-naṣṣ*), in accordance to what mention of it has passed, because there is no way to apply opinion (*ra'y*) when there is the possibility of acting upon the *naṣṣ* [of the Book and the Sunnah].

Thus, when the *qiblah* is doubtful to someone and a person informs him of it, investigation of it (*taḥarrī*) is not permitted for him.

If one finds water, and then someone of moral uprightness informs him that it is impure (*najis*), it is not permitted for him to perform *wuḍū'* with it, rather, he performs *tayammum*.

Material Doubt vs Conceptual Doubt[423]

On account of acting upon [one's] opinion being less than acting upon the *naṣṣ* [of the Book or Sunnah], we said: *Shubhah bi'l-maḥall*

---

421 This is due to *ʿadam al-qā'il bi'l-faṣl* though the source is the same, because if the conditional statement (*taʿlīq*) did not nullify the ruling when the condition was absent, then application of the ruling would be based on the depicted noun because of a depiction that does not oblige the attachment of the ruling.

422 The source of the disagreement in both is different.

423 There are various types of uncertainties and doubts (*shubhah*) that the *mujtahid* encounters when expending his efforts in pursuance of legal classification of the issues. Such uncertainties have similar, yet distinct, groupings and headings in their legal schools.

(material doubt)[424] is stronger than *shubhah fi'ẓ-ẓann* (conceptual doubt),[425] such that taking into account the presumption of a person would lapse in the first case [i.e. *shubhah bi'l-maḥall*].[426]

EXAMPLE

Its example is in when one has sexual intercourse with the slave-woman of his son, he will not be subjected to *ḥadd* [punishment], even though he says, 'عَلِمْتُ أَنَّهَا عَلَيَّ حَرَامٌ (I knew that she was unlawful to me),' but the lineage of the child will be established with him. That is because the doubt of his ownership in the property of the son is established by the *naṣṣ* [of the Book or Sunnah]. The Holy Prophet ﷺ said:

أَنْتَ وَمَالُكَ لِأَبِيكَ

'You and your property belong to your father.'[427]

Thus, the reckoning of his presumption in the lawfulness or unlawfulness of that [case] is omitted.

But if the son had sexual intercourse with the slave-woman of his father, his presumption in the lawfulness or unlawfulness would be taken into account, such that if he said, 'ظَنَنْتُ أَنَّهَا عَلَيَّ حَرَامٌ (I presumed that she was unlawful to me),' *ḥadd* [punishment] will be due [against him]. But if he said, 'ظَنَنْتُ أَنَّهَا عَلَيَّ حَلَالٌ (I presumed that she was lawful to me),' *ḥadd* [punishment] will not be due [to him], and that is because his doubt in the property of the father is not established by the *naṣṣ* [of the Book or Sunnah], and therefore his opinion is taken into account, and the lineage of the child is not established to him even if he claims it.

Conflict of Evidences

When two evidences mutually conflict for the *mujtahid*:

i. if the conflict is between two verses, he inclines towards the Sunnah,[428] and

---

424 *Shubhah bi'l-maḥall* is also known as *shubhah ad-dalīl* (doubt in evidence) and *shubhah ḥukmiyyah* (effective doubt). This occurs when evidence exists permitting or prohibiting an action or omission, but due to the presence of an impediment, it becomes doubtful whether such permission or prohibition is effective.

425 *Shubhah fi'ẓ-ẓann* is also known as *shubhah fi'l-fi'l* (active doubt) and *shubhah ishtibāh* (suspected doubt). This occurs when one takes evidence to perform or refrain from an action or omission, something that in reality is not evidence.

426 *Shubhah fi'ẓ-ẓann* is dependent on one's understanding, contrary to *shubhah bi'l-maḥall*. The latter, i.e. *shubhah bi'l-maḥall* would not be taken into account when a suitable case appears that contains both types of doubt, i.e. *shubhah fi'ẓ-ẓann* and *shubhah bi'l-maḥall*.

427 Ibn Mājah, *as-Sunan*, Kitāb at-Tijārāt, Bāb Mā li'r-rajuli min māli waladi-hī.

428 If there is an apparent clash of verses in the Book, and it is such that he finds it impossible to choose either or to reconcile between them, then he moves on to the Sunnah.

ii. if [the conflict] is between two Sunnah [narrations], he inclines towards the reports of the Noble Companions (Allah be pleased with them) and [then],

iii. authentic *qiyās* (analogical extrapolation).

iv. Thereafter, when two *qiyās* conflict for the *mujtahid*, he investigates and acts upon one of the two, because there is no legal evidence less than *qiyās* to which it may be resorted.

Acting by One's Own Opinion

Upon this [principle] we said: When there are two containers of water with the traveller, one impure and the other pure, he does not investigate to find out [the pure one] of the two, rather he performs *tayammum*, but if there are two garments with him, one pure and the other impure, he strives to find out [the pure one] of the two. [That is] because water has a substitute, and that is earth, but there is no substitute for garments to which it may be resorted.

By this it is established that acting by [one's own] legal reasoning (*ra'y*) legally only happens in the absence of any evidence other than it.

Thereafter, when he investigates and he affirms his investigation with action, it will not become annulled by mere investigation [again].

EXAMPLE

Its explanation is in when he investigates [to choose] between two garments, then performs *ẓuhr* prayer wearing one of them, and then his investigation takes place for *ʿaṣr* [prayer] [that he performs it] in the other garment, it is not permitted for him to perform *ʿaṣr* prayer with the other [garment], because the first [garment] has been confirmed through action, and so it does not become void by mere investigation.

This is contrary to when he investigated to ascertain the *qiblah*, and then his opinion changed and his investigation towards a new direction took place, he may face towards it [= the new direction], because the *qiblah* has the possibility of moving, and therefore it is possible to move the ruling [of investigation] to the status of the abrogation of *naṣṣ* [of the Book and Sunnah].[429]

Upon this [principle] are the issues mentioned in *al-Jāmiʿ al-Kabīr* regarding the *takbīrs* of *ʿĪd* prayer, if the opinion of the person changed,[430] as is known.[431]

---

429 If texts of the Book of Allah ﷻ and Sunnah of the Messenger of Allah ﷺ can be abrogated by texts of the same degree or superior to them, then so can rulings based on lesser statuses, such as the sayings of the Noble Companions (Allah be pleased with them), and decisions that have come about due to *taḥarrī* and *qiyās*, etc.

430 There is a possibility of a change in the number of additional *takbīrs* in *ʿĪd* prayers due to their number being differed on by the Noble Companions (Allah be pleased with them).

431 If someone begins the prayer of *ʿĪd* intending to perform ten extra *takbīrs* following the method taught by ʿAbdullāh ibn ʿAbbās (Allah be pleased with him), and after performing the five *takbīrs* for the first unit, he decides to perform the second unit according to the method taught by ʿAbdullāh ibn

QUESTIONS

1. What are the four 'ranks' of of *ijmāʿ*?
2. *Shubhah bi'l-maḥall* (material doubt) is stronger than *shubhah fi'ẓ-ẓann* (conceptual doubt). True or false?
3. When two evidences mutually conflict for the *mujtahid*, what is the process?
4. What is compound *ijmāʿ*?

❖

ʿAbbās (Allah be pleased with him) of six extra *takbīrs* (three in each unity), he shall perform three extra *takbīrs* in the second unit as opposed to the five he would have, had he continued with the first method. This is because it is possible to change the number of *takbīrs* in the *ʿĪd* prayer due to both claims coming from the Noble Companions (Allah be pleased with them).

QIYĀS (ANALOGICAL EXTRAPOLATION)

Qiyās[432] is one of the authoritative sources (*ḥujjah*) of the Sharīʿah, acting upon which is incumbent in the absence of whatever evidence is superior to it,[433] in [the event of] a new case. Certainly, [many] reports have been reported from the Prophet ﷺ and the Noble Companions (Allah be pleased with them) in this regard.

5.1: REPORTS FROM THE PROPHET ﷺ AND THE NOBLE COMPANIONS (ALLAH BE PLEASED WITH THEM) ON THE LEGAL STATUS OF QIYĀS

1. The Prophet ﷺ said to Mu'ādh ibn Jabal (Allah be pleased with him) when he dispatched him to Yemen:

بِمَ تَقْضِي يَا مُعَاذُ؟

'How will you adjudicate, O Muʿādh?'

He [= Muʿādh] (Allah be pleased with him) replied:

بِكِتَابِ اللهِ تَعَالَى

'With the Book of Allah.'

He [= the Messenger of Allah ﷺ] asked, 'What if you do not find [the ruling]?'

He [= Muʿādh] (Allah be pleased with him) replied:

بِسُنَّةِ رَسُوْلِ اللهِ صَلَّى اللهُ عَلَيْهِ وَسَلَّمَ

'With the Sunnah of the Messenger of Allah.'

He [= the Messenger of Allah ﷺ] then asked, 'What if you do not find [the ruling there either]?'

He [= Muʿādh] (Allah be pleased with him) replied:

أَجْتَهِدُ بِرَأْيِي

'I shall do my best with my opinion.'

The Messenger of Allah ﷺ approved him (Allah be pleased with him) and said, 'All praise to Allah Who enabled the envoy of the Messenger of Allah in that which pleases Allah and His Messenger.'[434]

2. It was reported that a woman from the Khathʿam [tribe] came to the Messenger of Allah ﷺ and said, 'My father is very old. Ḥajj is imposed on him, but he cannot undertake the journey. Is it permissible for me to perform *Ḥajj* on his behalf?'

He [= the Prophet] said, 'Do you think that if there was a debt on your father and you paid it for him, would it not be permitted for you?'

---

432 *Qiyās* literally means 'to value one thing with another' and 'to measure it'. In Islamic legal terminology, it is to attach the legal ruling (*ḥukm*) of a novel case (*far*ʿ) with an original case (*aṣl*) due to the effective cause (ʿ*illah*) of their ruling being the same.

433 The evidence that is superior to *qiyās* includes the Book, the Sunnah, *ijmā*ʿ and anything else that may or may not be connected to them, provided the Muslim legal theoreticians deem them to be stronger in evidence than *qiyās*.

434 Similar ḥadīths are found in: Abū Dāwūd, *as-Sunan*, Kitāb al-Aqḍiyah, Bāb Ijtihād ar-Ra'y fi'l-Qaḍā', Ḥadīth 3592, p.1489; At-Tirmidhī, *al-Jāmi*ʿ *al-Kabīr*, Kitāb al-Aḥkām, Bāb Mā Jā'a fī al-Qāḍī Kayfa Yaqḍī, Ḥadīth 1327, p.1785; At-Tibrīzī, *Mishkāt al-Maṣābīḥ*, Kitāb al-Imārah wa'l-Qaḍā', Ḥadīth 3737, p.14; also reported by ad-Dārimī, Aḥmad, etc.

She replied, 'Of course.'

So, he said [= the Prophet], 'Thus the debt of Allah is worthier and better.'[435]

The Messenger of Allah ﷺ attributed *Ḥajj* that was due on the decrepit old man (*shaykh fānī*) to financial rights, and he ﷺ indicated to the effective cause (*ʿillah*) that was operative in permitting [it]; [in this case] it is the fulfilment [of the right].[436] This is *qiyās*.

3. Ibn aṣ-Ṣabbāgh (Allah have mercy on him),[437] among the leading companions (i.e. students) of [Imam] ash-Shāfiʿī (Allah have mercy on him), reported in his book *ash-Shāmil* from Qays ibn Ṭalq ibn ʿAlī[438] that he said: A man came to the Messenger of Allah ﷺ – he was probably a Bedouin, and asked, 'O Prophet of Allah, what do you think of [the event when] a man touches his penis after he has performed *wuḍū'*?' He [= the Prophet ﷺ] replied, 'Is it not but a part of him?'[439]

This is *qiyās*.

4. Ibn Masʿūd (Allah be pleased with him) was asked about one who married a woman and did not determine any mahr for her. Her husband died before consummation of marriage [with sexual intercourse] with her. He [= Ibn Masʿūd (Allah be pleased with him)] sought one month to think over it before he said, 'I shall do my best to implement my opinion concerning it; if it is correct, it is from Allah ﷻ, but if it is incorrect then it is from the Son of Umm ʿAbd.'[440] Then he said, 'I adjudicate for her [that] her mahr is equal to women like her – nothing less in it and nothing more.'

5.2: CONDITIONS FOR THE VALIDITY OF QIYĀS

The conditions for the validity of *qiyās* are five:

i. one of them is that it must not be in opposition to the scripture,

ii. the second is that it must not warrant the changing of a ruling [established] by the scripture,

TERMINOLOGY

Qiyās: Analogical Extrapolation

Muḥṣar: Confined

Aṣl: Primary case

Farʿ: Novel case

Khamr: Grape juice that is rendered an intoxicant when it ferments and becomes strong, i.e. wine

ʿIllah: Effective cause

---

435 Al-Bukhārī, *al-Jāmiʿ aṣ-Ṣaḥīḥ*, Kitāb al-Ḥajj, Ch. 1, Ḥadīth 1513, p.120 (also Ḥadīths 1854, 1855, 4399, 6228); Muslim, *al-Musnad aṣ-Ṣaḥīḥ*, Kitāb al-Ḥajj.

436 To satisfy a debt is the primary case here, and the performance of Ḥajj is compared with the repayment of the debt. Therefore, Ḥajj is the matter in question/novel case (*farʿ*). The satisfaction of one's right by someone else has been permitted – such permission being the ruling (*ḥukm*), and the effective cause (*ʿillah*) is the performance that is due.

437 Ibn aṣ-Ṣabbāgh: He is 'Abdussayyid ibn Muḥammad ibn 'Abdulāḥād Abū Naṣr, *aka* Ibn aṣ-Ṣabbāgh ash-Shāfiʿī (d.477 AH / 1084 CE). He resided in Iraq and was one of the greatest jurists of his age. He authored *ash-Shāmil* and *al-Kāmil* on Islamic jurisprudence, and *al-'Uddah* on the principles of Islamic jurisprudence.

438 Qays ibn Ṭalq ibn 'Alī ibn al-Mundhar: He is from among the Successors.

439 See Abū Dāwūd; at-Tirmidhī; an-Nasa'ī.

440 Umm ʿAbd bint ʿAbd was the name of the mother of ʿAbdullāh ibn Masʿūd (Allah be pleased with him).

iii. the third is that the extended [ruling][441] must not be a ruling that cannot be comprehended,

iv. the fourth is that executing the effective cause (*'illah*) must take place for a legal ruling and not for a lingual matter, and

v. the fifth is that the matter in question must not be [already] mentioned in the scripture [of the Book or the Sunnah].

Qiyās Conflicting with the Scripture

An example of *qiyās* being in opposition to scripture is in what has been narrated that al-Ḥasan ibn Ziyād (Allah have mercy on him)[442] was asked about laughing in prayer (*ṣalāh*) and he replied, 'Purity is nullified by it.' The petitioner asked, 'If a man makes an unsubstantiated accusation of unlawful sexual intercourse against a *muḥṣanah*[443] during prayer (*ṣalāh*), his *wuḍū'* does not become null with it, whereas an unsubstantiated accusation of unlawful sexual intercourse against a *muḥṣanah* is graver a crime [than laughing], then how does it become null with laughing when it is less [serious] than it?'

This is *qiyās* in opposition to the scripture, and that [= scripture] is the ḥadīth of the Bedouin who was visually impaired.

Likewise, when we said that the Ḥajj of the woman is permitted with a *maḥram* (unmarriageable male relative), therefore, it is [also] permitted with a group of trustworthy women. This becomes *qiyās* in opposition to the scripture, and that [= scripture] is the saying of the Prophet ﷺ:

لَا يَحِلُّ لِامْرَأَةٍ تُؤْمِنُ بِاللّٰهِ وَالْيَوْمِ الْآخِرِ أَنْ تُسَافِرَ فَوْقَ ثَلَاثَةِ أَيَّامٍ وَلَيَالِيْهَا إِلَّا وَمَعَهَا
أَبُوْهَا أَوْ زَوْجُهَا أَوْ ذُوْ رَحْمٍ مَحْرَمٍ مِنْهَا

'It is not permitted for a woman, who believes in Allah and the Last Day, that she travels more than three days and their nights, unless [in the state that] with her is her father, her husband, or her dhū raḥim maḥram [cognate relative].'[444]

441 The extended ruling (*mu'addā*) is that which is found in the original case (*aṣl*) and extended to the matter in question (*far'*).

442 He is Al-Ḥasan ibn Ziyād al-Lu'lu'ī al-Kūfī (d.204 AH / 819 CE). Trading in pearls (*lu'lu'*), he was a great Ḥanafī jurist in Iraq who served as a judge in Kufa. He was known to be an erudite and immensely humble scholar. Some of his written works include *Adab al-Qāḍī*, *Ma'ānī al-Īmān* and *al-Kharāj*, etc.

443 *Muḥṣan*: Someone, male or female (*muḥṣanah*), who is married or has been married at some point, in a marriage that was consummated. The conditions for a *muḥṣan* (*iḥṣān*) are, to be: i. free, ii. adult, iii. sane, iv. Muslim, v. lawfully married, and vi. have had sexual intercourse with his wife when both had the characteristics of *iḥṣān*. (Al-Qudūrī, *Mukhtaṣar*, Ch. Ḥudūd: Contravention of the Limits, pp.541–542).

444 Muslim, *al-Musnad aṣ-Ṣaḥīḥ*, Kitāb al-Ḥajj, Ch. Travelling of a Woman with a Maḥram to Ḥajj, etc.

Qiyās Warranting the Changing of a Ruling Proven by the Scripture

An example of the second [condition] – that is what warrants the changing of a ruling [proven] by the scripture – is what is said that: Intention is a condition for *wuḍū'* (wudu) by an analogy with *tayammum*. This obliges a changing in the verse of *wuḍū'* from *muṭlaq* (unrestricted) to being *muqayyad* (constricted).

Likewise, when we said: Circumambulation of the House [of Allah ﷻ] is like prayer, based on [the Prophetic] report,[445] so purity and covering nakedness have been stipulated for it, like for prayer, and so this becomes *qiyās* that obliges changing the scripture [mentioning] circumambulation[446] from being *muṭlaq* to being *muqayyad*.

Qiyās When the Extended Ruling is Not Comprehensible

An example of the third [condition] – that is the meaning of that which cannot be comprehended – is in the favour of the permissibility to perform *wuḍū'* with *nabīdh*.[447] Thus, if one said: It [= *wuḍū'* (wudu)] is permitted with other forms of *nabīdh*, basing it on *qiyās* with the *nabīdh* of dates, [this is not correct] or if one said: If one suffers a head wound during prayer (*ṣalāh*),[448] or he has major ritual impurity,[449] he is to build upon his prayer [where he left off], basing it on *qiyās* with when someone becomes minor ritually impure – this is not correct [either].

That is because the ruling in the original case is not comprehensible, and so it is impossible to extend it [= the ruling] to the matter in question/new case (*far'*).

The companions of [Imam] ash-Shāfi'ī (Allah have mercy on him) said something like this: 'When two impure *qullahs*[450] come together, they become pure, and when they separate [after that], they remain pure,' basing it on *qiyās* with when filth falls into two *qullahs*. [This is not correct.] That is because the ruling, even if it is established in the original case, is not comprehensible.

Qiyās When Executing the Effective Cause ('illah) for a Legal Ruling and Not for a Lingual Matter

An example of the fourth [condition] – that is when executing the effective cause (*'illah*) takes place for a legal matter and not for a lingual matter – is in their [= the Shāfi'ī jurists (Allah have mercy on them)] saying: 'The half-cooked is *khamr* (wine)', and that

445 'Circumambulation of the House [of Allah ﷻ] is like prayer, except that Allah ﷻ has made it lawful to talk in it. Thus, whoever talks in it ought to only talk about what is good.' At-Tirmidhī, Ch. on Ḥajj.

446 وَلْيَطَّوَّفُوا بِالْبَيْتِ الْعَتِيقِ '... and they must perform circumambulation of the Ancient House.' Qur'an, 22:29.

447 A drink (potentially alcoholic) usually made from dates soaked in water.

448 In this case, the *wuḍū'* (wudu) is void and he must renew it.

449 In this case, he must bathe (*ghusl*) to achieve major ritual purity.

450 2 *qullahs* approximate 216 litres.

is because *khamr* is called *khamr* because it clouds the intellect.[451] Now, anything else that clouds the intellect is also *khamr*[452] by way of *qiyās*.[453]

The thief (*sāriq*) is a thief because he takes the property of others in a clandestine manner.[454] The grave-robber (*nabbāsh*)[455] associates him in this meaning, and so he is a thief by way of *qiyās*. This is a lingual *qiyās*, which he [= Imam ash-Shāfiʿī (Allah have mercy on him)] acknowledges – that the word is not lingually used for it.[456]

This Condition is Invalid

The evidence for this type of *qiyās* being invalid is that the Arabs call the horse *Adham* due to its blackness [of colour], and *Kumayt* due to its redness, but this noun is not applied to a person [of] black [coloured skin] and to red cloth.[457]

---

451 *Khamr*: خَمْرٌ: [Wine: or grape-wine:] what intoxicates, of the expressed juice of grapes: or the juice of grapes when it has effervesced, and thrown up froth, and become freed therefrom, and still: or it has a common application to intoxicating expressed juice of anything: or any intoxicating thing, that clouds, or obscures, (lit. covers) the intellect; [...]. خمر [in its proper acceptation] is so called because it veils the intellect: or because it infects the intellect. (Lane, Edward William, *Arabic-English Lexicon*. London: Williams and Norgate, 1863. p.808.)

452 Meaning, anything that clouds the intellect, be it known as wine, beer or anything as such, etc. It falls under the ruling of *khamr*, i.e. that which infects the intellect or intoxicates, and thus the prohibition of *khamr* extends to anything that has intoxicating effects.

453 According to the Ḥanafī scholars, this orientation of *khamr* is lingual, i.e. anything that produces the effects of *khamr* is and will be *khamr*. They disagree with the Shāfiʿī scholars in this regard and state that *khamr* is: raw grape juice that is rendered an intoxicant when it ferments and becomes strong (Al-Qudūrī, *Mukhtaṣar*, p.563). Thus, *khamr* is the name of a specific type of drink that is totally distinct from other types of prohibited beverages, and though other intoxicants may adopt its ruling [of prohibition] by way of *qiyās*, they will not adopt this name, i.e. *khamr*. Thus, one who consumes *khamr* is culpable, even if he only takes one drop, but the consumer of any other intoxicant is not culpable unless he becomes intoxicated with it.

454 *Sāriq:* سَارِقٌ: [Stealing; a thief; or] one who comes clandestinely to a place of custody and takes what does not belong to him. (Lane, Edward William, *Arabic-English Lexicon*. London: Williams and Norgate, 1863. p.1352.)

455 *Nabbāsh:* نَبَّاشٌ: One who rifles, or ransacks, graves; who takes forth the dead from them; or who uncovers graves. (Lane, Edward William, *Arabic-English Lexicon*. London: Williams and Norgate, 1863. p.2758.)

456 Imām ash-Shāfiʿī (Allah have mercy on him) admits that the word *sāriq* (thief) is not used for a bodysnatcher (*nabbāsh*); the latter has a specific name. However, he uses *qiyās* here, ruling the application of the *ḥadd* punishment applied to a thief to be applied to a bodysnatcher, also because the nature of both of them is the same; both of them take what does not belong to them in a clandestine manner.

The Ḥanafī scholars, however, deal with both names on a distinct basis. They argue that the hand of a thief is to be amputated due to the verse of the Qur'an:

وَٱلسَّارِقُ وَٱلسَّارِقَةُ فَٱقْطَعُوٓاْ أَيْدِيَهُمَا جَزَآءًۢ بِمَا كَسَبَا نَكَٰلًا مِّنَ ٱللَّهِ وَٱللَّهُ عَزِيزٌ حَكِيمٌ

'And the male thief and female thief: cut off their hands as a recompense for what they have earned, and an exemplary deterrent punishment from Allah.' Qur'an, 5:38.

The Ḥanafī scholars deem theft to be of something in custody whereas a shroud on a buried body is not in custody.

457 *Adham* comes from the word *duhmah* (دُهْمَةٌ) meaning deep black, and

If the [analogical] extension of *qiyās* continued in lingual names, then this would have been permitted due to the existence of the effective cause (*ʿillah*).[458]

But this contributes to the nullification of legal reasons (*asbāb sharʿiyyah*), and that is because the Sharīʿah has rendered theft a *sabab* for a [particular] category of rulings.[459]

When we attach the ruling to something that is more general than theft, and that is 'to take the property of another in a clandestine manner', it becomes clear that the *sabab* in the original case is a meaning other than theft.[460]

Likewise, the consumption of *khamr* is rendered a *sabab* for a [particular] category of rulings.

When we attach the ruling to a matter that is more general than *khamr*, it becomes clear that the ruling that was in the original case is attached to something other than *khamr*.[461]

Qiyās when The Matter in Question – or Novel Case (Farʿ) – is Already Mentioned in the Scripture [of the Book or the Sunnah]

An example of the fifth [condition] – that is when the matter in question/novel case (*farʿ*) is already mentioned in the scripture [of the Book and the Sunnah] – such as it is said [by the Shāfiʿī scholars (Allah have mercy on them)]:

---

kumayt comes from the word *kumtah* (كُمْتَة) meaning a red colour mixed with blackness. Although the words *adham* and *kumayt* refer to unspecified colours, they are specified with something particular. Hence, they cannot be used for something other than what the Arabs use them for, such as for someone who is of black-coloured skin, or for red-coloured cloth.

458 *Qiyās* does not extend the ruling of the original case to the subsidiary case/matter in question/novel case (*farʿ*) based on lingual commonality but on legal similarity, otherwise the word *adham* would be used for anything of black colour, and the same applies for the word *kumayt*. When something is used in a manner that may appear to be lending the word used specifically for something to something else, then that is not because of lingual *qiyās* but out of *majāz*.

459 If *qiyās* was used to extend the rulings of lingual names over one another, then that would extinguish the reasons and the effective causes of rulings; one would assume the ruling of one act or omission to another act or omission of a similar name by virtue of the names alone, without seeking the mutual reasons (*sabab*) or the mutual effective causes (*ʿillah*) within them.

460 There is a stark difference between the meaning of سَرَقَ (to steal; to take something in a clandestine manner; to commit theft; to rob, etc.) as aforementioned; the meaning of a *sāriq:* سَارِقٌ: [Stealing; a thief; or] one who comes clandestinely to a place of custody and takes what does not belong to him (Lane, Edward William, *Arabic-English Lexicon*. London: Williams and Norgate, 1863. p.1352), and what has been described here: *to take the property of another in a clandestine manner*. The latter meaning is more general than what theft entails, hence, if we take the latter meaning, it would render the reason (*sabab*) for amputation of hands to be something other than theft. This would lead to an alteration in the meanings of the textual commands [that are explicitly mentioned in the Book and the Sunnah].

461 As in the previous note, according to the Ḥanafī scholars, the ruling must remain within its parameter and not exceed its specified limit, otherwise if we were to render the *sabab* more *ʿāmm* (general) than its legal application, it would lead to an alteration in the meanings of the textual commands [that are explicitly mentioned in the Book and the Sunnah].

- The manumission of a non-Muslim slave, in the expiation for [the breach of] oath (*yamīn*), and in the expiation for [committing] injurious comparison (*ẓihār*), is not permitted by *qiyās* in the expiation for homicide.[462, 463]
- [According to the Shāfiʿī jurists (Allah have mercy on them)] If the man who makes the injurious comparison (*ẓihār*) has sexual intercourse during [the expiation of] feeding [sixty destitute people], he must restart the feeding afresh – by applying *qiyās* to fasting.[464]
- It is permitted for the *muḥṣar*[465] to release himself [from *iḥrām*] by fasting – by applying *qiyās* with the *mutamattiʿ* (someone performing *ḥajj tamattūʿ*).[466]

---

462 The expiation in quasi-intentional (*shibh al-ʿamd*) and unintentional (*al-khaṭaʾ*) homicide is to free one Muslim slave.

463 The Shāfiʿī jurists (Allah have mercy on them) ruled that the slave to be manumitted as expiation for the breach of an oath or for the commission of injurious comparison (*ẓihār*) must be a Muslim slave. They base this on the command to manumit a Muslim slave for the expiation of quasi-intentional (*shibh al-ʿamd*) and unintentional (*al-khaṭaʾ*) homicide, as stated in the Qur'an:

فَتَحۡرِيرُ رَقَبَةٖ مُّؤۡمِنَةٖ

'... then the freeing of a Muslim slave [is due from him].' (Qur'an, 4:92).

However, the Ḥanafī jurists (Allah have mercy on them) have argued against this, saying that the slave to be manumitted here need not be Muslim. They present the following Qur'anic verses for the expiation of committing injurious comparison (*ẓihār*) and breach of oath, respectively:

أَوۡ تَحۡرِيرُ رَقَبَةٖ '... or the freeing of a slave [is due from him].' (Qur'an, 5:89).

فَتَحۡرِيرُ رَقَبَةٖ '... the freeing of a slave [is due from them].' (Qur'an, 58:3).

These verses of the Qur'an are explicit in their not specifying the slave to be manumitted to be Muslim, but the Shāfiʿī jurists have specified them to be Muslim by analogy. The Ḥanafī jurists argue that since these verses explicate the expiation, *qiyās* is invalid.

464 The Ḥanafī and Shāfiʿī jurists (Allah have mercy on them) agree on the ruling of the following Qur'anic verse:

وَٱلَّذِينَ يُظَٰهِرُونَ مِن نِّسَآئِهِمۡ ثُمَّ يَعُودُونَ لِمَا قَالُواْ فَتَحۡرِيرُ رَقَبَةٖ مِّن قَبۡلِ أَن يَتَمَآسَّاۚ ذَٰلِكُمۡ
فَمَن لَّمۡ يَجِدۡ فَصِيَامُ شَهۡرَيۡنِ مُتَتَابِعَيۡنِ مِن قَبۡلِ أَن يَتَمَآسَّاۖ تُوعَظُونَ بِهِۦۚ وَٱللَّهُ بِمَا تَعۡمَلُونَ خَبِيرٞ (٣)
فَمَن لَّمۡ يَسۡتَطِعۡ فَإِطۡعَامُ سِتِّينَ مِسۡكِينٗاۚ ... (٤)

'And those men who commit injurious comparison (*ẓihār*) with their wives and then they revoke what they have said, the freeing of a slave [is due from them] before that they touch one another [in sexual intercourse]. That is what you [all] have been advised to conform; and Allah ﷻ is well aware of what you do. And whoever does not find [a slave to free], the fasting of two months consecutively before they touch one another [in sexual intercourse]; and whoever is not able to [fast], the feeding of sixty destitute people...' (Qur'an, 58:3-4).

This verse mentions the fasting of two months consecutively, i.e. sixty days without missing a day in between, for someone who commits injurious comparison (*ẓihār*) with his wife. However, when it comes to feeding, no such restriction of continuity is mentioned. In other words, one may feed twenty people in one go, and then ten over the next ten days, followed by five a few days later, and then the remaining twenty-five in due course. Thus, the Ḥanafī jurists (Allah have mercy on them) have refuted the Shāfiʿī stance on performing *qiyās* of feeding sixty destitute people consecutively with consecutive fasts of two months – the latter requires a daily continuation, but the former does not.

465 One who is under siege, confinement, restraint or is hindered by an enemy, or is ill and cannot perform such rites is, in the legal meaning of the term *iḥṣār* (confinement), a *muḥṣar* (confined).

466 The *muḥṣar* is someone who was confined and therefore restricted from completing his Ḥajj. In order to release himself from *iḥrām*, he must send forth

- The *mutamattīʿ*, if he does not fast during the Days of *Tashrīq*, may fast after them – by *qiyās* with the delayed performance of [the fasts of] Ramadan.[467]

QUESTIONS

1. Mention three of the five conditions for the validity of *qiyās*.
2. Give an example of when extending the ruling of *qiyās* is not comprehensible.
3. Give an example of when the matter in question/novel case (*farʿ*) is already mentioned in the scripture [of the Book and the Sunnah].

❖

an animal to be sacrificed. The *mutamattīʿ* is someone who performs Ḥajj *tamattuʿ* (i.e. he performs umrah and then Ḥajj without leaving Makkah but in separate *iḥrāms* for each), and because of that, he needs to sacrifice an animal. If he cannot do that, then he must fast for ten days; three during his Ḥajj and seven when he returns home after Ḥajj.

According to the Shāfiʿī jurists (Allah have mercy on them), someone who was restricted from completing his Ḥajj (i.e. the *muḥṣar*) may also fast if he does not find an animal to sacrifice, by way of *qiyās* with the *mutamattīʿ*. The Ḥanafī jurists (Allah have mercy on them) argue that this *qiyās* is invalid because it is discussing something that the Qur'an has already explicated:

وَأَتِمُّوا۟ ٱلْحَجَّ وَٱلْعُمْرَةَ لِلَّهِ ۚ فَإِنْ أُحْصِرْتُمْ فَمَا ٱسْتَيْسَرَ مِنَ ٱلْهَدْيِ ۖ وَلَا تَحْلِقُوا۟ رُءُوسَكُمْ حَتَّىٰ يَبْلُغَ ٱلْهَدْىُ مَحِلَّهُۥ ۚ فَمَن كَانَ مِنكُم مَّرِيضًا أَوْ بِهِۦٓ أَذًى مِّن رَّأْسِهِۦ فَفِدْيَةٌ مِّن صِيَامٍ أَوْ صَدَقَةٍ أَوْ نُسُكٍ ۚ فَإِذَآ أَمِنتُمْ فَمَن تَمَتَّعَ بِٱلْعُمْرَةِ إِلَى ٱلْحَجِّ فَمَا ٱسْتَيْسَرَ مِنَ ٱلْهَدْيِ ۚ فَمَن لَّمْ يَجِدْ فَصِيَامُ ثَلَٰثَةِ أَيَّامٍ فِى ٱلْحَجِّ وَسَبْعَةٍ إِذَا رَجَعْتُمْ ۗ تِلْكَ عَشَرَةٌ كَامِلَةٌ

'And complete the Ḥajj and the umrah for Allah ﷻ. But if you are confined, then whatever of offering is easy [for you to send]. And do not shave your heads until the offering reaches its destination. And whoever among you is sick or has an ailment of the head [must pay] a ransom of fasting or charity or sacrificing. If you are in safety, then whosoever is content with [combining] the umrah with the Ḥajj then whatever of offering is easy [for you to send]. And whosoever cannot find [such offering], then fasting of three days during Ḥajj, and of seven when you have returned; that is ten in total...' (Qur'an, 2:196).

467 The Shāfiʿī jurists (Allah have mercy on them) have used *qiyās* permitting the *mutamattīʿ* not to fast during the Days of *Tashrīq*, and that he may make up for those fasts by way of delayed performance (*qaḍāʾ*), with the fasts of the days missed during the month of Ramadan. The Ḥanafī jurists (Allah have mercy on them) have discounted this ruling and rejected this form of *qiyās* due to the availability of the scripture on this issue:

A man came to ʿUmar ibn al-Khaṭṭāb (Allah be pleased with him) on the Day of Sacrifice [10th Dhu'l-Ḥijjah] saying that he was a *mutamattiʿ* and could not sacrifice an offering [i.e. animal], and nor could he fast the tenth [day of Dhu'l-Ḥajj]. ʿUmar (Allah be pleased with him) told him to ask for an animal from his tribe, and then said, 'O Muʿayqīb, give him a goat.' (Aṭ-Ṭaḥāwī, *Sharḥ Maʿānī al-Āthār*, 2:248).

ʿUmar (Allah be pleased with him) did not allow the man to make up for the fasts at a later date but assisted him in finding an animal to sacrifice – an option easier for that man than fasting.

The existence of this scripture does not allow for *qiyās* to be applied.

5.3: LEGAL QIYĀS (QIYĀS SHARʿĪ)[468]

Definition of Legal Qiyās (Qiyās Sharʿī)

It is the application of the ruling to something which does not have a text-based ruling with a meaning that is the effective cause (*ʿillah*) for that text-based ruling.[469]

Thereafter, the meaning being the effective cause (*ʿillah*) is only known via:

i. the Book,

ii. the Sunnah,

iii. *ijmāʿ* (scholarly consensus)

iv. *ijtihād* (juristic reasoning), and *istinbāṭ* (juridical inference).[470]

Effective Cause (ʿIllah) Known by the Book

Thus, an example of the effective cause (*ʿillah*) being made known via the Book is [that of] making frequent visits, because it has been rendered an effective cause (*ʿillah*) for removing the inconvenience [existing] in [repeatedly] seeking permission,[471] in the saying of Allah ﷻ:

---

468 *Qiyās* (analogical extrapolation) is attributed with *sharʿī* (legal) to particularise it, and to identify it as that analogical extrapolation which is concerned with law and legal extraction so as to give the benefit of legislation. General *qiyās* has already been understood to be the evaluation of a novel case with a principal case due to a mutually common element. However, as we learn here, *qiyās* is specified in order to understand it in a respective context, such as *qiyās lughawī* (linguistic *qiyās*) – the use of one word for something that has a similar effect to it, i.e. wine is a specific drink that contains alcohol, but all intoxicating drinks can be known as wine; *qiyās shibhī* (quasi *qiyās*) – the similarity of one with another though their rulings may differ, i.e. the two sitting postures in a prayer consisting of more than two units, where the first sitting is *wājib* and the last sitting is *farḍ*, but due to the apparent similarity of the postures, one might presume them both to be *farḍ*; and *qiyās ʿaqlī* (intelligential *qiyās*) – the acceptance of one statement leads to the acceptance of another as if they were mutually dependent on one another, i.e. the world is ever-changing; anything that ever-changes is finite; (hence) the world is finite.

469 The ruling for an act or omission (i.e. case) given in scripture [of the Book or the Sunnah] has an effective cause (*ʿillah*). A new case that is not explicitly mentioned in the text of the Book or Sunnah could be subject to the same ruling, provided it also has an effective cause (*ʿillah*) that is common with that of the case mentioned in the text (i.e. scripture of the Book or the Sunnah). The ruling shall thereby extend from the original case (i.e. the *aṣl*) to the new case, also known as the *far'* (matter in question/subsidiary case/novel case).

470 The effective cause (*ʿillah*) must be common between the original case (*aṣl*) and the subsidiary case/novel case (*far'*). Furthermore, such effective cause (*ʿillah*) may only be extracted from the authoritative sources of the Sharīʿah; the Book of Allah ﷻ, the Sunnah of the Messenger of Allah ﷺ, the *ijmāʿ* (scholarly consensus), *ijtihād* (juristic reasoning) and *istinbāṭ* (juridical inference), respectively – mere opinions or linguistic commonness do not qualify.

471 It is imperative for servants and maids to seek the permission of their masters and mistresses at three times of the day: before *fajr* prayer, at midday and after *'ishā'* prayer. The Holy Qur'an terms these 'the three times of privacy'. During these times, one is either asleep, or preparing for sleep after having removed the clothes of the day, or in a relaxed mood, and so it is understandably inappropriate for anyone to enter upon another who is in such a condition without permission. However, those who make frequent visits to

لَيْسَ عَلَيْكُمْ وَلَا عَلَيْهِمْ جُنَاحٌ بَعْدَهُنَّ

'There is no sin on you and nor on them besides these (three times); (they are) frequent visitors to you, some of you (make frequent visits) to others.'
Qur'an 24:58

Thereafter, the Messenger of Allah ﷺ removed the inconvenience of [ritual] filth from the leftover of the cat by the ruling of this effective cause (*'illah*),[472] as he ﷺ said:

اَلْهِرَّةُ لَيْسَتْ بِنَجِسَةٍ، فَإِنَّهَا مِنَ الطَّوَّافِيْنَ عَلَيْكُمْ وَالطَّوَّافَاتِ

'The cat is not (ritually) filthy because it is among those males and females who frequent you.'

So our Companions [= the Ḥanafī jurists (Allah have mercy on them)] performed a *qiyās* with the cat on everything that lives in houses, such as mice and snakes, due to the effective cause (*'illah*) of frequent visitation.

Likewise, is the saying of Allah ﷻ:

يُرِيدُ ٱللَّهُ بِكُمُ ٱلْيُسْرَ وَلَا يُرِيدُ بِكُمُ ٱلْعُسْرَ

'Allah desires ease for you, and He does not desire for you hardship.'
Qur'an 2:185

The Sharī'ah has explained that exemption from fasting for the sick and the traveller is in order to ease the matter for them, and that is so they may enable themselves to fulfil that which is priority in their view between performing the due obligation of the time or postponing it to other days.[473]

On account of this meaning, [Imam] Abū Ḥanīfah (Allah have mercy on him) said: 'The traveller, when he intends to perform other incumbent [fasts][474] during the days of Ramadan, they shall take effect regarding [those] other incumbent [fasts], because when a dispensation (*rukhṣah*) has been established for him that relates to the welfare of his body – that is the exemption from fasting, then it is also established for him that relates to the welfare of his religion – that is the discharging the self from the responsibility of what is incumbent [upon him], to a higher degree.[475]

---

their masters, mistresses or family members are relieved of seeking permission during other than the aforementioned times, so as to remove the burden of repeatedly seeking permission for the frequent visitor and the inconvenience of repeatedly granting permission by those frequently visited.

472 The effective cause (*'illah*) here is the frequentation.

473 It is difficult for the sick and the traveller to fast, and so they have been given a choice whether to fast in such a condition or postpone it until after Ramadan. This choice only exists because fasting during the month of Ramadan might prove relatively easier for them than on other days due to other people also fasting in Ramadan. However, they may have to make up for the missed fasts of Ramadan on their own after Ramadan, and observing others eating and drinking could cause discomfort to the one fasting. However, the primary reason for the exemption from fasting during sickness and travel is to create ease and remove difficulty that comes with sickness and travelling.

474 Other incumbent fasts include specific vows (*nadhr*), etc.

475 Imam Abū Ḥanīfah (Allah have mercy on him) is of the opinion that when

Effective Cause (ʿIllah) Known by the Sunnah

An example of the effective cause (*ʿillah*) being made known by the Sunnah is in the saying of the Holy Prophet ﷺ:

لَيْسَ الْوُضُوْءُ عَلَى مَنْ نَامَ قَائِمًا أَوْ قَاعِدًا أَوْ رَاكِعًا أَوْ سَاجِدًا، إِنَّمَا الْوُضُوْءُ عَلَى مَنْ نَامَ مُضْطَجِعًا، فَإِنَّهُ إِذَا نَامَ مُضْطَجِعًا إِسْتَرَخَتْ مَفَاصِلُهُ

'There is no wuḍūʾ due on someone who slept standing, sitting, bowing, or prostrating. Wuḍūʾ is only due on the one who slept [lying down] on his side, because when he sleeps [lying down] on his side, his joints become loose.'[476]

Thus, loosening of the joints is rendered the effective cause (*ʿillah*), and so the ruling, due to this effective cause (*ʿillah*), extends to sleeping whilst leaning or reclining on something such that if it were removed from him, he would fall.

Likewise, the ruling, due to this effective cause (*ʿillah*), extends to unconsciousness and intoxication.

Likewise, is the saying of the Prophet ﷺ [to a woman experiencing chronic menstrual bleeding]:

تَوَضَّئِي، وَصَلِّي، وَإِنْ قَطَرَ الدَّمُ عَلَى الْحَصِيْرِ قطرا فإنه دَمُ عِرْقٍ اِنْفَجَرَ

'Make wuḍūʾ and perform the prayer (ṣalāh), even if the blood drips onto the mat, it is [merely] the blood of a vein that has outpoured.'

The outpouring of the blood is rendered the effective cause (*ʿillah*), and so the ruling, due to this effective cause (*ʿillah*), extends to phlebotomy and cupping.

Effective Cause (ʿIllah) Known by Ijmāʿ

An example of the effective cause (*ʿillah*) being made known by *ijmāʿ* (scholarly consensus) is in what we [= the Ḥanafī jurists (Allah have mercy on them)] said:

- Infancy (*ṣighar*) is the effective cause (*ʿillah*) for the guardianship of the father with regards to the male minor, and so this ruling is [also] established in the right of the female minor due to the existence of the effective cause (*ʿillah*).
- Maturity of intellect is the effective cause (*ʿillah*) for the lapsing of the father's guardianship with regards to the male child, and so the ruling extends to the female child due to this effective cause (*ʿillah*).

---

one has been given a dispensation not to fast in Ramadan for the betterment of his body, it is even more important to provide betterment to one's religion. In this case, the betterment provided to one's religion is the discharging of an act of incumbency, and that is the fast of a specific vow (*nadhr*), etc. Thus, if one is exempted from the obligatory fasting of a day in Ramadan, he may fast that particular day to discharge himself of a fast of a specific vow (*nadhr*), etc. – the exemption is beneficial to his body and the fasting is beneficial to is religion.

476 Abū Dāwūd, *Sunan*, Kitab aṭ-Ṭahārah, Ch. Performing Wuḍūʾ after Sleeping.

- The outpouring of blood is the effective cause (*ʿillah*) for the invalidity of purity with regards to the woman who experiences chronic menstrual bleeding, and so the ruling extends to another [issue] due to the existence of the effective cause (*ʿillah*).

Further Divisions of Qiyās

Thereafter, we say that *qiyās* is of two types:

i. one of the two is that the extended ruling is of the kind of ruling [that is] established in the original/primary case (*aṣl*) [i.e. *ittihād fi'n-nawʿ*], and

ii. the second is that it is of its genus [i.e. *ittiḥād fi'l-jins*].

Examples of the Unity of Kind

An example of the unity of the kind (*ittiḥād fi'n-nawʿ*) is what we [= the Hanafī jurists (Allah have mercy on them)] said: Infancy is the effective cause (*ʿillah*) in the guardianship for enforcing marriage with regards to the male child, and so the right of guardianship for enforcing marriage with regards to the female child is [also] established due to the existence of the effective cause (*ʿillah*) in her. With this, the ruling is established with regards to the female minor who was previously married and had consummated her marriage (*thayyib*).

Likewise, we said: [Frequentation of] visits are the effective cause (*ʿillah*) for the absence of [ritual] impurity of remnant water in the remnant water of the cat, and so the ruling extends to the remnant water of [all animals that] inhabit houses due to the existence of the effective cause (*ʿillah*).

The male child's maturity of intellect is the effective cause (*ʿillah*) for the lapsing of the [father's] guardianship for enforcing marriage, and so the guardianship [for enforcing the marriage] with [regards to] the female child [also] lapses due to the ruling of this effective cause (*ʿillah*).

Examples of the Unity of Genus

An example of the unity of the genus (*ittiḥād fi'l-jins*) is what is said: The frequency of visits is the effective cause (*ʿillah*) for the lapsing of the inconvenience when seeking permission, with regards to what our right hands possess (i.e. slaves). Therefore, the inconvenience in [ritual] impurity of remnant water [also] is omitted due to this effective cause (*ʿillah*). Thus, this inconvenience is of the genus of that inconvenience, and not of its kind.

Likewise, infancy is an effective cause (*ʿillah*) in the father's guardianship of disposal in the property [of the minor], so the guardianship of disposal in the life [of the minor] is [also] established with the ruling of this effective cause (*ʿillah*).

Indeed, the female child's maturity of intellect is the effective cause (*ʿillah*) for the lapsing of the father's guardianship with regards to property, so therefore his guardianship [also] lapses with regards to the person, due to this effective cause (*ʿillah*).

TERMINOLOGY

Istinbāṭ: Juridical inference

Ittiḥād fi'n-naw': Unity of kind

Ittiḥād fi'l-jins: Unity of genus

Ghalabat aẓ-ẓann: Inclination of the mind

Rukhṣah: Dispensation

Homogeneity of the Effective Cause (ʿIllah)

Thereafter, regarding this type of *qiyās*, it is imperative for the effective cause (*ʿillah*) to be of the same genus, such that we say: The father's guardianship is established in the property of the female child because she is incapable of [its] disposal by herself, and hence, the Sharīʿah establishes the guardianship of the father so that her [welfare and] benefits connected to that [property] are not suspended, and [therefore,] she is [also] incapable of disposal in her own person which is why the statement regarding the guardianship of the father over her comes into implementation. There are many illustrations on this.

Ruling of the Unity of Kind

The ruling of the first *qiyās* [= *ittiḥād fi'n-nawʿ*] is that it does not become void by [an unrestricted] difference, because as long as the original/principal case (*aṣl*) is united with the novel case (*farʿ*) in the effective cause (*ʿillah*), their unity in the ruling shall be incumbent, even if they do differ in [areas] other than this effective cause (*ʿillah*).

Ruling of the Unity of Genus

The ruling of the second *qiyas* [= *ittiḥād fi'l-jins*] is its invalidity due to the inconsistency of the homogeneity and the specific difference – this is the explanation that the influencing of minority [of age] in the guardianship of the disposal of property is above its influencing with regards to the guardianship of disposal in the person.

On the Effective Cause (ʿIllah) Known by Ijtihād (Juristic Reasoning) and Istinbāṭ (Juridical Inference)

The explanation of the third type[477] is apparent, and that is *qiyās* where the effective cause (*ʿillah*) is deduced by legal reasoning and *ijtihād*.

Its substantiation is:

i. when we find a suitable characteristic for the ruling,
ii. in a state that necessitates the establishing of the ruling, and
iii. it necessitates the ruling via observation of it, and
iv. the ruling is associated with it in an area of *ijmāʿ*, and
v. the ruling shall be assigned to it out of suitability and
vi. not because of the Sharīʿah testifying to it being an effective cause (*ʿillah*).

EXAMPLE

Its illustration is when we see a man giving a dirham to a poor man, the mind is inclined [to believe] that the giving was to alleviate the need of the poor man and to achieve the benefits of reward.

---

477 The author probably refers to the Book and the Sunnah as one type of analogical legal source, hence he has categorised this as the third, whereas we have already studied three such legal sources of analogy: i. the Book, ii. the Sunnah, and iii. *ijmāʿ*, in which case this should be number four.

Thus, when this is known, we say: When we see a suitable characteristic for the ruling, and the ruling is associated with it in an area of *ijmāʿ*, the mind is inclined [to believe] in the association of the ruling to that [particular] characteristic.

The inclination of the mind (*ghalabat aẓ-ẓann*) in the Sharīʿah obliges action in the absence of any evidence stronger than it. In the status of the traveller when his mind is inclined [to believe] that there is water near him, it is not permitted for him to perform *tayammum*.

Upon this [principle] are the issues pertaining to *taḥarrī*.

Ruling of the Effective Cause (ʿIllah) Known by Ijtihād and Istinbāṭ

The ruling of this [type of] *qiyās* is that it is rendered void by a suitable difference [between the *aṣl* and the *farʿ*] because at that point, a suitable [characteristic] other than it [= the previous suitable characteristic] may be found in the form of the ruling. Thus, there remains no presumption (*ẓann*) for the ruling to be associated to it, and so the ruling is not established by it for it was based on reasonable doubt (*ghalabat aẓ-ẓann*), which has since become void due to the difference.

Upon this [principle]:

i. acting on the first type is in the status of issuing a decree with testimony after the witness has been attested (*tazkiyat ash-shuhūd*) and declared morally upright (*taʿdīl*),[478] whereas

ii. the second type is in the status of [issuing a decree with] the testimony at the appearance of the moral uprightness [of the witness] but prior to [his] attestation,[479] and

iii. the third type is in the status of [issuing a decree] with the testimony of a witness who is *mastūr* (whose outward character conforms to the Sharīʿah but the inward is not known).[480]

QUESTIONS

1. What are the four ways to derive the effective cause (*ʿillah*)?
2. The definition of legal *qiyās* is the application of the ruling to something which does have a text-based ruling with a meaning that is the effective cause (*ʿillah*) for that text-based ruling. True or false?
3. What happens when there is a suitable difference between the *aṣl* and the *farʿ*?
4. The inclination of the mind (*ghalabat aẓ-ẓann*) in the Sharīʿah obliges action in the absence of any evidence stronger than it. True or false?

---

478 The first type of *qiyās* occurs when the effective cause (*ʿillah*) is known by the Book of Allah ﷻ or the Sunnah of the Messenger of Allah ﷺ.

479 The second type of *qiyās* occurs when the effective cause (*ʿillah*) is known by *ijmāʿ* (scholarly consensus).

480 The third type of *qiyās* occurs when the effective cause (*ʿillah*) is known by *ijtihād* (juristic reasoning) and *istinbāṭ* (juridical inference).

5.4: OBJECTIONS AGAINST QIYĀS[481]

The objections preventing [valid] *qiyās* are eight:

i. *mumānaʿah* (prevention)
ii. *al-qawl bi mūjab al-ʿillah* (arguing the effect of the effective cause)
iii. *qalb* (circular reasoning)
iv. *ʿaks* (disparity)
v. *fasād al-waḍʿ* (misuse/misapplication)
vi. *farq* (difference)
vii. *naqḍ* (infraction)
viii. *muʿāraḍah* (conflict)

Mumānaʿah (Prevention)

As for *mumānaʿah* (denial), there are two types:

i. one of the two is the denial in the characteristic,[482] and
ii. the second is the denial of the ruling.[483]

The Denial of the Characteristic and Its Examples

Its example is in the saying [of the Shāfiʿī jurists (Allah have mercy on them)]: [The payment of] *ṣadaqat al-fiṭr* is incumbent because of the [Day of] al-Fiṭr, and so it does not lapse by one's dying on the eve of al-Fiṭr.[484]

We [= the Ḥanafī jurists (Allah have mercy on them)] said: We do not accept it being incumbent due to the [Day of] al-Fiṭr, but rather it becomes incumbent, according to us, by [*per*] head that he provides for and has guardianship over.[485]

Likewise, when it is said:[486] The amount of *zakāh* is incumbent in [one's] liability, and so it is not omitted due to the perishing of the *niṣāb*, just like the debt, we [= the Ḥanafī jurists (Allah have mercy on them)] said: We do not accept that it is the amount of *zakāh* that is incumbent in [one's] liability, but rather its payment is incumbent.

The Denial of the Ruling and Its Examples

If one said: The incumbent aspect is paying it [= *zakāh*], and therefore it is not omitted by perishing, just like the debt [is] demanded, we said: We do not accept that payment is incumbent in the form of

---

481 This section highlights the erroneous ways that *qiyās* is employed.

482 This is to deny the existence of the description that is present in the area of debate, i.e. both parties differ whether a particular description exists in both cases – the *'aṣl* and the *far'* – so as to serve as the effective cause (*'illah*).

483 This is to deny the existence of the ruling even though the description and its capacity to serve as an effective cause (*'illah*) are not denied.

484 The eve of al-Fiṭr is the night before.

485 In this case, *ṣadaqat al-fiṭr* is not obliged on one who dies on the eve of al-Fiṭr, because the reason (*sabab*) for the obligation is the capital, which has lapsed due to his demise.

486 This is the opinion of the Shāfiʿī jurists (Allah have mercy on them).

a debt, but rather it is unlawful to withhold [it] until one discharges [himself] from responsibility by submitting [it]. This [example] is of the denial of the ruling.

Likewise, when [the Shafi'ī jurists (Allah have mercy on them)] said: Wiping is an integral in the category of *wuḍū'*, and so it ought to be tripled, as a sunnah performance, like washing, we [= the Ḥanafī jurists (Allah have mercy on them)] said: We do not accept that tripling is a sunnah in washing, but rather to extend the action in the place of the obligation is an addition to what is obliged, inasmuch as prolonging the standing and the recitation in the category of prayer (*ṣalāh*), except that to extend, in the category of washing, cannot be imagined except by repetition in order to fully cover the [whole] area with the action. Similar to it we say, in the category of wiping, that the extension [of wiping the head] is a sunnah action via the means of covering [the head] fully.

Likewise, it is said:[487] Mutual taking of possession is a condition in the sale of food for food, just like [in an exchange of] currencies, [but] we [= the Ḥanafī jurists (Allah have mercy on them)] said: We do not accept that mutual taking of possession is a condition in the category of currencies, but rather the condition is to specify them so that it does not become a credit (*nasī'ah*) for credit sale, except that according to us currencies cannot be specified except by taking of possession.

Al-Qawl bi Mūjab al-ʿIllah (Arguing the Effect of the Effective Cause)

As for *al-qawl bi mūjab al-ʿillah* (arguing the effect of the effective cause), it is to accept the characteristic to be the effective cause (*ʿillah*), but the explanation that its *maʿlūl* (effective outcome)[488] is other than what the *muʿallil* (the person identifying the effective cause) claims it to be.[489]

EXAMPLE

Its example is the elbow being the limit in the category of *wuḍū'* and so it does not enter into [the rule of] washing because the limit does not enter what is delimited. We [= the Ḥanafī jurists (Allah have mercy on them)] said: The elbow is the cut-off limit (*ḥadd as-sāqiṭ*), and so it does not enter the ruling of the cut-off because the limit does not enter the delimited.

Likewise, it is said: The fasting of Ramadan is obligatory fasting, and so it is not permitted without specification, like those [fasts that are] made up by way of delayed performance (*qaḍā'*). We [= the

487 This is the opinion of the Shāfi'ī jurists (Allah have mercy on them).

488 The *maʿlūl* is the ruling in the *far'* (subsidiary/novel case), i.e. that which is based on the effective cause (*ʿillah*) of the *aṣl* (primary/principal case).

489 The *muʿallil* (the person identifying the effective cause) would identify the effective cause (*'illah*) and then base the ruling upon that effective cause (*'illah*). However, if one was to accept the same effective cause (*'illah*) and yet challenge the ruling by purporting it to be other than what has been claimed, this would be an instance of *al-qawl bi mūjab al-'illah* (arguing the effect of the effective cause).

Ḥanafī jurists (Allah have mercy on them)] said: Obligatory fasting is not permitted without specification, except that specification is found here [made] by the Sharīʿah [itself].

If [the Shāfiʿī jurists (Allah have mercy on them)] said: [The fasting of Ramadan] is not permitted without specification from the person, like those made up by way of delayed performance (*qaḍā'*), we [= the Ḥanafī jurists (Allah have mercy on them)] said: Delayed performance (*qaḍā'*) is not permitted without specification, except that as long as specification is not established by the Sharīʿah with regards to delayed performance (*qaḍā'*), it is thus stipulated that specification is made by the person. So specification is found here [made] by the Sharīʿah [itself] and so it is not stipulated for the person to specify.

Qalb (Circular reasoning)

As for *qalb*, there are two types:

i. One of the two is: what the *muʿallil* has rendered the effective cause (*ʿillah*) in the ruling, [another] renders it a *maʿlūl* (effective outcome) for that particular ruling.

EXAMPLE

Its example in legal matters [according to Imam ash-Shāfiʿī (Allah have mercy on him)] is that the existence of interest in a large amount necessitates its existence in a little amount, such as payments [i.e. cash]. Thus, the sale of one handful of food for two handfuls of it is unlawful.

We [= the Ḥanafī jurists (Allah have mercy on them)] said: No, but rather the existence of interest in a little amount necessitates its existence in a large amount, such as payments.[490]

Likewise, in the issue of the one who seeks refuge in the Ḥaram,[491] the unlawfulness of destroying a life necessitates the unlawfulness of destroying a limb, such as hunting.

---

490 In this argument, the effective cause (*ʿillah*) and the *maʿlūl* (effective outcome) have been swapped by the two schools.

491 He is someone who is guilty of homicide. The Ḥanafī scholars (Allah have mercy on them) are of the view that if someone who is guilty of culpable homicide enters the Ḥaram (in Makkah), he is not subjected to punishment therein, in accordance with the Qur'anic verse: وَمَن دَخَلَهُۥ كَانَ ءَامِنًا 'And whoever enters it shall be secure,' (Qur'an, 3:97), though he may be forced out of the Ḥaram by placing a ban on his food, drink, meeting others, buying and selling, etc. He may only be punished once he has left the Ḥaram. The Shāfiʿī scholars (Allah have mercy on them), on the other hand, opine that the offender may be punished inside the Ḥaram. Both schools agree that retaliatory punishment (*qiṣāṣ*) may be exacted from someone who has destroyed the limb of someone, even if he seeks refuge inside the Ḥaram. The Shāfiʿī scholars (Allah have mercy on them) have taken this as an extension of the prohibition of killing inside the Ḥaram and decreed that, similar to hunting inside the Ḥaram, it is prohibited to injure a human limb, but if exacting punishment for injuring a human is permitted inside the Ḥaram, then so is exacting punishment for culpable homicide. Thus, they have based the permissibility of retaliatory punishment inside the Ḥaram for culpable homicide on the permissibility of exacting retaliatory punishment for harming a human limb. The Ḥanafī scholars (Allah have mercy on them), however, have taken a different view on this. They claim a significant difference between harming

We [= the Ḥanafi jurists (Allah have mercy on them) said: [No,] but rather the unlawfulness of destroying a limb necessitates the unlawfulness of destroying a life, such as hunting. Thus, when its effective cause (*ʿillah*) is rendered the *maʿlūl* (effective outcome) for that particular ruling, it does not remain an effective cause (*ʿillah*) for it, due to the impossibility of the same thing being an effective cause (*ʿillah*) as well as a *maʿlūl* (effective outcome) for it.

ii. The second type of *qalb* is that the objector renders what the *muʿallil* has rendered the effective cause (*ʿillah*) in what he [= the *muʿallil*] claims in the ruling, the effective cause (*ʿillah*) opposite to that particular ruling, and so it becomes an authoritative source (*ḥujjah*) for the objector after it had been an authoritative source for the *mu'allil*.[492]

TERMINOLOGY

Muʿāraḍah: Conflict
Maʿlūl: Effective outcome
Fasād al-waḍʿ: Misuse
Nasī'ah: Credit/Delayed payment

EXAMPLE

Its example is: the fasting of Ramadan is obligatory fasting, and it is conditional to specify it, like that [which is] made up by way of delayed performance (*qaḍā'*).

We [= the Ḥanafi jurists (Allah have mercy on them)] said: Since the fasting [in Ramadan] is obligatory, it is not conditional to specify it after the day has [already] been specified for it, such as that [which is] made up by way of delayed performance (*qaḍā'*).

ʿAks (Disparity)

As for *ʿaks* (disparity), by it we mean that the objector commits to the original/primary case (*aṣl*) of the *muʿallil* in a way that the *muʿallil* is forced into accepting the disparity between the original/primary case (*aṣl*) and the derivative/novel case (*farʿ*).

EXAMPLE

Its example is jewellery prepared for common use – there is no *zakāh* on it [according to the Shāfiʿī jurists (Allah have mercy on them)], like common clothing.

We [= the Ḥanafi jurists (Allah have mercy on them)] said: If jewellery was in the [legal] status of clothing, then *zakāh* would not be incumbent on men's jewellery, just like common clothing.[493]

a human limb and taking a human life, and they too compare it to hunting; just as it is forbidden to hunt inside the Ḥaram – that is, to kill an animal – it is also prohibited to kill a human, be that for punishment or otherwise. As far as exacting retaliatory punishment for injuring a human limb is concerned, it is permitted because it does not lead to taking a life.

492 In this case, the objector renders the effective cause (*'illah*) a proof opposite to the ruling that the *mu'allil* has rendered.

493 In this case, the *muʿallil* is forced to incline to the mutual disparity between jewellery and common clothing.

Fasād al-Waḍ' (Misuse)

As for *fasād al-waḍ'* (misuse), it refers to one rendering the effective cause (*'illah*) such a characteristic that is not appropriate for that ruling.

EXAMPLE

Its example is the saying of [the Shāfi'ī scholars (Allah have mercy on them)] regarding the acceptance of Islam by one of the two spouses, that difference in religion befalls the marriage and invalidates it, similar to one of the spouses reneging [on Islam]. This renders [one's acceptance of] Islam to be an effective cause (*'illah*) for the loss of ownership.

We [= the Ḥanafi jurists (Allah have mercy on them)] said: Islam is known to be a protector of ownership, and so it [= Islam] is not effective in removing ownership.

Likewise, in the issue of the [man's] ability [to marry] a freewoman, he is free and able to marry, and so it is not permitted for him [to marry] a slave-woman [according to the Shāfi'ī jurists (Allah have mercy on them)], [just] like when he is already married to a freewoman.

We [= the Ḥanafi jurists (Allah have mercy on them)] said: His being described as free and able entails the permissibility of marriage, [in which case] it does not have an effect [to enforce] impermissibility.

Farq (Difference)

[*Farq* (difference) is missing from the text; however, it has been touched on previously. Also, the discussion can be found in other texts.[494]]

Naqḍ (Infraction)

As for *naqḍ* (infraction),[495] it is like what is said [by the Shāfi'ī jurists (Allah have mercy on them)]: *Wuḍū'* is purification for which intention is conditional, as [it is] for *tayammum*.[496]

We [= the Ḥanafi jurists (Allah have mercy on them)] said: It [= the stipulation of the intention] becomes invalid by washing clothes and pots.[497]

---

494 See the end of the section on Mu'āraḍah in *Ifāḍah al-Anwār*.

495 *Naqḍ* occurs when the effective cause (*'illah*) is present yet the ruling is absent, and therefore, the evidence is proven wrong.

496 The Shāfi'ī jurists (Allah have mercy on them) deem intention a prerequisite to purification by *tayammum* or *wuḍū'*. The Ḥanafī scholars (Allah have mercy on them) believe that intention is obliged in *tayammum* but not *wuḍū'*, hence, it is not a prerequisite for purification.

497 The Ḥanafī jurists (Allah have mercy on them) give an example of washing clothing and pots to achieve their purity without the condition for an intention, hence refuting the claim made by the Shāfi'ī scholars (Allah have mercy on them). Here, the effective cause (*'illah*) is present, and that is the objective of achieving purity, but the ruling is absent; the condition of intention.

Muʿāraḍah (Conflict)

As for *muʿāraḍah* (conflict),[498] it is like what is said [by the Shāfiʿī jurists (Allah have mercy on them)]: Wiping (*masḥ*) [over the head] is an integral of *wuḍū'*, so tripling it is sunnah, just like washing.[499]

We [= the Ḥanafi jurists (Allah have mercy on them)] said: Wiping [over the head] is an integral but tripling is not sunnah, just like wiping over *khuffs* and in *tayammum*.[500]

QUESTIONS

1. Name four objections against *qiyas*.
2. Name the two types of *mumānaʿah* (denial) and give an example of one of them.
3. How do Ḥanafis respond to the opinion of there being no *zakāh* on jewellery?

❖

---

498 *Muʿāraḍah* occurs when the ruling is proven wrong.

499 The Shāfiʿī jurists (Allah have mercy on them) claim that because wiping over the head in *wuḍū'* is one of its four integrals – the other three being washing the face, washing the arms and washing the feet – it ought to be done thrice as are the other three.

500 The Ḥanafī jurists (Allah have mercy on them) do not deny wiping over the head in *wuḍū'* being one of its four integrals, except that they compare it to wiping over *khuffs* – done only once or wiping during *tayammum* – also done once and not thrice.

SUBSTANTIATING **WITHOUT PROOF**

Substantiating without proof is of many types.

6.1: INFERENCE (ISTIDLĀL) WITHOUT AN 'ILLAH (EFFECTIVE CAUSE)

[One] of them is inference (*istidlāl*) without an *'illah* (effective cause) results in absence of ruling (*ḥukm*).

EXAMPLE

Its example is:

i. vomiting does not invalidate [*wuḍū'*] because it does not exit from the two [excretal] passages, and
ii. a brother is not manumitted due to a brother because there is no [relationship of] parentage (*wilād*) between them.

[Imam] Muhammad (Allah have mercy on him) was asked: 'Is *qiṣāṣ* due from the one who collaborated with a minor [in committing a murder]?' He (Allah have mercy on him) replied, 'No, because the minor is not legally responsible [literally: The pen of accountability has been lifted from him].'

The petitioner asked, 'Then it must be due from someone who collaborated with the father, because the father is legally responsible [literally: The pen of accountability has not been lifted from him].'

This adherence to the absence of the ruling due to the lack of an *'illah* (effective cause) is in the status of when it is said: 'So-and-so did not die because he did not fall from the roof.'

When Inference Can Be Made in the Absence of a Ruling Due to the Lack of an 'Illah

Inference cannot be made in the absence of a ruling due to the lack of an *'illah* (effective cause)] except when the *'illah* (effective cause) of the ruling depends on a single meaning, in which case that [particular] meaning becomes binding for the ruling [to apply], and therefore, evidence of its negation may be inferred from the absence of the ruling.

EXAMPLE

Its example is that which was reported from [Imam] Muhammad (Allah have mercy on him), that he said: 'The child of the misappropriated [slave-woman] is not under the liability [of the usurper], because he [= the child] was not misappropriated. There is no [liability of] *qiṣāṣ* due from the witness in the issue of *qiṣāṣ* if they go back [on their testimony], because he is not the murderer.' That is because the misappropriation necessitates the liability for it, and murder necessitates the obligation for *qiṣāṣ*.

NOTES

6.2: ISTIṢḤĀB (PRESUMPTION OF CONTINUITY)

Likewise, [a second type,] adherence to *istiṣḥāb al-ḥāl* (presumption of continuity in the state of affairs) is adherence to a lack of proof, since the existence of a thing does not necessitate its continued existence [in the past]; it is fit for repelling (*daf*ʿ) rather than enjoining (*ilzām*).

EXAMPLE

It is on this [principle] that we [= the Ḥanafī jurists (Allah have mercy on them)] said: A freeman whose ancestry is unknown and someone claims him to be [his] slave, then he [= the claimant] commits an offence against him [= the alleged slave], the compensation of a freeman shall not be liable on him [= the claimant] because the obligation of the compensation of a freeman is enjoinment (*ilzām*); it cannot be established without proof.

It is on this [principle] that we said: If the bleeding exceeds beyond ten [days] during menstruation (*ḥayḍ*), and that woman has a known regular [menstrual cycle], it is resorted to the days of her regular [cycle], and the excess is *istiḥāḍah* (irregular bleeding), because any excess to the regular [cycle] is connected to the menstruation and also to *istiḥāḍah*, and thus it carries both possibilities simultaneously. If we decree the termination of the regular [menstrual cycle], we enjoin an act without proof.

Likewise, if [a minor] commenced her puberty in the state of *istiḥāḍah*, her menstruation is ten days, because anything under ten days carries [the possibility of being] menstruation as well as *istiḥāḍah*. So if we decreed the ending of menstruation [and beginning of *istiḥāḍah*], we enjoin an act without proof, as opposed to what [bleeding flows] after the ten [days], due to the existence of evidence that menstruation does not exceed beyond ten [days].

6.3: LACK OF EVIDENCE IS PROOF FOR REPELLING (DAFʿ)

As for the proof that it [= *istiṣḥab al-ḥāl*] is not an authoritative source but for repelling and not for enjoining (*ilzām*), is the issue of the missing person; no other person is entitled to his inheritance, and if any of his close relatives die while he is missing, he does not inherit from them. Hence, the right of another is repelled without evidence whereas his [= the missing person's] right is not established without evidence.

If it is said: It was reported from [Imam] Abū Ḥanīfah (Allah have mercy on him) that he said: 'There is no fifth [due] in ambergris because a report (*athar*) has not been mentioned about it,' and this is adherence [to it] without evidence.

We said: He [= Imam Abū Ḥanīfah (Allah have mercy on him)] mentioned that in explaining his excuse that he did not claim there was a fifth [due] in ambergris, and therefore it was reported that (Imam) Muhammad (Allah have mercy on him) asked him regarding the fifth [due] in the ambergris and said, 'What is it with the ambergris that there is no fifth [due] in it?' He [= (Imam Abū Ḥanīfah (Allah

TERMINOLOGY

Istidlāl: Inference

Istiṣḥāb: Presumption of continuity

Istiḥāḍah: Irregular bleeding

Ilzām: Enjoinment

have mercy on him)] replied, 'Because it is like fish.' He [= Imam Muhammad (Allah have mercy on him)] asked, 'Then what is it with fish that there is no fifth in it?' He [= Imam Abū Ḥanīfah (Allah have mercy on him)] replied, 'Because it is like water, and there is no fifth in that.'

And Allah ﷻ knows best what is correct.

QUESTIONS

1. What is the outcome of inference (*istidlāl*) without an *'illah* (effective cause)? Can we make inference in the absence of a ruling due to the lack on an *'illah* (effective cause)?
2. What is adherence to *istiṣḥāb al-ḥāl* (presumption of continuity in the state of affairs)?
3. Give an example of *istiṣḥāb al-ḥāl*.

❖

THE SABAB (REASON) FOR THE ḤUKM (RULING)

The ruling (*ḥukm*) is connected to its [own] reason (*sabab*); it is established by its [own] effective cause (*ʿillah*), and it exists with [the fulfilment of] its [own] conditions.

7.1: THE REALITY OF THE SABAB (REASON)

The *sabab* is a path to something by a means, such as a passage – it is a *sabab* to reach the destination by the means of walking, and a rope – it is a *sabab* of reaching the water by casting buckets.

Upon this [principle], everything that is a path to the ruling by a means is called a *sabab* for it in the Sharīʿah, and the means [itself] is the *ʿillah* (effective cause).

EXAMPLE

Its example is: opening the gate of a stable, [door] of a cage, or unbinding the shackles of a slave; [this action] is a *sabab* for destruction by the means of what exists in the [stable] animal,[501] the bird[502] and the slave.[503]

Types of Sabab

[There are four types of *sabab*:

i. *sabab* on its own
ii. *sabab* in the meaning of *ʿillah*
iii. *sabab* as a substitute to *ʿillah*
iv. metaphorical *sabab*]

Sabab on its Own

The *sabab* with the *ʿillah* (effective cause), when they combine, the ruling is ascribed to the *ʿillah* and not the *sabab*, unless the ascription to the *ʿillah* is impossible, in which case it shall then be ascribed to the *sabab*.

EXAMPLE

Upon this [principle], our companions [= the Ḥanafī jurists (Allah have mercy on them)] have said: When a knife is given to a minor and he kills himself with it, he [= the one who gave the knife] is not liable, but if it falls from the hands of the minor and injures him, he [= the one who gave the knife] is held liable.

---

501 When someone opens the gate of a stable, the animal will wander out and become lost or perish. In this case, its destruction is by the means of its leaving the stable, whereas its leaving the stable is the *ʿillah* (effective cause) for its being destroyed.

502 When someone opens the door of a cage in which there is a captive bird, the bird will fly out and escape, resulting in it perishing. Thus, its escaping is the means between the opening of the cage door and the bird perishing.

503 The slave might flee if he is unshackled, and so the flight of the slave is the means between the shackles being removed and his perishing.

If one mounts a minor upon an animal and he [= the minor] drives it [himself], and the animal rocks to the right and left, and he falls, he [= the one who mounted the minor upon the animal] is not liable.

If one directs another person to someone else's property and he [= the one who was directed] steals it [himself], or [he directs him] to the person, and he [= the one who was directed] kills that person [himself], or [he directs him] to a convoy and he [= the one who was directed] intercepts its path[504] [himself], liability is not due on the one who directed [to them].

This is contrary to the depositary when he directs the thief to the deposit, who [subsequently] steals it, or the one in a state of *iḥrām* (*muḥrim*) who directs someone else to a game of the Ḥaram and the latter kills it.

[And that is] because the liability falls:

i. on the depositary on account of [his] omission to protect what is incumbent on him and not [on account of his] granting directions, and

ii. on the *muḥrim* on account of granting directions being prohibited by his *iḥrām* – in the status of wearing perfume and donning stitched clothing – and so he is liable for pursuing what was prohibited and not for granting directions.

except that the offence is only ascertained when the killing [of the game] actually materialises, whereas prior to that there is no ruling for it due to the possibility of the effects of the offence[505] disappearing, in the status of healing in the category of wounds.

Sabab in the Meaning of ʿIllah

Sometimes the *sabab* is in the meaning of *ʿillah* (effective cause), and so the ruling is ascribed to it.

EXAMPLE

Its example is where the *ʿillah* (effective cause) is established by the *sabab*, in which case the *sabab* is in the meaning of the *ʿillah* (effective cause) – because when the *ʿillah* (effective cause) is established by the *sabab*, the *sabab* will be the medium of effective cause (*ʿillah*) of the effective cause (*ʿillah*) (*ʿillat al-ʿillah*), and so the ruling is ascribed to it.

Thus, we [= the Ḥanafī jurists (Allah have mercy on them)] said: When one drives an animal and it destroys something, the driver is liable.

The witness, when he destroys some property because of his [false] testimony, and then the nullification of [the testimony] becomes apparent by [his] revocation, he [= the witness] is liable.

That is because the movement of the animal is ascribed to the driving and the legal judgement delivered by the judge is ascribed

504 Intercepting the path refers to acts of brigandry.

505 The offence in this regard is the directing of the *muḥrim* for a non-*muḥrim* to game, and its effects are the non-*muḥrim* killing it.

to the testimony – for it is not in his [= the judge's] capacity to omit the judgement after the truth has appeared to him due to the testimony of one morally upright person, and [as such,] he is like someone who is compelled to do that, in the status of the animal that is [compelled to follow] the action of the driver.

Sabab as a Substitute to the ʿIllah

Thereafter, the *sabab* is sometimes put in the place of the *ʿillah* when acquaintance with the real *ʿillah* is difficult. [This happens] to make ease in the affair of the legally responsible person, and because of it, consideration of the *ʿillah* is omitted and the ruling revolves around the *sabab*.

EXAMPLE

Its example in legal rulings is deep sleep; when it is put in the place of impurity (*ḥadath*)[506] consideration of real impurity (*ḥadath*) is omitted, and the annulment [of *wuḍū'* (wudu)] revolves around the absoluteness of the sleep.[507]

Likewise, valid seclusion (*khalwah ṣaḥīḥah*), when it is put in the place of sexual intercourse, consideration of real sexual intercourse is omitted, and the ruling (*ḥukm*) revolves around the validity of privacy for the purpose of [the payment of] full mahr and the obligation of the waiting period (*ʿiddah*).[508]

Likewise, travel, when it is put in the place of hardship (*mashaqqah*) in relation to dispensation (*rukhṣah*), consideration of real hardship (*mashaqqah*) is omitted and the ruling (*ḥukm*) revolves around the travel itself, such that if the sovereign were to travel around in the regions of his kingdom intending thereby the [legal] distance of the journey,[509] he shall be granted dispensation (*rukhṣah*) in not fasting and in shortening [prayer].[510]

Metaphorical Sabab

Sometimes something other than the *sabab* is metaphorically called a *sabab*.

---

506 This refers to passing wind, as one who is asleep does not sense that he has passed wind due to his lack of consciousness, and also due to the looseness of the joints when one is sleeping.

507 When one experiences deep sleep, his *wuḍū'* is considered annulled, irrespective of whether or not he has passed wind in that state.

508 Though sexual intercourse legally consummates the marriage, so does *khalwah ṣaḥīḥah* as it substitutes the former as the *'illah*; this obligates *'iddah* on the woman were she to be divorced after *khalwah ṣaḥīḥah* as well as her entitlement to the full payment of mahr.

509 According to the Ḥanafī scholars, the minimum legal distance of a journey that causes a change in certain legal commands is the travelling of three days and three nights, i.e. 72 hours, by medium pace on foot or any other means of travel. This approximates 61 terrestrial miles (98 kilometres).

510 The *'illah* for curtailing the prayer and for not fasting is hardship, and this also takes place when one is travelling. However, merely travelling the legally specified distance will also allow for this dispensation, whether any hardship was experienced or not.

EXAMPLE

Like the oath (*yamīn*) is called the *sabab* for the expiation (*kaffārah*) even though, in reality, it is not the *sabab* [for it]. [This claim is incorrect because] the *sabab* does not negate the existence of the *musabbab* (effect of the *sabab*) whereas the oath negates the obligation of the expiation, and that is because the expiation occasions out of the violation [of the oath], and with that the oath terminates.

Likewise, is the attaching of the ruling (*ḥukm*) to the condition, such as divorce and manumission are metaphorically called the *sabab* even though, in reality, it [= the attachment] is not the *sabab*, because the ruling (*ḥukm*) is established with the [existence of the] condition whereas the attachment terminates by the existence of the condition. Hence, it cannot be a *sabab* when there exists mutual incompatibility between them.

7.2: ASBĀB (REASONS) FOR LEGAL COMMANDS

Legal commands are connected to their *asbāb* (reasons), and that is because the obligation[511] is hidden from us, and so therefore it is indispensable to have a distinguishing mark by which the person may recognise the obligation of the ruling (*ḥukm*) [upon him] and [it is] on account of this that the rulings are ascribed to the reasons.

Thus, the *sabab* for the obligation of prayer (*ṣalāh*) is the time, with the proof that the divine instruction (*khiṭāb*) regarding the performance of prayer (*ṣalāh*) does not apply prior to the beginning of the time; it only applies after the time begins.

The divine instruction (*khiṭāb*) is something that establishes the obligation of performance, and it makes the person aware of the *sabab* of the obligation prior to it [= the obligation of performance].

This is like our saying: 'أَدِّ ثَمَنَ الْمَبِيعِ (Pay the price of the product),' and, 'أَدِّ نَفَقَةَ الْمَنْكُوحَةِ (Pay the maintenance of the wife).'[512] Therefore, except for the beginning of the time, nothing exists here that would make the person aware [of the obligation], and this explains that the obligation is established with the beginning of the time. Also, the obligation is established for someone whom the divine instruction (*khiṭāb*) does not include, such as the one sleeping and the unconscious. Thus, there is no obligation [to perform] prior to [the beginning of] the time; it is established with the beginning of the time.

On this basis, it becomes apparent that the first part [of the time] is the *sabab* for the obligation.

Two Methods for Explaining the Sabab

Then, after that, there are two methods:

---

511 This may refer to the Lawgiver, Allah ﷻ, as He is not visible to us.

512 The payment of goods and of maintenance is made when they are demanded, respectively, after purchase or marriage.

TERMINOLOGY

Sabab: Reason
Mashaqqah: Hardship
Musabbab: Effect of the sabab
Khiṭāb: Divine address/ instruction
Kharāj: Land-tax

Method One

One of the two is that the *sabab* is relocated from the first portion [of the time] to the second portion if it is not performed in the first portion, and thereafter [it is relocated] to the third and then the fourth [respectively], until it terminates in the end portion of the time, where the obligation shall then become certain at that point. In that [= end] portion,

i. the state of the person is considered, and [also],
ii. the description of that [end] portion is [also] considered.

Considering the State of the Person

The explanation of considering the state of the person in it [= the last portion of the time] is that:

i. if one was a minor during the first portion of the time and adult in that [end] portion, or
ii. he was a disbeliever in the first portion of the time and a Muslim in that [end] portion, or
iii. the woman was experiencing menstruation or postnatal bleeding in the first portion of the time and she was in [a state of] purity in that [end] portion,

the prayer is obligatory.

Upon this [principle] are based all the scenarios of [when] capacity takes place in the end [portion] of the time.

On the contrary, such that menstruation or postnatal bleeding, overwhelming[513] insanity or unconsciousness occurs that extends throughout that portion [of the time], then [the obligation of] prayer is omitted from them.

If one was a traveller during the first [portion] of the time and a resident in the last [portion] of it, he prays four [units].

If he was a resident during the first [portion] of the time and a traveller in the last [portion] of it, he prays two units.[514]

Considering the Description of the End Portion of the Time

The explanation of considering the description of that [end] portion [of the time], is that if that [end] portion [of the time] is perfect (*kāmil*), the task (*waẓīfah*) is certainly inclusive [in its obligation to perform], and so one does not discharge himself from responsibility to perform it during the times repugnant [for prayer].

EXAMPLE

Its example is in what is said: Indeed, the end [portion] of the time for the *fajr* is inclusive, but the time becomes invalid (*fāsid*) with sunrise,

513 This refers to a period spanning more than the conventional day (i.e. twenty-four hours).

514 When someone takes up a journey of more than the minimum distance required to be legally declared a *musāfir* (traveller), certain rules and regulations change, such as the curtailment of the obligatory prayers of four units to two units, etc.

and that [invalidity occurs] after the time has elapsed, in which case the obligation becomes certain with the attribute of perfection. So, when the sun rises during prayer (*ṣalāh*), the obligation becomes void, because it is not possible for one to complete the prayer except with the attribution of defectiveness (*nāqiṣ*) on account of time.

If that [end] portion [of time] was defective, as in the *ʿaṣr* prayer, because the end [portion] of the time is [indicated by] the time of the redness of the sun, and the time is invalid (*fāsid*) during that [= redness of the sun], and so therefore the task is certainly with the attribution of defect. Therefore, it is incumbent [to accept] the statement regarding [its] permissibility during that time [= when the sun has turned red] even though the time is invalid (*fāsid*).

Method Two

The second method is that each portion of the [various] portions of the time are rendered a *sabab*, and not by way of relocation, for surely, the statement in [supporting the relocation] is one that purports the nullification of the *sabab* established by the Sharīʿah.

Compounding of the incumbent act is not a necessary outcome based on this [compounding of the *sababs*], for surely the second portion [of the time] establishes exactly what the first portion [of the time] establishes [and nothing more], being from the category of a succession of *ʿilal* (effective causes) and [from the category of] a multitude of witnesses with regard to disputes.

- The *sabab* for the obligation of fasting is presence in the month [of Ramadan], due to the application of the divine instruction (*khiṭāb*) at [the time of] presence in the month [of Ramadan] and [also] due to the ascription of fasting to it.

- The *sabab* for the obligation of [paying] *zakāh* is ownership of progressive *niṣāb* – either actually (*ḥaqīqī*)[515] or [only] legally (*ḥukmī*)[516] and on account of the obligation of the *sabab*, it is permitted to make haste in terms of [its] performance.

- The *sabab* for the obligation of the [performance of] Ḥajj is the House [of Allah ﷻ], due to it [= the Ḥajj] being ascribed to the House[517] and the non-repetition of its task during the [rest of one's] life. Upon this [principle], if one performs Ḥajj prior to attaining capacity, it corresponds to the Ḥajj of Islam due to the existence of the *sabab*. With this [principle], the payment of *zakāh* prior to the existence of the *niṣāb* is differentiated [from the Ḥajj] due to the absence of the *sabab*.

---

515 Real ownership in *niṣāb* results from real investments such as in trades, etc., without the condition of the passing of a complete year on the *niṣāb*; the capital may have dropped below the *niṣāb* level but that is immaterial to the obligation of paying it once a year.

516 Legally effective form of ownership in *niṣāb* results from the passing of a complete lunar year on one's wealth, the surplus of 2.5% of which must be paid, irrespective of whether that *niṣāb* has increased since the previous year or not, provided the total amount of wealth does not fall below the *niṣāb* level at any point.

517 وَلِلَّهِ عَلَى ٱلنَّاسِ حِجُّ ٱلْبَيْتِ مَنِ ٱسْتَطَاعَ إِلَيْهِ سَبِيلاً

'It is a right of Allah, [as an obligation] on the people [to perform] the Ḥajj of the House – on everyone who is able to afford a way to it.' (Qur'an, 3:97).

- The *sabab* for the incumbency of *ṣadaqat al-fiṭr* is the person that he provides for and has guardianship over. On account of the *sabab*, it is permitted to hasten [it] inasmuch that it is [even] permitted to pay it prior to the Day of [*ʿĪd*] *al-Fiṭr*.
- The *sabab* for the obligation of [paying] the *ʿushr* is the lands that are progressive through actual produce.
- The *sabab* for the obligation of *kharāj* (land-tax) are the lands that are suitable for cultivation, in which case the progression shall be [only] legally effective (*ḥukmī*).
- The *sabab* for the obligation of *wuḍū'* is, according to some, prayer (*ṣalāh*),[518] and so therefore *wuḍū'* is obligatory on whomever prayer (*ṣalāh*) is obligatory, and *wuḍū'* is not due on whomever prayer (*ṣalāh*) is not obliged. Some [others] said: 'The *sabab* for it [= *wuḍū'*] being obligatory is minor ritual impurity (*ḥadath*), whereas the obligation of the prayer (*ṣalāh*) is a condition [for it]. This [opinion] has been reported from [Imam] Muhammad (Allah have mercy on him) in a [legal] text.
- The *sabab* for [the major ritual purification by] bathing (*ghusl*) being obligatory is menstruation, postnatal bleeding, and major ritual impurity (*janābah*).

QUESTIONS

1. Explain the reality of the *sabab* (reason/cause).
2. What are the four types of *sabab*?
3. What is one method for explaining the *sabab*?
4. What is the *sabab* for the incumbency of *ṣadaqat al-fiṭr*?

❖

NOTES

518 This is the majority opinion.

IMPEDIMENTS

8.1: THE TYPES OF IMPEDIMENTS

Al-Qāḍī al-Imam Abū Zayd said: Impediments are of four types:[519]

i. the impediment that prevents the enactment of the *'illah* (effective cause),

ii. the impediment that prevents the completion of it [= the *'illah* (effective cause)],

iii. the impediment that prevents the inception[520] of the ruling (*ḥukm*), and

iv. the impediment that prevents the continuation of it [= the ruling (*ḥukm*)].

Impediment Preventing the Enactment of the 'Illah (Effective Cause)

EXAMPLE

An illustration of the first type is selling a freeman, carrion and blood, because the lack of suitability impedes the enactment of management to be an *'illah* so as to give the benefit of the ruling (*ḥukm*).[521]

Upon this [principle] are all the conditional [statements] – according to us [= the Ḥanafīs].[522] Indeed, the conditional [statement] impedes the enactment of management as an *'īllah* prior to the existence of the condition, according to what we have [previously] mentioned.

Due to this [principle], if one swears an oath that he will not divorce his wife, and then he attaches the condition of his wife's divorce to [her] entering a building, he does not violate [his oath].[523]

---

519 A fifth type has also been reported by the Ḥanafī scholars (Allah have mercy on them), and that is the impediment that prevents the injunction from being binding despite completion of transaction, such as the option to rescind a sale due to a blemish in the object of sale.

520 According to some, this is not 'the commencement' but rather 'the completion'.

521 A freeman, carrion and blood are such types that cannot be rendered objects of a sale. Hence, they are unsuitable for such a transaction. In such a case, the sale would be the *'illah* and the ownership would be the ruling (*ḥukm*). Anything that cannot be the object of a sale cannot be sold, hence, it cannot be the *'illah* as the sale would not take place. The purpose of any sale transaction is the exchange of ownership from the seller to the purchaser, but in this case that is not possible due to the seller's lack of ownership in the first place, hence, the lack of the ruling (*ḥukm*).

522 All illustrations of conditional statements rest on this particular principle, such that if Mr. A promises to give item X to Mr. B on the condition that Mr. B gives item Y to Mr. A, then Mr. A shall not be obliged to give item A to Mr. B until Mr. B gives item Y to Mr. A. In this case, the impediment that is preventing item A from entering the possession of Mr. B is the latter's lack of giving item Y to Mr. A.

523 If a husband states he will not divorce his wife and he subsequently attaches to it the condition of her entry into a particular building, saying that he will not divorce her unless she enters that particular building, he will not have violated his oath of not divorcing her unconditionally. In this case, her entry into the building would be the *'illah* and the divorce would be the ruling (*ḥukm*).

Impediment Preventing the Completion of the ʿIllah (Effective Cause)

An example of the second type is the perishing of the *niṣāb* during the course of the year, the refusal of one of two male witnesses from testifying, and the rejection of [one of the two parties to] the contract.[524]

Impediment Preventing the Inception of the Ruling (Ḥukm)

An example of the third type is the sale wherein is an option stipulated in the contract [to approve or rescind], and the remainder of the time for someone with a legal excuse.[525]

Impediment Preventing the Continuation of the Ruling (Ḥukm)

An example of the fourth type is the *khiyār al-bulūgh* (option of deciding the continuation of a marriage secured when the spouse was a minor by someone other than the father or grandfather when the spouse attains majority age), [*khiyār*] *al-ʿitq* (option of the manumitted married slave-woman on deciding whether or not to continue her marriage secured by her master prior to her manumission), [*khiyār*] *ar-ru'yah* (option to purchase subject to examination), *ʿadam al-kafā'ah* (marital incompatibility), and healing – in the category of wounds – is on this principle.[526]

TERMINOLOGY

Khiyār al-bulūgh: Option of deciding at maturity

ʿAdam al-kafā'ah: Marital incompatibility

Khiyār ar-ru'yah: Option to purchase subject to examination

Takhṣīṣ al-ʿillah: Restricting the legal effective cause

Kharāj: Land-tax

---

524 The *niṣāb* is the *ʿillah* for the obligation to pay *zakāh* upon completion of an entire year. If the *niṣāb* perishes prior to the completion of the year, the obligation to pay *zakāh* also lapses from the owner of the *niṣāb*. Likewise, when it is stipulated for two male witnesses to testify in order to complete the quorum of testimony, such quorum of testimony shall be the *ʿillah*. If one of the two refuses to testify, the ruling cannot take place. Also, when two parties are required as an *ʿillah* to complete a transaction and one of the parties rejects the offer made by the other party, the transaction cannot be enacted. In all three cases, the *ʿillah* is incomplete, therefore, the ruling (*ḥukm*) cannot be applied.

525 A sale is concluded with the exchange of considerations from either party. However, where there is an option stipulated in the contract, the object of sale remains the ownership of the seller until the stipulation lapses. This option stipulated in the contract is the impediment that prevents the commencement of the ruling (*ḥukm*). Likewise is the case when someone suffers from urinary incontinence or a continuous nosebleed; his *wuḍū'* is not nullified due to his being legally excused, and so his *wuḍū'* extends until the end of the time for prayer even though he may have performed his obligatory prayer. His legal excuse is the impediment that prevents the commencement of the ruling (*ḥukm*), i.e. the violation of his *wuḍū'* due to that particular legal excuse in the duration of the time that remains for that prayer.

526 *Khiyār al-bulūgh* is the option given to someone who was married as a minor by someone other than his or her father or grandfather. Upon attaining majority age, he or she has the option of whether or not to continue the marriage.

Khiyār al-ʿitq is the option given to a slave-woman who was married to someone by her master. Upon her manumission, she has the option whether to continue the marriage or not.

Khiyār ar-ru'yah is the option given to the purchaser on whether to keep the commodity after he or she has examined it after the sale.

ʿAdam al-kafā'ah occurs when a woman marries someone not of her status. In such a case, her legal guardians have the option of whether to let that marriage

This [classification] is on account of the permissibility of *takhṣīṣ al-'illah* (specifying the legal effective cause).[527] As for the opinion of those who do not speak in favour of the permissibility of *takhṣīṣ al-'illah*, the impediment with them is of three types:[528]

i. the impediment that prevents the inception of the *'īllah* (effective cause),

ii. the impediment that prevents the completion of it [= the *'īllah* (effective cause)],

iii. the impediment that prevents the continuation of the ruling (*ḥukm*).

As for when the *'īllah* (effective cause) is complete, the ruling (*ḥukm*) is established unequivocally.[529]

Then upon this [principle] everything that the first group [of jurists (Allah have mercy on them)] rendered an impediment in order to establish the ruling (*ḥukm*), the second group [of jurists (Allah have mercy on them)] have rendered it an impediment for the completion of the *'īllah* (effective cause). On this principle does the debate between both groups [of jurists (Allah have mercy on them)] rotate.

QUESTIONS

1. What are the four types of impediments?
2. Explain one of the types of impediments.

❖

continue or not.

When someone wounds another, if the wound is healed such that it is unnoticeable and leaves no traces, either visibly or in any other form, the offender is not obliged to pay the victim for the injury caused.

In all the aforementioned cases, *khiyār al-bulūgh, khiyār al-'itq, khiyār ar-ru'yah, 'adam al-kafā'ah* and the healing are impediments that prevent the continuation of the ruling (*ḥukm*).

527 Imām al-Karkhī (Allāh have mercy on him) and the jurists of Iraq (Allāh have mercy on them) are of the opinion that the *'illah* (effective cause) may be specified, i.e. it may exist independently of the ruling (*ḥukm*). They have proposed four types of impediments.

528 Those jurists (Allāh have mercy on them) who claim that the *'illah* (effective cause) cannot be specified, i.e. that it cannot exist independently of the ruling (*ḥukm*), claim there to be only three types of impediments.

529 This second group of jurists (Allah have mercy on them) are of the opinion that impediment no. 3 (the impediment preventing the inception of the ruling (*ḥukm*)) of the first group of jurists (Allah have mercy on them) does not exist, because once the *'illah* (effective cause) is present, the ruling (*ḥukm*) must also exist; they are mutually dependent.

GLOSSARY

A

adā':	performance of something in its due time or place (see *qaḍā'*); due fulfilment of an act or due omission of what must be omitted
adā' kāmil:	perfect performance, complete performance
adā' qāṣir:	imperfect performance, incomplete performance
ʿādah:	recurrent practice, habit
'ādālah:	moral uprightness, justice; *leg.* the condition of being a witness in legal proceedings, esp. in a court of law, or for acceptance for reporting a ḥadīth
adhān:	Muslim call to prayer
ajnabī (fem. *ajnabiyyah*):	foreign, alien; non-relative, stranger
āḥād:	solitary; see *khabar al-āḥād*
Ahl al-Kitāb:	The People of the Book, referring to Christians and Jews
amānah:	a trust, something placed as a trust
ʿāmm:	general, common, non-specific
amr:	command, esp. to do an action
amr muṭlaq:	unrestricted imperative;
amr muṭlaq ʿan al-waqt:	the enjoined act that is unconstructed by time (see *muṭlaq an al-waqt*)
ʿanbar:	ambergris; amber
ʿaql:	mind, mindset, intelligence, sanity (*law*), discernment
arsh:	compensation
aṣl:	origin; source; principal case in *qiyās* when determining the rule of a novel case; upon which something rests; preponderant, preferred; rule, criterion, maxim; proof, evidence; continuity, *status quo*
athar (pl. *āthār*):	report; news; narration attributed to one of the earliest generations of Muslims; narration attributed to the Prophet Muḥammad ﷺ
ʿayn al-wājib:	the required due; the specific obligation.
ʿazīmah:	regular act; resolution to act or omit something

B

badal: subordinate, substitute, proxy

baʿḍ : part or portion of a whole, some or one of a few

bā'in: separate (esp. irrevocable divorce – see *ṭalāq bā'in*)

bāṭil: null, void, absurd, futile, terminated

bayʿ: sale, transaction

bayʿ fāsid: invalid sale; vitiated transaction

bayān: expression, explanation, elaboration, explication, to make clear*esp.* meanings in texts

bayān al-ʿaṭf: conjunctive explanation, connected expression

bayān aḍ-ḍarūrah: compulsive explanation, necessary expression

bayān al-ḥāl: circumstantial explanation, expression of the state

bayān at-tabdīl: abrogative explanation, conditional expression

bayān at-tafsīr: interpretive explanation, elaborating expression

bayān at-taghyīr: transformative explanation, excluding expression

bayān at-taqrīr: determinative explanation, complementary expression

baynūnah: separation (esp. irrevocable divorce – see *ṭalāq bā'in*)

D

ḍabṭ: certainty; accurate retention

dafʿ: to repel or rid of something

dalālah: indication

dalālat al-ḥāl: circumstantial evidence, contextual indication, the context of something occurring or being said

dalālat an-naṣṣ: indicative text, implication of the text, the inferred meaning of the text

dalīl: indication, something that indicates; evidence, proof

dalīl qaṭʿī: definitive evidence, such proof as does not entertain any doubt

dam: animal sacrificed as atonement

ḍamān: liability, compensation, guarantee, surety

dār al-ḥarb: non-Muslim countries and states

ḍarūrah: compulsive necessity

dhū (fem. *dhāt*) *raḥm maḥram:* male relative of the prohibited degree for marriage due to consanguinity, cognate relative

diyah (pl. *diyāt*): compensation paid to the victim or to his successors for the loss of limbs or of life; wergild

F

fāʿil: the doer of something; the subject, as opposed to the object; one who executes an action or verb

fajr: the true dawn when the light spreads across the eastern horizon prior to sunrise

faqīr: needy, poor; someone who owns less than the *niṣāb*.

farʿ:	branch; the novel case, subsidiary case or new casein *qiyās* when determining the extendability of the rule of a principal case to it, the matter in question
faraq:	a measurement of 36 riṭls
fard muṭlaq:	unrestricted clause
fasād:	invalidity, vitiation; corruption
fāsiq:	deviant, dissolute, morally wayward, sinner
fatwā:	decree, ruling, esp. religious (i.e. on beliefs) or legal.
fidyah:	redemption, ransom

G

ghalabat aẓ-ẓann:	inclination of the mind, overwhelming thought or belief
ghāyah:	extent, the utmost limit of space or time.
ghayr-murakkab:	non-compound; *ijmāʿ ghayr-murakkab* (non-compound scholarly consensus) is when many opinions have agreed upon the ruling of a novel case with there being agreement on the same *ʿillah*
ghusl:	bathing, esp. ritual bathing performed when one is in a state of major ritual impurity (*janābah*), or at the end of menses and postnatal bleeding

H

ḥadath:	minor ritual impurity requiring *wuḍū'*
ḥadd as-sāqiṭ:	cut-off limit
ḥadīth:	narrations from the Prophet Muhammad ﷺ
ḥajj:	pilgrimage to the House of Allah ﷻ in Makkah
ḥājjah:	need, requirement
ḥajr:	interdiction, legal incompetence
ḥāl:	a denotative of state of the agent or of the objective complement
ḥaqīqah:	real, literal, actual, physical
ḥaqīqah mahjūrah:	archaic, that *ḥaqīqah* which has been abandoned by the people even though it may be easy to achieve it.
ḥaqīqah mustaʿmalah:	that *ḥaqīqah* which has not been abandoned by the people and it is easy to achieve.
ḥaqīqah mutaʿadhdhirah:	that *ḥaqīqah* which cannot be achieved without difficulty.
ḥaqīqah qāṣirah:	imperfect original meaning, when only some portions or some categories of the conventional are intended
ḥaqīqī:	what is actual, real, physical, and practical, as opposed to legal and ritual
ḥarbī :	enemy combatant, belligerent.
ḥasan:	good, noble, preferred, commendable.
ḥayḍ:	menstruation
ḥinth:	violation, esp. of oath
ḥiss:	sense - as in the five human senses
ḥissī:	perceptible to the senses

ḥujjah:	evidence, proof; authoritative source
ḥukm:	legal ruling, command
ḥukmī:	pertaining to the law or to ritual, as opposed to physical, real, actual and practical

I

ʿibārat an-naṣṣ:	the explicit and plain meaning of the text
ibhām:	vague, unclear, having an indefinite meaning.
ʿiddah:	waiting period before a woman can remarry following divorce or the death of her husband.
ifrāṭ:	squandering, being excessive, lacking moderation
iḥrām:	state of prohibiting oneself from acts that are otherwise permitted *esp.* during *ḥajj*
iḥṣār:	confinement; restriction
ijārah:	hire, lease, rent; letting out on rent
ijmā' :	the consensus of Muslim jurists (*mujtahids*), within a specific point in time, after the death of the Prophet ﷺ, on a rule of law
ijtihād :	the intense effort exerted by a qualified jurist in the quest to deduce laws from legal sources. In Islam, those agreed-upon legal sources are the Qur'an, the Sunnah, the consensus of jurists and analogy; juristic reasoning
ikhbār:	informative, as in *jumlah ikhbāriyyah* (informative sentence)
'illah:	effective cause, *ratio legis*, the reasoning behind whether a rule in the principal case (*aṣl*) in *qiyās* ought to extend to the novel case *(far')*
ilṣāq:	adhesion, association, adherence
ilzām:	enjoining, to oblige, to make compulsory
imsāk:	restraint; abstinence
iqāmah:	call for the commencement of prayer congregation
iqtiḍā':	exigency, requirement
iqtiḍā' an-naṣṣ:	the required meaning of the text (*esp.* out of necessity)
istidlāl:	inference (*juristic*)
istiḥāḍah:	irregular vaginal bleeding and discharge, *esp.* if less than three days ormore ten days of menstrual bleeding, and more than forty days of postnatal bleeding
istithnā':	exclusion, exception
iʿtikāf:	religious seclusion, esp. during the last ten days of Ramaḍān
iʿtirāḍ:	inhibition, restraint; opposition
ʿillah:	effective cause or operative cause in *uṣūl al-fiqh* (principles of Islamic jurisprudence), esp. one that extends the rule of the principal case to the novel case due to its commonality in both; *ratio decidendi*
inshā':	performative, as in *jumlah inshā'iyyah* (performative sentence)
ishārat an-naṣṣ:	the allusive meaning of the text
ism al-jins:	generic noun

isti'ārah:	metaphorical borrowing
istinbāṭ:	juridical inference; deduction
istiṣḥāb al-ḥāl:	presumption of continuity in the state of affairs; status quo
iṭlāq:	unrestricted.
ittisāq:	harmony, congruence, agreement

J

janābah:	state of ritual defilement, major ritual impurity requiring *ghusl*
jarr:	the genitive state (*grammar*)
jazā':	consequence or outcome; consequent clause, or apodosis of a conditional sentence
Jihād:	war waged by Muslims according to the rules laid down for it, military campaign; to struggle, to strive
jins:	genus, type, kind
jumlah:	all, entire; sentence, statement
jumlah ikhbāriyyah:	informative sentence or informative statement, giving information
jumlah inshā'iyyah:	performative sentence or performative statement, issuing a command for proscription or prescription
junūn:	insanity

K

kaffārah:	atonement, expiation
kāmil:	inclusive, complete, whole
karāhah:	abhorrence, repugnance, reprehension
kayl :	a dry measure for identifying the quantity of commodities that are measured by a three-dimensional object, like wheat, salt, etc.; a dry measure of volume
khabar:	report; narration from the Prophet Muhammad ﷺ
khabar al-āḥād:	solitary report, one that does not reach the qualification of it being *mutawātir* (continuously mass-transmitted) (see *mutawātir, mash'hūr*) – it is also known as *āḥād*
khafī:	obscure
khalaf:	substitute
khalwah ṣaḥīḥah:	valid privacy; seclusion of a couple such that in legal terms it equates to sexual intercourse
khamr:	wine made from grapes
kharāj :	tax levied on the produce of land owned by non-Muslims living under Muslim governance.
khāṣṣ:	specific, particular, determined
khiṭāb:	speech; instruction
khuffs:	leather socks.
khul':	divorce at the instance of the wife.
kināyah:	allusive, implicit, implied meaning

kitāb:	book; the Book of Allah ﷻ
kurr:	a dry volumetric measure equal to 60 *qafīzs*

L

laghw:	null, void, false
liʿān:	imprecation by both parties with regards to the accusation of unlawful sexual intercourse made by the husband against the wife, where the former is unable to produce four witnesses; sworn allegation of adultery against spouse; imprecation

M

mabīʿ:	sold commodity, the object of a sale
mabtūtah:	a woman who has been issued an irrevocable divorce by her husband
ma'dhūn:	authorised slave, a slave who has been authorised by his master to carry out specific tasks on the behalf of the latter, such as trade, etc.
mafʿūl:	object (*grammar*)
maḥall:	Site, place, location, locus; subject of a legal command.
mahjūrah:	a type of *ḥaqīqah* which has been abandoned by the people even though it may be easy to achieve it
mahr:	mahr paid by the husband to the wife at the time of marriage
mahr al-mithl:	mahr a woman of her standing would receive
maḥram:	relative of the prohibited degree of marriage
majāz:	metaphorical, figurative
majhūl an-nasab:	one whose ancestry, or parentage, is unknown
majnūn:	insane person, possessed
makrūh:	detested, reprehensible, disliked, abhorrent, repugnant
maʿlūl:	the ruling in the *far'* (novel case), i.e. that which is based on the effective cause (*illah*) of the *aṣl* (primary/principal case).
mamlūk:	property or a person owned by another
ma'mūr bihī:	objective of the command, that which is enjoined, commanded
maʿnā:	meaning; intended sense; denotation
manāfiʿ al-biḍʿ:	a term used for sexual pleasure derived from marriage
manṣūṣ ʿalayhi:	that which is determined by the text
mastūr:	a Muslim whose outward conforms to the Sharīʿah but his inward self is not known; *esp.* a witness in Islāmic Law
ma'ṭūf:	conjoined word (used after 'and', 'but', 'or', etc.) (grammar). In Arabic grammar, it usually appears after the conjunctive word and is known as the second conjunct (in a conjunctive sentence).
ma'ṭūf 'alayhi:	conjoined to (used prior to 'and', 'but', 'or', etc.) (grammar). In Arabic grammar, it appears prior to the conjunctive word and is known as the first conjunct (in a conjunctive sentence).
mawlā:	master; freedman

mawṣūf:	something that is described, depicted, or qualified with an attribute
mithl:	fungible; reasonable; similar; customarily, equivalent, reasonable.
mithl al-wājib:	similar of what is due. (See: *ʿayn al-wājib*)
mithlī:	fungible item
muʿallil:	the person identifying the effective cause (*ʿillah*)
mu'awwal:	construed, interpreted
mubham:	see *ibhām*
mūda':	bailee; trustee; custodian
mudabbar(fem. *mudabbarah*):	a slave who is set free at the death of his master
muḍārabah :	trade contract in which the capital provider shares the profits with the trader but the former alone bears the losses (also known as *qirāḍ*), silent partnership, speculative partnership.
muḍārib:	trader (i.e. the working partner) in a contract of *muḍārabah*
mufaṣṣal:	elaborated, described in detail
mufassar:	interpreted, succinct
mufassir:	someone or something that interprets, elaborates, and clarifies, *esp.* ambiguous texts
mufriṭ:	squanderer, one who exceeds all bounds - see *ifrāṭ*
mughayyā:	the object to which the limit is set (see *ghāyah*)
muḥkam:	conclusive; perspicuous
muḥrim:	one in the state of *iḥrām*
muḥṣan:	someone, male or female (*muḥṣanah*), who is married or has been married at some point, in a marriage that was consummated
muḥṣar:	confined; one who is under siege, confinement, restraint or is hindered by an enemy, or is ill and cannot perform such rites is, in the legal meaning of the term *iḥṣār*, a *muḥṣar*
mūjab aṣlī:	primary obligation; that which is initially prescribed before it is replaced by something else
mujmal:	ambiguous, summary, or summarised, general concept, word or text that needs further elaboration
mujtahid:	independent distinguished jurist, a jurisconsult who has the legal liberty to exercise *ijtihād*
mukallaf:	legally responsible person, on whom the law is applicable
mukātab:	a slave who has entered a contract with his master to purchase his freedom
mukhaffaf:	abbreviated; non-geminated (*see takhfīf*)
mulāmasah:	touch, palpate, fondle; also referred to sexual intercourse
mumānaʿah:	denial, prohibition, proscription
muqarr lahū:	someone in whose favour the confession or the acknowledgement is made
muqayyad:	restricted, constricted, qualified, determinate, fixed, reserved
muqayyad bi'l-waqt:	qualified by time, time-restricted, time-constricted

muqtaḍā: exigency, or that which is exigent; requirement, that which is demanded or required as a condition

murakkab: compound, one made of two or more distinct parts; *ijmāʿ murakkab* (compound scholarly consensus) is when many opinions have agreed upon the ruling of a novel case with there being disagreement on the *ʿillah*

mushaddad: geminated (see *tashdīd*)

mash'hūr: famous, well-known; a ḥadīth that is reported by a large number of people in the second generation and thereafter, but in the first generation there are fewer than the minimum required to render it *mutawātir*

mushkil: complex

mushtarak: homonymous, a word with multiple meanings

mustaʿmalah: a type of *ḥaqīqah* which has not been abandoned by the people and it is easily achievable

musta'nif: beginner; beginning sentence (*grammar*), as in *jumlah musta'nifah* (*isti'nāfiyyah* or *istīnāfiyyah*)

mutaʿadhdhirah: a type of *ḥaqīqah* which is achieved but with difficulty

mutʿah: temporary marriage forbidden to Muslims; gift of consolation

mutamattīʿ: someone performing umrah and then Ḥajj with two *iḥrāms*

mutashābih: allegorical, unintelligible

mutawātir: continuously flowing; a ḥadīth that is transmitted by such a large number of people in each generation that their agreement on something false cannot be conceived

muṭlaq: unrestricted, unrestricted, unreserved, independent, general, indeterminate

muṭlaq ʿan al-waqt: unrestricted by time, unrestricted by time, time-independent

muttaṣil: connected; a ḥadīth that is traced all the way back and connected to the Prophet Muhammad ﷺ

muwakkil: someone who appoints the agent or attorney; the principal in a contract of agency

muwaqqat: restricted to time, that which is contingent on a time limit, time-contingent

muzāḥamah: opposition, competition, rivalry; confluence

muzāḥim: opposite, competitor, rival; conflux

muẓāhir: one who makes injurious comparison (see *ẓihār*)

muzāra'ah: crop sharing (also sharecropping) - an agreement between two parties in which one agrees to allow a portion of his land to be used by the other in return for a part of the produce of the land

N

nabbāsh: bodysnatcher; one who ransacks graves

nabīdh: mead, *esp.* of dates

nadhr: specific vow, pledge

nafaqah: maintenance, financial payment made by the husband to the wife for the wife and children and other dependents

nafl: supererogatory, optional, additional, extra

nafy: banishment, exile; negation

naḥr: sacrifice; to slaughter an animal, especially a camel, by stabbing into a vein at the base of the neck

nahy: prohibition: command to omit an action.

nahy ḥissī: moral proscription, such as adultery, backbiting, lying, etc.

nahy shar'ī: legal proscription, such as praying at times repugnant for prayer, etc.

nāqiṣ: defective, imperfect, incomplete, shortfalling

naṣb: the accusative state (*grammar*)

nasī'ah: credit; a sale transaction wherein one of the considerations from either party is delayed; this is not the same as *salam*

naṣṣ: when a word conveys a clear meaning that is also in harmony with the context in which it appears; textual evidence yet is still open to *ta'wil*

nayf: used for amounts above and beyond, and referring to a number between one and three, such as 'ten plus *nayf* (1 – 3)'

nifās: postnatal bleeding, lochia

niṣāb: minimum amount of property obliging payment of *zakāh*

niyyah: intention, determination, resolve, will

nushūz: discord (marital); violation of marital duties on the part of the husband or the wife

Q

qabīḥ: ugly; abhorrent, repulsive

qaḍā': discharge, perform; to make up for something missed from its due time or place (see *adā'*); delayed performance of an act or delayed omission of something that must be omitted; judgement

qadhf: unsubstantiated accusation of unlawful sexual intercourse.

qāḍī: judge, arbitrator, legal authority

qafīz: a volumetric measure equal to twelve *ṣā's*, Ḥanafī 40.344 litres; others 32.976 litres.

qarīnah: contextual indicator, contextual reference, contextual evidence, external factor

qaṭ'ī: definitive; having no doubt; proof by conclusive evidence (*law*)

qīmī: item of value but not quantified by volume, weights, or measures.

qiṣāṣ: *lex talionis*; legally supervised retaliatory punishment for bodily injury or killing

qiyās: to measure; analogical extrapolation, the attachment or extension between the ruling of that which does not appear in the texts with the ruling of that which does appear because the two things share in the effective cause (*'illah*)of that ruling (*law*)

qullah:	a volume of measurement, equal to approximately 108 litres. (2 *qullahs* would approximate 216 litres, as mentioned in ḥadīths for the minimum amount of water that does not become impure if any of its three characteristics does not change.)
qur':	menstruation

R

rabb al-māl:	owner of the property, of the capital, of the stock; investor
raḍā':	suckling, breastfeeding.
raj'ī:	returnable: retractable (esp. divorce) (see *ṭalāq*)
rājiḥ:	preponderant; the most preferred opinion in a legal issue
ra'y:	attitude, personal opinion
ray':	actual produce, land that produces crop
ribā:	interest, interest
riṭl:	a dry volumetric measure equal to 128.57 dirhams.
rukhṣah:	dispensation in legal prescription, as opposed to *'azīmah*

S

ṣā':	a dry volumetric measure equal to 3.362 litres (Ḥanafī)
sabab:	reason; the effective condition of a rule of law
ṣadaqah:	charity; includes *zakāh*, *'ushr*, *khums*, as well as supererogatory charity.
ṣadaqatal-fiṭr:	incumbent charity to be paid on the Day of 'Īd al-Fiṭr
sajdah:	prostration (see *sujūd*)
Ṣāḥābī (pl.*Ṣaḥābah*):	Companions (Allah be pleased with them) of the Prophet Muḥammadﷺ – those who lived and died as Muslims
ṣaḥīḥ:	sound, authentic, correct, accurate
sahw:	forgetfulness, error
salam:	a contract of advance payment – when the consideration from either party is advanced prior to the payment of the consideration from the other party; this is not the same as *nasī'ah*
ṣarīḥ:	explicit, the clear and unambiguous meaning of a text, be it written or spoken
ṣarīḥ an-naṣṣ:	explicit text
sāriq:	thief
ṣawm:	abstinence; fasting
shafī':	pre-emptor; the executor of pre-emption.
sharṭ:	condition; dependent clause or protasis in a conditional sentence.
shaykh fānī:	enfeebled, decrepit old man
shuf'ah :	pre-emption (*law*)
ṣifah:	characteristic, depiction, description, attribute, quality of something
ṣīghah:	mode, manner, fashion, form, shape, wording

ṣighar:	infancy, having young age
sujūd:	prostration
suqūṭ:	lapse, elimination, drop off

T

ta'addī:	extend; extension of one ruling on to another issue (*law*)
ta'adhdhur:	excuse, unfeasibility, impracticality, etc.
Ṭābi'ī:	Successor, a Muslim who encountered a *Ṣaḥābī* (Allah be pleased with them)
Ṭabi at-Tābi'ī:	a Muslim who encountered a *Ṭābi'ī*
ta'dīl:	appraisal; to declare someone to be morally upright (*law*), *esp.* as a witness in a legal proceeding
tafrīṭ:	negligence
tafsīr:	interpretation, to interpret; explanation, elaboration
taḥarrī:	inquiry, investigation; guesswork, to work something out
taḥrīm:	prohibition, to proscribe, to render unlawful
taḥrīmah:	the initial saying of *'Allahu Akbar'* whilst raising both hands to the ears, indicating the formal entry into the prayer
takhfīf:	abbreviation; non-gemination (*gram.*), occlusion
takhṣīṣ:	specification, to specify
takhṣīṣ al-'illah:	specifying the legal effective cause
taklīf:	legal responsibility, the application of the law
ṭalāq:	separation; divorce
ṭalāq bā'in:	irrevocable divorce including the final divorce
talāq bā'in baynūnah ṣughrā:	irrevocable divorce not amounting to final divorce
ṭalāq bā'in baynūnah kubrā:	irrevocable divorce amounting to final divorce
ṭalāq raj'ī:	revocable divorce, any divorce not amounting to *ṭalāq bā'in*
ta'līq:	attachment; conditional statement (*law*)
tarākhī:	indolence; to lag behind another.
ṭarrār:	pickpocket
taṣarruf:	disposal, disposition, having the capacity, power, and authority to perform or oblige
tashdīd:	intensification; (*gram.*) intensified pronunciation, gemination, doubling (of a consonant); doubling sign over a consonant
tashrīq:	cutting meat into strips and drying them in the sun, referring to the three days after the Day of Sacrifice (i.e. 11th, 12th and 13th of Dhu'l-Ḥijjah)
ta'wīl:	construe (*esp.* the meaning), interpret
tawjīh:	orientation; understanding of something in a given context
tazkiyat ash-shuhūd :	the process of inquiry that the court employs to ascertain the eligibility and standard of a witness, and whether the witness is just or unjust, the attestation of witnesses.
thaman:	price; payment.

thayyib:	a woman who was previously married and her marriage was consummated

U

ukht:	sister
ukht min ar-raḍā':	milk sister, female who was breastfed by the same woman as the principal
umm al-walad:	the slave-woman who is mother of her master's child
'umūm:	generality, holistic, the state of being common or general
'urf:	custom, usage, tradition
'ushr:	a tenth, taxation paid by Muslims as *zakāh* on the produce of their land property, tithe.

W

wadī'ah:	deposit; a trust, bailment.
wājib:	incumbent, something the action of which is proven by non-definite evidence.
wakālah:	agency, representation.
walā':	clientage (or contract of) between a freed slave and his former master, amity (or treaty of), succession.
walī:	guardian; heir.
wāsiṭah:	means; extrinsic circumstance
wasq:	a camel's load; a volumetric measure equal to 60 *ṣā's*
waẓīfah:	task; something appointed *esp.* on daily basis
wilād:	parentage, birth
wujūb:	incumbency, proof by non-definite evidence

Y

yamīn:	right side; oath
yamīn al-fawr:	momentary oath

Z

ẓāhir:	apparent, revealed; manifest; obvious – that has a clear meaning and yet is open to *ta'wil*, primarily because the meaning that it conveys is not in harmony with the context in which it occurs; linguistically determined meaning; something that is commonly practised
ẓāhir ar-riwāyah:	legal opinions and inferences of Imam Abū Ḥanīfah, Imām Abū Yūsuf and Imām Muḥammad (may Allah have mercy on them); manifest rulings.
zānī:	fornicator, adulterer
ẓann:	thought, speculation, presumption,
ẓannī:	speculative; that has a degree of uncertainty or doubt
zakāh:	mandatory poor-due
zakat al-fiṭr:	incumbent poor-due paid on or prior to 'Īd al-Fiṭr

ẓarf:	receptacle, time condition, place condition, container
zawj:	partner, mate
ẓihār:	injurious comparison, the husband's unlawful comparison of his wife, equating her with the back of his own mother and, thereby, prohibiting intercourse with her. Someone who makes *ẓihār* is a *muẓāhir*.
zinā:	unlawful sexual intercourse

www.ingramcontent.com/pod-product-compliance
Lightning Source LLC
Chambersburg PA
CBHW040438190426
43202CB00042B/2993
* 9 7 8 1 9 1 2 3 5 6 9 2 8 *